MW01222778

Digital Document Management

William Saffady

INTERNATIONAL®

ARMA International
Lenexa, Kansas

Consulting Editor: Mary L. Ginn, Ph.D.
Composition: Rebecca Gray Design
Cover Art: Brett Dietrich

ARMA International
13725 West 109th Street, Suite 101
Lenexa, KS 66215
913.341.3808

ISBN-13: 978-1-931786-35-5
ISBN-10: 1-931786-35-6

Contents

Appendices

Preface

Digital Document Management is a reconceptualized, updated, and expanded version of *Electronic Document Imaging: Technology, Applications, Implementation* that was published by ARMA International in 2001. That book was a reconceptualization and revision of *Electronic Document Imaging: A State of the Art Report* published by ARMA International in 1996. The title of this book reflects the most important change: Although its predecessors were limited to document imaging, this book deals with digital documents in all formats. The book is otherwise intended for the same audience as its predecessors: records managers, information systems analysts, office automation specialists, librarians, archivists, and other information professionals who want a systematic introduction to computer-based document management and who are responsible for planning, selecting, and implementing document management systems and services.

Digital Document Management is divided into six chapters that cover the most important aspects of digital document technology, implementations, and applications:

- Chapter 1 explains the scope of the book, defines essential terminology, provides an overview of the major categories of digital documents, reviews the history of digital document technology, and surveys its benefits for records management applications.

- Chapter 2 discusses technologies and methods for creating digital documents. The chapter begins with a survey of preparation, scanning, and related requirements and methods for digital imaging implementations. Later sections examine available options for creating character-coded text from nondigital sources.

- Chapter 3 deals with document indexing and data-entry concepts and methods. It also examines technologies and methodologies for entry of index information into systems that manage digital documents.

- Chapter 4 discusses storage requirements, file formats, devices, and media for digital documents. It also explains retrieval capabilities supported by digital document technologies.

- Chapter 5 reviews commonly encountered issues, complications, and concerns in digital document implementations. Topics include strategic considerations, procurement procedures, the legal status of digital documents, and the implications of digital document technology for records retention.

- Chapter 6 deals with the cost of digital document implementations. It features a step-by-step, worksheet-based method for calculating implementation costs for records management applications with defined characteristics.

Building on the discussion of procurement procedures in Chapter 5, Appendix A presents a model Request for Proposals for a digital document implementation. Appendix B presents a cost-calculation example using the worksheet-based method explained in Chapter 6. Appendix C presents a cost-justification example, based on costs calculated in Appendix B. Appendix D presents suggestions for additional reading.

William Saffady

Chapter 1

Introduction

Most information specialists agree that a *digital document* is a document in computer-processible form. However, these specialists agree less about the definition of a *document*. Dictionary definitions that predate widespread computerization equate documents with paper records. The *Random House Dictionary of the English Language*, College Edition, published in 1968, is typical of its time in defining a document as "a written or printed paper furnishing information or evidence." This definition encompasses business and legal documents as well as books, periodicals, and other information-bearing objects, provided they are paper-based. Electronic documents, a rarity in the 1960s, are not mentioned, but modern usage remedies this omission. The *Oxford Compact English Dictionary*, Second Edition, published by Oxford University Press in 1996, defines a document as "a piece of written, printed, or electronic matter that provides information or evidence."

Records management authorities generally agree that document status is independent of physical form. Australian Standard AS A390, *Records Management*, defined documents as "structured units of recorded information, published or unpublished, in hard copy or electronic form, and managed as discrete units of information systems." Its successor, ISO 15489, *Information and Documentation—Records Management—Part 1: General*, defines a document more succinctly as any "recorded information or object which can be treated as a unit"; format is not even mentioned as a defining characteristic. ISO 5127, *Documentation and Information – Vocabulary* provides a similar definition of a document as "recorded information or material object which can be treated as a unit in a documentation process."

Although a document continues to be defined as "a written or printed paper," the *American Heritage Dictionary of the English Language*, Fourth Edition, published in 2000 by Houghton Mifflin, provides two additional meanings from the field of computer science: one defines a document as "a piece of work created with an application, as by a word processor"; the other broadly equates a document with "a computer file that is not an executable file." *MSN Encarta*, the dictionary provided with Microsoft

Word, provides a similarly broad definition that encompasses any "computer file created using an applications program, for example, a database, spreadsheet, illustration, or text file." Comparable definitions are found in dictionaries of computing and information science. The *Free On-Line Dictionary of Computing* (FOLDOC), for example, defines a document as "any specific type of file produced or edited by a specific application." The Webopedia, a popular online dictionary for computer and networking terminology, notes that personal computer users initially equated documents with word processing files, but the term is increasingly used to denote files produced by any computer application.

As their principal difficulty, these definitions reject the historical link between documents and paper records. They simply equate "document" and "record," rendering the two terms synonymous rather than treating documents as a type of record. More specifically, they equate digital documents with computer-processable records. According to these definitions, MP3 audio files, digitized video clips, and computer animation files are considered digital documents. This usage is confusing and inconsistent with records management practice for nondigital records with similar content. Voice dictation tapes, analog video recordings, and animated motion pictures, for example, are not commonly described as documents.

To obtain a manageable focus and more clearly address the role of digital documents in records management, this book adopts a narrower definition based on the relationship of digital documents to paper and photographic documents. For purposes of this discussion, **digital documents** are computer-processable records that have *both* of the following characteristics:

- They are created by computer programs for purposes that would otherwise be served by paper or photographic documents. If a digital document did not exist, the same information would and could be created and maintained in nonelectronic form.

- They can be printed to produce paper or photographic documents of comparable content, appearance, and functionality.

This definition is not perfect, but it is meaningful and useful. It obviously encompasses digital documents that are modeled after paper documents. Examples include electronic document images, which are produced by scanning paper or photographic documents; word processing files, which simplify the typing of paper documents; e-mail messages, which are electronic versions of correspondence and memoranda; computer-aided design (CAD) files, which are the digital counterparts of architectural plans, engineering drawings, surveys, and other schematics; and radiological images generated by CT scanners, MRI devices, and other medical systems as alternatives to conventional photographic X-rays.

Further, this definition differentiates digital documents from other types of computer-processable records. It clearly rules out audio and video files, which have characteristics that cannot be replicated in paper documents. The definition does not apply to web pages. Although sometimes described as documents, web pages are created for purposes for which paper documents are unsuitable; in particular, they incorporate features and functions, such as hyperlinks, that are clearly absent from paper records. The definition covers databases that consist of simple lists, which can be printed without loss of functionality. However, databases with more complex structures are excluded; in such cases, printouts cannot fully replicate the content, appearance, or functionality of a database. The definition applies to spreadsheets, provided that calculated values may be substituted for formulas when spreadsheets are printed.

Types of Digital Documents

From a records management perspective, the most numerous types of digital documents are digitized images and character-coded text. **Digitized images** may be produced by document scanners, microfilm scanners, digital cameras, or other devices, including specialized scientific and medical instruments that are outside the scope of this book. **Character-coded text** may be generated by word processing programs, e-mail systems, optical character recognition (OCR) programs, or other software. Other digital documents, such as CAD-generated drawings and documents produced by graphic arts programs, are difficult to categorize. Sometimes described as vector files, they consist of mathematical formulas that represent images as lines, circles, arcs, and other geometric objects.

With the notable exception of photographs produced by digital cameras, digitized images are duplicate records. They are produced by scanning existing documents or microfilm images that were produced from paper documents. By contrast, most character-coded digital documents are original records. The principal exception, described more fully in a later chapter, involves character-coded text produced by OCR from digitized images of paper documents. Much less commonly, character-coded digital documents may be created by key-entry of information from existing documents. Like character-coded digital documents, most CAD-generated drawings and other vector files are original records. As an exception, vector files may be produced by software that converts digitized images of drawings or other graphic documents to vector formats, in which case the vector files would be considered duplicate records. CAD software and graphic arts programs can also be used to create vector files through manual entry of information from existing documents, thereby creating digital copies of them.

The following sections summarize basic characteristics of digitized images, character-coded text, and vector files as digital documents. More detailed information is provided in subsequent chapters.

Digitized Images

Digitized images produced by document scanners and, less commonly, film scanners have played an important role in records management applications since the 1980s. Digitized images produced by digital cameras have attracted less records management attention—possibly because photographic records are less numerous than office documents and engineering drawings in government agencies, corporations, and other organizations—but they are increasingly supplanting conventional photographs in organizations that have large image collections. The increase in the use of digitized images is the case, for example, in engineering and construction companies that maintain photographs of facilities under construction, repair, or inspection; in press relations departments that publish and distribute photographs of products, persons, and events for publicity or other purposes; in museums that create photographs of objects in their collections for identification, reference, or publication; in zoos, botanical gardens, and arboreta, that photograph animals, plants, and their surroundings; and in libraries and archives that acquire and preserve photographs for scholarly purposes.

Whatever their sources, digitized images are computer-processible pictures of objects or scenes. As such, they are the electronic counterparts of conventional photographic images. Each digitized image is composed of microscopically small units called **picture elements** or **pixels**, which represent areas of an object or scene. A typical digitized image produced by a document scanner or digital camera consists of millions of pixels. The exact number depends on equipment characteristics, the nature of the object or scene being digitized, and other factors. A digitized image produced from a letter-size page by a scanner operating at 200 dots per inch, for example, contains 3.74 million pixels (megapixels), while images produced by widely available digital cameras contain two to eight megapixels, depending on the model.

Digitized images are encoded by predetermined sequences of "zero" and "one" bits that represent the tonal values of individual pixels. The bit sequences are based on the way in which areas of an object or scene reflect light. The simplest digitization scheme uses a single bit to represent each pixel. It is typically associated with scanning of black-and-white office documents and drawings that contain text or line art. With most office documents and drawings, the information areas contain ink, pencil lines, or other dark marks that absorb light, while the background areas, which are white or another light color, are highly reflective. For scanning purposes, a page is divided into a grid of pixels, which are exposed to light. Pixels that reflect light in excess of a predetermined threshold amount are considered white and are each encoded as a zero bit; such pixels are likely to be in the background areas of the page. Where the amount of reflected light is lower than the threshold amount, the pixels are considered black and are each encoded as a one bit; such pixels are likely to be in the information areas of the page. The resulting images consist of one and zero bits that represent the tonal values of successively encountered pixels within the scanned page. Images produced in this manner are variously described as digitized or digitally-coded. They are also termed *bit-mapped images*, because the bits correspond to specific locations and tonal values within the scanned page, or *raster images*, because the pixels conform to a rectangular array of parallel lines. These terms are used interchangeably and synonymously.

Although single-bit coding is suitable for scanning black-and-white office documents and drawings that contain text or line art, it cannot represent gray tones or colors. It renders them as either black or white, depending on their relative lightness or darkness. This limitation is inconsequential for documents that incorporate gray tones or colors as insignificant decorative elements, but it is unacceptable for photographs, drawings with shaded areas, and other documents where meaningful grayscale or color content must be accurately reproduced in digitized images. Grayscale and color-coding schemes address this limitation by using multiple bits to represent each pixel. The most popular grayscale coding scheme uses eight bits per pixel, which is sufficient to differentiate 256 shades of gray. Color-coding schemes use 24 or more bits to represent each pixel. A 24-bit coding scheme can differentiate almost 16.8 million colors. A 36-bit coding scheme, used by some scanners, can differentiate over 68 billion colors. Color photography is a standard capability of digital cameras. Once rare and expensive, color scanners for documents and slides are now commonplace; their prices have declined steadily and significantly since the 1990s. Color scanners also support grayscale coding.

Character-Coded Text

Digitized images are computer-processable pictures of documents or scenes. When business records or publications are scanned, alphabetic characters, numbers, punctuation marks, and other textual symbols are reproduced as dark or colored tones within a page, as they would be in a photocopy or microfilm image produced from the same page. Digitized images thus reproduce the appearance of textual information within the source documents from which the images were made. In character-coded digital documents, by contrast, each letter of the alphabet, numeric digit, punctuation mark, and other textual symbol is represented by a predetermined sequence of bits. As textual information is typed at a computer keyboard or processed from digitized images by OCR software, bit sequences that represent specific characters are automatically generated. These bit sequences are defined by standardized coding schemes that have evolved over several decades:

- The best-known and most widely encountered example is the American Standard Code for Information Interchange (ASCII), which was developed in the early 1960s and has been revised several times over the years. Applicable standards are *ASCII INCITS-4, Information Systems—Coded Character Sets—7-Bit American National Standard Code for Information Interchange (7-Bit ASCII) and ISO 646, ISO 7-Bit Coded Character Set for Information Interchange.* Redundantly termed the *ASCII code*, it uses seven-bit sequences, ranging from 0000000 to 1111111, to represent upper- and lowercase alphabetic characters, numeric digits 0 through 9, punctuation marks, and certain mathematical symbols, as well as control codes and other characters that are not printed. Thus, the seven-bit sequence 1000001 represents the uppercase A, the seven-bit sequence 1100001 represents the lowercase a, and so on.

- Seven-bit ASCII can encode 128 different characters. This number of characters is sufficient for most English-language documents—a typewriter keyboard contains about 95 printable characters—but it is not enough for documents written in other languages that use the Roman alphabet. Such languages include accented characters or other symbols that have no English counterparts. For this reason, 7-bit ASCII is sometimes described as *US-ASCII*. To accommodate a broader range of recorded information, extended versions of the ASCII code use eight bits, which increases the number of encodable characters to 256. These extended versions can encode accented characters and special symbols. The most widely cited standard is ISO/IEC 8859-1, *8-Bit Single-Byte Coded Graphic Character Sets—Part 1: Latin Alphabet No. 1*, which covers most Western European languages. Other standards in the ISO/IEC 8859 series extend the ASCII code to accommodate Central European, South European, Nordic, and Celtic languages. Over time, new characters, such as the Euro symbol, have been added to extended ASCII coding schemes, but other characters remain excluded. Examples include ligatures, em dashes, and directional quotation marks. ANSI/NISO Z39.47, *Extended Latin Alphabet Coded Character Set for Bibliographic Use* provides a table of character codes for 35 languages that use the Latin alphabet and 51 Romanized languages.

- Most extended versions of ASCII are limited to the Latin (Roman) alphabet. Some standards in the ISO/IEC 8859 series can accommodate Greek, Cyrillic, Hebrew, Arabic, and Thai characters, but they may be interpreted incorrectly by some computer programs, including text retrieval software discussed later in this book. Extended versions of ASCII are incompatible with Chinese, Japanese, Korean, and other Asian languages, which may contain thousands of characters. ANSI/NISO Z39.64, *East Asian Character Code for Bibliographic Use* addresses this problem by defining a coding structure for Chinese, Japanese, and Korean characters, but Unicode provides a broader approach to computer-processible representation of non-Roman characters. Introduced in the early 1990s as an international replacement for other character-coding schemes, Unicode is designed to accommodate every symbol in every written language. It employs the universal character set specified in ISO/IEC 10646, *Information Technology—Universal Multiple-Octet Encoded Character Set (UCS)*, a multipart standard. Unicode began as a 16-bit coding scheme, which could accommodate 65,536 different characters. It has since been expanded to include 32 bits with the potential to encode millions of different characters. The latest versions of Windows® and the Macintosh operating system employ Unicode rather than the ASCII coding scheme. Given the increased globalization of the software industry, the number of applications that support Unicode is likely to increase.

- The Extended Binary Coded Decimal Interchange Code (EBCDIC) is an eight-bit character-coding scheme developed by IBM in the 1960s. Used by IBM mainframe and mid-range computers, it has limited significance for digital document implementations. With the demise of mainframe-based word processing software and e-mail systems, few applications generate EBCDIC-coded documents.

- Older character codes—such as the Baudot code, a five-bit coding scheme used in telex communications, or the binary coded decimal (BCD) code, a six-bit code used in the 1960s by IBM computers—are no longer encountered.

By definition, **character-coded digital documents** are limited to textual information that can be represented by one of the coding schemes described previously or by other character-coding schemes that may be developed in the future. By contrast, digitized images, which replicate the appearance of paper documents from which they were made, can contain textual and/or graphic information, including signatures, handwritten annotations, and illustrations. The inability to accommodate significant graphic information is a limiting factor for character-coded digital documents, but, as discussed later in this book, compound document formats, such as the portable document format (PDF), support combinations of character-coded text and digitized graphics.

Vector Files

Vector files are not as widely encountered as digitized images and character-coded text, but they play an important role in certain records management applications, especially those associated with architectural, engineering, construction, and land surveying activities. In most organizations, for example, CAD software has replaced manual drafting as a method of creating architectural plans, engineering drawings, and similar documents. Vector files are also encountered in advertising, packaging, publishing, commercial printing, textile design, and other industries and activities with a graphic arts component.

As digital documents, vector files emphasize images rather than text. Consequently, they are sometimes compared to digitized images, but they store image information in a different way. Unlike digitized images, which are composed of bit patterns that represent the tonal values of scanned pages, vector files contain mathematical statements that represent images as lines, circles, arcs, rectangles, polygons, or other geometric objects. The statements define a series of points and provide instructions about how they are to be connected to produce geometric objects with specific characteristics, including shape, color, fill, and outline. Vector files can also contain text with information about fonts, sizes, and other attributes.

Vector files are usually created by direct entry of mathematical statements using computer software designed for that purpose. Examples include CAD programs, such as AutoCAD® and Microstation,® and graphic arts programs, such as Adobe Illustrator® and CorelDraw.® Vector files can easily be converted to digitized images in a bit-map or raster format. Most CAD and graphics programs provide such "rasterization" capability as a standard feature. Conversion of digitized images to vector files is a more difficult task. Although vectorization software is available for that purpose, it can require considerable operator intervention to achieve usable results.

History of Digital Document Technology

Long discussed at professional meetings and in a diverse group of publications, the concept of fully automated alternatives to paper recordkeeping systems predates the commercial availability of computers and digital storage technologies.

Writing in 1945,* Vannevar Bush, an influential science administrator, proposed "a mechanized private file and library. . .[for] books, records, and communications." Bush termed this imaginary mechanized file the "Memex," which he conceptualized as a personal workstation with internal storage and indexing capabilities. Bush suggested computer-like mechanisms for the entry of retrieval commands and search terms by Memex users. Rather than employing digital technology, however, the Memex would store documents on microfilm. It was the conceptual precursor of computer-assisted retrieval (CAR) systems, which combine computer and micrographic technologies, rather than of true digital document systems, which are completely computer-based. Given the primitive nature of computer storage technology in the mid-1940s, a completely digital library would have been impossible. Hard disk drives did not become commercially available until the 1950s, and capacities of the earliest models were much too low for voluminous document storage.

Following Bush's lead, CAR systems were introduced in the 1960s and widely implemented during the 1970s. At the same time, a number of vendors and users experimented with systems that combined computer hardware and software components with other technologies such as video or micrographics. Viewed by their developers as necessary compromises imposed by the technical and economic limitations of completely computerized systems, these hybrid forerunners of digital document technologies attracted considerable attention and stimulated market interest in technology-based alternatives to conventional records management methodologies.

For some researchers, however, fully computerized implementations offered the best prospects for improvements in document storage and retrieval. In 1965, an influential study sponsored by the Council on Library Resources outlined the advantages of digital storage, emphasizing the potential of innovative indexing and retrieval concepts made possible by computerization.** During the mid-1960s, several demonstration projects explored the potential of digital storage and full-text indexing for selected library materials. They converted the textual content of journal articles, technical reports, and other documents to character-coded form for computer storage. Designed to test the efficacy of specific indexing and retrieval methodologies, these research projects were experimental rather than operational in nature. They involved small quantities of documents, narrowly circumscribed applications, and tightly controlled user groups. These research initiatives were soon followed, however, by practical implementations and commercially available products. The following sections survey the historical development of systems and technologies for storage and retrieval of digital documents in text and image formats.

---

*   Vannevar Bush, "As we may think," *The Atlantic Monthly*, vol. 176, no. 7 (July 1945), pp. 101-8. A shorter version subsequently appeared in the September 10, 1945, issue of *Life* magazine.

**   J. Licklider, *Libraries of the Future*. Cambridge, MA: MIT Press, 1965.

Text Indexing and Retrieval

The first practical implementations of digital document technology were intended for full-text storage and retrieval of legal statutes and cases, an application that remains important today. The Legal Information Thru Electronics (LITE) system, developed by for the U.S. Air Force in 1967, stored and indexed the complete text of the U.S. Code along with legal and judicial interpretations and related information. In the same year, the Ohio Bar Automated Research (OBAR) system provided full-text indexing of Ohio statutes and cases. OBAR was the precursor of the LEXIS system, introduced in 1973. NEXIS, its news-oriented counterpart, was introduced in 1980. By that time, other information services were offering full-text indexing and online searching of journal articles, technical reports, patents, and other documents. Today, such offerings are commonplace.

The text retrieval implementations described previously relied on customized programming for specific document collections. During the mid-to-late 1970s, several computer manufacturers and software developers introduced prewritten programs for digital storage, full-text indexing, and online retrieval of character-coded documents. Well-known examples included the Storage and Information Retrieval System (STAIRS) from IBM and the Battelle Automated Search Information System (BASIS). Variously described as text storage and retrieval systems (TSRS), full-text retrieval systems (FTRS), text information management systems (TIMS), and text-based management systems (TBMS), these programs were intended for mainframe and larger mid-range computer installations. Government agencies, corporations, universities, and other large organizations used them to store, index, and retrieve a variety of documents, including scientific, technical, and business reports; laboratory notebooks; patent case files; material safety data sheets; standard operating procedures; and conference presentations, preprints, and reprints.

Text indexing and retrieval programs for personal computers were introduced in the early 1980s. Early products intended for the MS-DOS operating system have been replaced by Windows versions, which are available from many software developers and resellers. Competitively priced and easily implemented, these programs simplify indexing and retrieval of word processing documents, e-mail messages, PDF files, and other character-coded documents stored on local and network drives in law firms, libraries, technical information centers, and other work settings.

Since the late 1990s, widespread utilization of Web search engines has made full-text indexing a commonplace approach to information retrieval. Millions of computer users are accustomed to searching for Web pages that contain specific words or phrases. Some search engines and computer manufacturers offer software that extends these retrieval capabilities to local hard drives. Text indexing and retrieval, no longer considered unusual or innovative, are increasingly viewed as a functional attribute of digital document products and services rather than a self-contained technology. Full-text indexing and retrieval capabilities are routinely incorporated into the document and content management products discussed next.

Digital Imaging

Well into its third decade, digital document imaging has experienced a similar transition from innovative technology to routine functionality. Digital imaging components are no longer remarkable. Document scanners, for example, are commonplace computer peripherals in offices and homes. Digitization of documents for attachment to e-mail messages, incorporation into word processing documents, or other purposes has become an everyday business task. Software to display digital images is installed on most personal computers. Organizations of all types and sizes are using digital imaging technology to facilitate storage and retrieval of office records, engineering drawings, and other documents. The technology is well understood and well accepted.

In the early 1980s, when the first digital document imaging systems were implemented, digital imaging was considered unusual and innovative. However, as with other information management technologies, its introduction was an evolutionary rather than a revolutionary development. Document imaging concepts and components predated the technology's commercialization by several decades. As noted above, the characteristics and advantages of automated document storage and retrieval methods were discussed in the 1950s, and pre-computer systems, most of which relied on micrographics rather than electronic technology, were introduced during the 1960s.

The earliest electronic imaging systems intended specifically for document storage and retrieval employed a combination of computer and video technologies. Introduced in the late 1960s and early 1970s, these systems featured specially designed video cameras that recorded documents as analog rather than digital images on videotape. Like their digital successors, these video-based configurations relied on computer databases to index and locate images for display, printing, or distribution. Retrieval performance was severely constrained, however, by the serial access limitations of videotape; in order to retrieve a particular image, a videotape drive must physically pass all preceding images. Few video-based imaging systems were installed, and their brief period of commercial availability is seldom recalled in historical surveys of automated document storage and retrieval technology. Tape-based document imaging configurations resurfaced briefly in the mid-1980s when several companies introduced digital imaging systems that employed eight-millimeter data cartridges (which are based on eight-millimeter videocassette technology) as storage media. Given their performance limitations, those systems attracted few customers.

During the late 1970s and early 1980s, various researchers and product developers explored the document imaging potential of videodisk technology, which stored television images on a platter-shaped medium that resembled a phonograph record. Although it was conceptually attractive, this approach fared little better than its videotape predecessor. Videodisk images, recorded in analog rather than digital format, were generated by video cameras or transferred from other video sources such as videotapes. A 12-inch videodisk—the most popular size—stored the equivalent of 54,000 television images on each of two sides. When used to record feature films or interactive training materials, a videodisk provided 30 to 60 minutes of full-motion video programming per side. For document storage and retrieval, the images could be treated as a series of still frames to be individually retrieved and displayed, either manually or under computer control.

By providing direct access to recorded information, videodisks addressed the performance limitations of videotape-based systems—any image could be retrieved within a few seconds—but significant limitations made videodisk technology impractical for records management applications:

- As read-only media, videodisks contained prerecorded information produced by a mastering process. The information had to be formatted in a prescribed manner for submission to a videodisk factory where multiple disk copies were produced from a specially prepared master. The economics of mastering and replication favored applications that required many copies of videodisks for distribution or sale (a limitation shared by CD-ROM and DVD-ROM, which are likewise produced by mastering and replication). Most records management applications, however, require just one or two copies of a document collection. In network implementations, multiple users are served by online access to a centralized image repository rather than physical distribution of copies.

- As an additional complication, off-premises mastering and replication of videodisks presented unacceptable delays in records management applications with stringent turnaround time requirements or where new document images must be added at frequent intervals. These limitations were partially addressed by videodisk recorders, which supported the direct recording of video images. Introduced in the early 1980s, they were demonstrated at document management conferences as potential alternatives to micrographics technology, but they attracted few customers for such applications.

- Document imaging implementations based on videodisk technology were further impeded by limited image quality. Television signal formats employed by videodisk components did not provide sufficient detail for consistently legible reproduction of the typewritten or typeset text contained in most office documents and publications. In the United States, prevailing video standards specified television frames consisting of 525 horizontal scan lines. As discussed in Chapter 2, digital document imaging systems support scanning formats with more than 2,000 lines per letter-size page. Given these quality constraints, videodisk systems were limited to imaging applications that involved pictorial documents such as photograph collections.

Another early approach to electronic document imaging combined computer, micrographics, and facsimile technologies in complex implementations that provided online access to document images recorded on microfilm, microfiche, or aperture cards. Variously described as microfacsimile, videomicrographic, microimage transmission, or electronic micrographic systems, the typical configuration included a computer-based index to microimages. The microforms themselves were stored in a computer-controlled retrieval unit—a kind of microform jukebox—that incorporated a microimage selection mechanism and an image scanner. Images identified by an index search were automatically located and positioned for scanning. The resulting electronic images, which might be in digital or analog formats, were transmitted to desktop workstations where they were displayed on computer monitors or printed onto paper.

Although early implementations of microfacsimile date from the 1960s, the technology gained considerable notoriety in the late 1970s, when it was viewed as a leading-edge solution for complex records management problems. Impressive installations in large corporations and government agencies were widely publicized in conference papers and information management publications. By the late 1970s, microfacsimile capabilities were being advertised by more than a dozen companies. When completely computerized document imaging systems became available, however, customer attention quickly shifted to the new technology, and interest in hybrid computer-micrographics-facsimile configurations faded. No vendor currently promotes microfacsimile as its core technology, but micrographics components can be effectively incorporated into digital imaging installations. Backfiles, for example, may be stored on microfilm, while newly received documents are recorded on computer media as digital images. A single index can provide integrated access to both formats. At retrieval time, microimages can be scanned to produce digital images for transmission, display, or printing. This approach is discussed in subsequent chapters.

In the United States, the earliest operational examples of fully computerized document imaging were implemented on a customized basis for government agencies and corporations by consulting firms, information service companies, and other systems integrators. The Optical Disk Pilot Project, initiated by the Library of Congress in 1982, was one of the most widely publicized examples. It involved digitized images of books, journals, and other research materials from the library's collections. Designed to explore the preservation and reference implications of digital imaging and optical storage technology, the Optical Disk Pilot Project attracted considerable attention, both within and outside the library community. Other widely publicized digital imaging systems were implemented during the early 1980s by other government agencies, including the National Archives and Records Administration, National Library of Medicine, U.S. Patent and Trademark Office, and the Internal Revenue Service. In the private sector, customized digital imaging systems were implemented by General Electric Company and American Express.

Between 1980 and 1984, several Japanese and European manufacturers introduced digital imaging systems composed of preconfigured combinations of computer hardware and software intended for automated document storage and retrieval in a paperless office environment. Described as "turnkey systems," these products included a proprietary computer, a document scanner, a high-resolution monitor, and a laser printer, plus prewritten software for document indexing, recording, and retrieval. All these components were commercially available—though, admittedly, not commonplace—in the 1970s; high-resolution displays and laser printers, for example, were utilized in the video-based document imaging configurations and microfacsimile installations described previously.

Historically, the principal impediment to the development of completely computerized document imaging systems was the lack of reasonably priced, direct-access storage devices and media with sufficient capacity to accommodate digital images. Magnetic disks can satisfy high-speed retrieval requirements, but hard drives available in the early 1980s had limited storage capacity. As their most distinctive feature, turnkey digital imaging systems incorporated optical disk drives and media with sufficient capacity to satisfy image storage requirements. Such optical storage components became commercially available in the early 1980s. Described by their developers as "optical filing systems," turnkey digital imaging systems initiated a close association between imaging technology and optical storage components. Even in their third decade, electronic document imaging systems continue to be described as optical disk systems, the computer application being confused with the storage medium. Digital images are now more likely to be stored on hard drives than on optical disks.

Initial availability of turnkey digital imaging systems was limited to Japan and Europe where a small number of installations were reported in the early 1980s. Some models were eventually exported to North America where they were demonstrated before large audiences at professional conferences and trade shows. By the mid-1980s, several U.S. companies, including micrographics and filing system vendors, began actively marketing turnkey systems obtained from foreign suppliers. In late 1984, FileNet Corporation became the first U.S. company to offer a preconfigured digital imaging system that was not based on a foreign product line, although it did incorporate certain Japanese and European hardware components. Like the turnkey optical filing systems previously described, the original FileNet Document Image Processor System incorporated a proprietary minicomputer, a document scanner, and high-resolution display and printing components. It also supported a high-capacity optical disk jukebox, an innovative storage component that Japanese and European vendors advertised but had yet to deliver. The first digital imaging systems to utilize personal computers were introduced in 1985. Over the next several years, similar products were announced by several dozen companies.

At least 50 companies demonstrated digital imaging and optical storage products at the 1988 conference of the Association for Information and Image Management (AIIM), the leading North American venue for the introduction and demonstration of document imaging systems and capabilities. Greatly aiding the technology's visibility, mainframe and minicomputer manufacturers exhibited digital imaging systems as additions to their product lines. By the end of the decade, the number of AIIM exhibitors offering digital imaging products and services had surpassed micrographics vendors—formerly the core group of AIIM exhibitors—in both numbers and prominence. That trend continued and intensified during the 1990s. At the 1995 AIIM conference, for example, more than 300 companies exhibited digital imaging products and services. After a decade of mergers, acquisitions, and other industry consolidations, the 2005 AIIM conference still had over 350 exhibitors involved in some aspect of digital imaging technology. Digital imaging products and services are now sold by several thousand companies, including software developers, value-added resellers, systems integrators, imaging service bureaus, and manufacturers of document scanners, high-resolution displays, and other imaging hardware components.

Document / Content Management

Digital imaging is now viewed as a function rather than a technology. Conceptualization and marketing of digital imaging products has changed as well. Software developers and other vendors increasingly characterize their digital imaging offerings as document management products to reflect their broader capabilities, but document management is not a new product designation. It dates from the late 1980s and early 1990s when PC DOCS (subsequently acquired by Hummingbird Ltd.*), Documentum (now part of EMC Corporation), and other companies introduced software to create and maintain organized, searchable repositories of digital documents in text and image formats. Going beyond document storage and retrieval, however, document management products offered additional functionality to support the document preparation and approval process. As their most notable innovation, they integrated document storage and retrieval with word processing programs, spreadsheet software, presentation aids, desktop publishing tools, and other document-authoring components.

Successive generations of document management products have enhanced this capability. Digital documents can be saved in a designated repository from within their originating applications at the time they are created. When a document is retrieved through full-text indexing or assigned index terms as described in later chapters, it can be reviewed and edited by authorized persons within its originating application. Among their other features, document management products allow digital documents to be annotated, and they will track changes and conclusively identify the latest versions of documents subject to multiple revisions. As discussed later in this book, these capabilities are particularly useful for legal briefs, contracts and agreements, engineering specifications, regulatory submissions, standard operating procedures, and other documents subject to multiple revisions and a prescribed approval process.

Since the late 1990s, document management vendors have reconceptualized and enhanced their products to accommodate a wide variety of digital content, including Web pages, video clips, audio clips, and other files outside the scope of digital documents as defined earlier in this chapter. These broader configurations are collectively described as *electronic content management (ECM) products*. Document management, including digital imaging and text-retrieval functionality, is one of their components. In addition to document storage and retrieval, ECM products permit the creation and maintenance of multiple repositories with digital content from a variety of sources. Content in different file formats can be co-mingled in organized folders and subfolders within a repository. Among their other capabilities, full-featured ECM products support the conversion of digital documents and other content from one file format to another; incorporation of digital content into Web pages on the public Internet and organizational intranets; version control for Web site content; preparation of presentation aids with media content; and managing rights and permissions for video presentations, conference call recordings, artworks, and audio-visual media.

---

*   Hummingbird Ltd. was acquired by Open Text Corporation in October 2006.

Benefits of Digital Documents

Digital document technologies offer computerized alternatives to paper recordkeeping systems and, to a lesser extent, microfilm produced from paper documents. The paper-to-microfilm capability is the principal attraction for records management applications. Compared to their paper or photographic counterparts, digital documents can simplify records management operations and improve the efficiency and effectiveness of information-dependent business processes. The following sections summarize the benefits of digital documents in relation to the traditional responsibilities of records management: the organization, storage, retrieval, retention, and protection of recorded information. The cited benefits address significant limitations of paper recordkeeping methods. They are particularly important for government agencies, corporations, and other organizations that have large quantities of records that are subject to demanding retrieval requirements. Benefits introduced here are examined more fully in subsequent chapters.

Enhanced Retrieval

Enhanced retrieval, with associated improvements in employee productivity, is the principal motive for many digital document implementations. Many business operations require fast access to documents in order to complete transactions, to respond to inquiries, to make decisions, to perform services, or for other purposes, but paper records can be difficult to locate when needed. The organization of paper files for responsive retrieval is one of the most difficult records management tasks. Although they have been steadily refined over many decades, paper filing methods are only effective in a narrow range of applications. Familiar alphabetic and numeric filing arrangements are best suited to records that are requested by a single identifier, such as a name or account number, and where an entire folder of documents will be retrieved at one time. Examples include personnel files, student records, patient files, customer files, legal case records, and insurance claims.

Paper filing methods are less effective for documents that may be requested in several different ways—by a customer's name, account number, or date of a transaction, for example, depending on the circumstances—or where the requestor wants a specific document rather than a complete folder. In such cases, labor-intensive, time-consuming searches through cabinets and folders are often required to locate documents needed for a given purpose. Paper filing systems are also poorly suited to subject filing of documents that treat multiple topics. In some organizations, such documents are photocopied for filing in multiple subject folders, thereby increasing the quantity of records that must be stored. Alternatively, cross-references must be inserted into or among folders to refer users to related subject headings where relevant documents may be filed. This time-consuming procedure is difficult to sustain in busy filing installations where support staff are often hard-pressed to keep up with other filing tasks.

Digital document technologies can address these limitations. Compared to paper filing systems, they can accommodate a broader range of records management applications, including those with demanding retrieval requirements. They provide convenient, fast retrieval of records needed for specific purposes, thereby expediting business processes and improving employee productivity for information-dependent tasks. As explained in subsequent chapters, digital document technologies employ indexing rather than filing methods. Instead of grouping related documents in folders, an **index database** keeps track of digital documents that relate to a given person, account, case, claim, subject, or other matter. Assuming that an appropriate indexing plan is utilized, digital documents can be quickly identified and retrieved at personal computer workstations for display or printing.

Paper records are filed in a predetermined sequence. Digital documents are not limited to a single file arrangement. Instead, they can be indexed for retrieval by multiple parameters. A medical record, for example, can be indexed by the patient's name, the patient's identification number, the name of the attending physician, the date the document was created, the type of document, the medical conditions for which the patient was treated, or other attributes. Similarly, correspondence, reports, and other narrative documents can be indexed by multiple subject headings or, where full-text indexing is employed, every word the documents contain, thereby eliminating the need for duplicate filing or cross-references. As discussed in subsequent chapters, powerful search software can execute complex retrieval commands to conclusively identify the exact documents needed for a given purpose. Tedious file browsing to locate specific documents in cabinets or within folders is eliminated.

Remote Access

In addition to improving retrieval through flexible indexing capabilities, digital document technologies can provide convenient online access to document collections. In particular, they remove a significant limitation in paper filing systems: the requirement that users be in the same location as documents in order to retrieve them. (Admittedly, a paper document can be faxed to a remote user, but someone must be in the same location as the document in order to fax it.) Assuming that appropriate computing and networking arrangements are made, digital documents can be accessed by authorized persons at any time from any location, including international locations.

Digital documents can be available during the evening, on weekends, or at other times when offices and file rooms are closed. Digital documents can be retrieved by authorized persons who are working at home or traveling. Sales representatives can access order documents and product information from customer locations. Engineers and technicians can retrieve drawings, specifications, and technical manuals from field locations. Rather than going to a medical records room, health care providers can consult patient records from their offices or from a patient's bedside. Rather than going to a library, college students can access assigned readings from their homes or dormitory rooms.

Centralized Document Repositories

As a related benefit, remote access facilitates the creation and maintenance of central files as complete, authoritative repositories of documents relating to specific business processes, projects, products, clients, or other matters. Broadly defined, **central files** consolidate documents in a designated location where multiple persons can access them. Commonly encountered examples include student transcripts in a university, patient records in a hospital or medical clinic, deeds and mortgages in a county clerk's office, client files in a social services agency, incident reports in a police department, claims files in an insurance company, litigation files in a law firm, case files in a courthouse, laboratory notebooks and safety assessment reports in a pharmaceutical company, customer account records in a credit union, merger and acquisition files in an investment bank, and engineering drawings in a manufacturing company.

As their most widely recognized advantage, central files promote information sharing among members of workgroups, project teams, committees, or other cooperative endeavors where participants must consult documents that are created or received by others. Where recorded information must be available to more than one person, consolidated document repositories are preferable to **decentralized filing arrangements** in which documents are kept in the work areas of individual employees or are otherwise scattered in multiple locations. A centralized repository gives authorized persons a single access point for documents pertaining to specific business processes, operations, activities, or other matters. Among their other advantages, centralized files facilitate the implementation of uniform filing practices, make efficient use of support personnel, and minimize duplicate recordkeeping.

Digital document technologies simplify the implementation and use of centralized document repositories. In particular, online access to digital documents stored on network servers overcomes a longstanding objection to centralized paper files—that the centralized filing area is not located in convenient proximity to all authorized users, some of whom may work in distant locations. This objection causes them to keep some documents close at hand for convenient access when needed, but such precautionary measures are unnecessary where centralized files are stored digitally. Further, centralized repositories of digital documents can be accessed from branch offices and field locations, thereby eliminating the need to maintain satellite files at those sites.

File Completeness

Office records, engineering drawings, and other documents contain information needed for an organization's day-to-day business operations as well as for decision-making, long-term planning, and other analytical activities. To be useful for these purposes, document collections must be complete and reliable. Missing documents are unacceptable but unfortunately commonplace in paper filing installations. Individual documents or entire folders may be removed from filing areas and not returned. Few unsupervised filing installations have effective methods of tracking the locations of documents in such situations. Manual tracking procedures rely on out-guides or charge slips that are supposed to be completed whenever documents or folders are removed from filing areas. However, such procedures are difficult to enforce. Barcode folder checkout systems, modeled on computer-based library circulation procedures, are available for supervised filing installations, but they require careful planning for effective implementation, and they provide no assurance that documents removed from a filing area will be returned. (Recognizing this problem, libraries, which have had computerized circulation control systems for decades, periodically offer amnesty from fines to encourage the return of overdue items.) File tracking aside, misfiling of documents within folders and misplacement of folders within cabinets is inevitable and difficult to detect. Color-coded folders can help locate misplaced folders, but they cannot detect documents filed in the wrong folders.

Digital document technology can successfully address these problems. Assuming that they are properly indexed and barring accidental destruction by hardware or software malfunctions, digital documents cannot be lost or misfiled. Because digital documents are not physically removed from files for reference or distribution, file completeness is maintained and document tracking requirements are eliminated, as is refiling of previously removed documents with its attendant potential for misfiling. As an added advantage, digital document implementations eliminate contention for recorded information. Because users do not take exclusive physical possession of digital documents when they retrieve them, the same documents can be accessed simultaneously by multiple persons.

Version Control

Many policy documents, reports, engineering drawings, technical specifications, product formulations, standard operating procedures, and other records are subject to revisions that affect their content and business value. Effective recordkeeping systems must provide reliable methods for identifying the latest versions of documents, thereby preventing the use of superceded or otherwise inaccurate information for decision-making, transactions, or other purposes. In paper filing installations, strictly enforced procedures and significant administrative effort are required to manage the succession of documents, date and label the latest revisions or final versions, and maintain a history of changes to specific documents. Even then, such version control procedures are far from foolproof. They cannot eliminate the possibility that a superceded document will be mistaken for the current version. Documents distributed to many recipients are particularly problematic: Revised versions may not be sent to all recipients of superceded documents; even if they are, nothing assures that all recipients will discard their obsolete copies.

Digital document technologies, by contrast, offer simpler, more effective version control functionality for documents that are subject to revision. Software can conclusively identify and limit retrieval to the latest versions of digital documents stored in centralized repositories. Document revision histories can be displayed during the retrieval process. Superceded, withdrawn, or otherwise obsolete documents are clearly identified. They can be rendered unretrievable or, where appropriate, deleted. If desired, authorized users can be notified when new versions of documents are released.

Improved Security

Although secure file rooms can be established, important paper documents are often kept in unlocked cabinets in unsupervised locations where they may be accessible to unauthorized persons. By contrast, digital documents are stored in secure locations on network servers. Access can be restricted to specific employees or other authorized persons on a need-to-know basis. Retrieval can be strictly controlled by password privileges or other computer-based security measures. When employees rely on digital documents for reference or other purposes, the number of paper records maintained in office areas is greatly reduced, thereby minimizing the exposure of sensitive or proprietary information to unauthorized employees or visitors. If desired, printing of specific digital documents can be prohibited or limited to designated users. Downloading of digital documents for local storage can likewise be prohibited.

Space Savings

Compared to paper files, digital documents reduce space requirements and costs for in-office storage of large quantities of records. Digital documents can also limit or eliminate continuing purchases of new filing cabinets and supplies. Since the early 1990s, innovations in computer storage technology have dramatically reduced the cost of storing digital information while the cost to store paper documents has remained steady or risen a bit as prices for certain filing equipment and supplies have increased. Straightforward calculations confirm the cost advantages of storing documents digitally. A four-drawer letter-size vertical filing cabinet requires about eight square-feet of floor space, costs about $300, and can store approximately 12,000 pages. When stored as digitized images on a hard drive, the same quantity of documents will occupy about 600 megabytes of computer storage space, which costs less than $2.50. Stored as character-coded text, 12,000 single-spaced typewritten pages will occupy about 40 megabytes of hard drive space at a cost of less than 20 cents.

Document Conservation and Backup

In government agencies, corporations, and other organizations, certain paper documents are subject to physical wear and tear due to frequent retrieval, photocopying, or other handling. This wear and tear is especially the case with documents—such as deeds, mortgages, employee records, birth and death records, technical manuals, and engineering drawings—that may be handled repeatedly over a period of many years. Digital documents, by contrast, are not physically handled by users. Consequently, digital document technology can prevent damage to important records and limit further damage to older documents.

Digital document technology also provides a convenient method for creating backup copies of essential documents through duplication and offsite storage at remote locations. Compared to paper records, digital documents can be duplicated much more quickly and economically. Magnetic tapes and optical disks are inexpensive backup media. The resulting backup copies also occupy less space in offsite storage.

Automated Workflow

Although the previously cited benefits address traditional records management concerns about the organization, storage, retrieval, and protection of recorded information, digital document technologies can also improve the efficiency and effectiveness of an organization's business processes. Broadly defined, a **business process** consists of interrelated activities and procedures that accomplish a specific objective such as the completion of transactions, creation of products, or performance of services. Recordkeeping is an integral aspect of every business process. Of particular relevance for this discussion, certain business processes require the routing of documents among authorized persons in a prescribed sequence in order to complete transactions or other operations. In a bank, for example, mortgage applications and supporting documents, such as credit reports and property appraisals, are typically routed from loan officers to underwriters and others for review, approval, and preparation of customer notifications and loan agreements. Documents requiring special attention may be referred to supervisors or fraud-prevention personnel, accompanied by the loan officer's questions or comments. Similar document routing requirements are encountered in insurance claims processing, customer order fulfillment, loan payment processing, accounts payable, enrollment processing, and other transaction-based activities that require review of documents by multiple persons.

Performed manually, document routing procedures are subject to errors and delays. Documents may be referred to the wrong parties or lost in transit. Recipients may fail to act on received documents in a timely manner, thereby delaying the completion of transactions or tasks. Supervisors are often unaware of problems until customers complain about them. Digital document technologies address these difficulties through automated workflow capabilities, which route documents electronically and monitor the progress of specific activities to ensure timely completion of transactions or tasks.

As defined by the Workflow Management Coalition, a nonprofit group concerned with workflow standards and practices, **workflow** automates the routing of documents among designated recipients according to user-defined rules and relationships. Workflow capabilities are incorporated into many digital document software products. They are often implemented in the context of business process reengineering, which involves the analysis and improvement of existing methods of accomplishing specific operational objectives. In addition to speeding the completion of transactions, workflow implementations can streamline business procedures and eliminate unnecessary work steps. Photocopying and hand delivery of routed documents will be discontinued or minimized. Because workflow software maintains an audit trail for routed documents, and supervisors can be automatically notified when specific tasks are completed or delayed, supervision will be improved as well.

Document Distribution

Because digital documents are accessible online, document distribution procedures can be automated. Organizations need not produce multiple copies of documents for manual distribution to employees or others. Instead, digital document can be routed automatically to designated recipients as e-mail attachments. Alternatively, digital documents intended for a specific audience can be stored in shared folders or posted on Internet or intranet web sites for viewing or downloading, with password protection if controlled access is desired. If documents are accessible online, photocopying requirements and costs will be reduced. Faxing of documents will likewise be minimized or simplified. If e-mail distribution is unacceptable, software can transmit digital documents to designated fax machines. The documents need not be printed prior to faxing.

Issues and Concerns

Digital document technology offers a completely computerized alternative to paper recordkeeping systems. As such, it is an extension of innovations in office automation that, since the 1970s, have computerized commonly encountered office tasks. Not surprisingly, the potential market for digital document products and services is enormous. Ultimately, it encompasses every business, government agency, not-for-profit institution, or other organization that maintains paper files or uses microfilm for any purpose. In this respect, digital document technology occupies the same position in relation to paper filing that word processing technology once did in relation to typewriting. Like word processing, digital document technology automates a pervasive and necessary office operation that has significant limitations when performed manually. Paper documents are difficult to organize, store, retrieve, control, protect, and distribute.

Since the 1980s, digital imaging, text retrieval, and document management products have been successfully implemented in thousands of applications. Yet, compared to word processing at the same stage in its developmental history, digital document technology is underutilized, even in organizations that make extensive use of computers for other purposes. Although digital document products and services have been commercially available for more than two decades, paper recordkeeping remains widespread. Within twenty years of its introduction, word processing technology had virtually supplanted conventional typewriters. Where they are still encountered, typewriters are relegated to occasional tasks such as the preparation of envelopes and business forms. By contrast, filing cabinets remain commonplace fixtures in modern offices. Although government agencies, corporations, professional service firms, academic institutions, healthcare facilities, and other organizations create millions of documents digitally each year, many are printed out for filing, retrieval, and retention.

This practice may be regressive, but it is not inexplicable. Over the past two decades, significant questions have been raised about the records management implications and limitations of retaining documents digitally rather than in paper form or on microfilm. Records managers and others responsible for the retention of information needed for legal reasons, operational uses, or other purposes are understandably concerned about the continued acceptability and viability of digital documents over time. The legal status of digital documents has been widely discussed, as has the limited stability of digital storage media and the impact of product obsolescence on the future retrievability of digital documents. Further, the cost of digital document implementations is a longstanding concern. Although digital document technology can reduce costs when compared to paper recordkeeping systems, its implementation often involves substantial initial expenses that can be difficult to justify in some circumstances. The following sections examine these issues and concerns. Specific points are discussed more fully, where applicable, in subsequent chapters.

Legally Mandated Recordkeeping Requirements

Space savings through elimination of paper files and cost reduction through discontinuation of microfilming operations are frequently cited motives for digital document implementations. Such motives assume the substitution of digital documents for original paper records or microfilm copies. Specifically, word processing documents, e-mail messages, CAD-generated drawings, and other records that originate in digital form will be retained electronically rather than printed out for retention, while paper records will be scanned then discarded following inspection of digitized images. Microfilm operations, where they exist, will be discontinued in favor of electronic document imaging. If these substitutions are not legally acceptable, paper copies must be retained and/or microfilming operations continued.

Since the early 1980s, two concerns about the legal status and associated records management implications of digital documents have been widely expressed:

1. Various legal statutes and government regulations specify recordkeeping requirements and retention periods for documents associated with particular business activities. Corporations, government agencies, and other organizations want reasonable assurance that digital documents will satisfy those recordkeeping requirements to which they are subject.

2. Corporations, government agencies, and organizations retain certain documents for their possible use as evidence in litigation, government investigations, administrative hearings, and other judicial or quasi-judicial proceedings. They want reasonable assurance that digital documents, or printouts made from them, will be admissible as evidence in such situations.

These concerns are obviously greatest where paper documents are destroyed following creation of digital versions or, in the case of documents that originate in digital form, are not produced at all. In such situations, digital documents are the only available versions to satisfy evidentiary or recordkeeping requirements. As discussed elsewhere in this book, space savings through elimination of paper files and cost reduction through discontinuation of microfilming operations are frequently cited justifications for digital document implementations. Such justifications assume the substitution of digital documents for original paper records or microfilm copies. If such substitution is not legally acceptable, paper copies must be retained and/or microfilm operations continued. Anticipated cost savings will be reduced or forfeited.

Operational Retention Requirements

Legal considerations aside, records managers are understandably concerned about the ability of digital documents to satisfy their organizations' operational retention requirements, which are based on the concept of an information life cycle. Decades of records management theory and practice indicate that the operational value of many, if not most, records varies inversely with the age of the records. Typically, records maintained by businesses, government agencies, and other organizations are referenced frequently for a relatively brief period of time following their creation or receipt. As the records age, reference activity diminishes, either gradually or abruptly. When, and if, reference activity falls to zero, the records may be discarded. Operational requirements are often longer than legally mandated recordkeeping requirements. Multidecade operational retention periods are common, and indefinite or permanent retention may be specified for some records series.

Potentially significant complications can affect the implementation of digital document technology in applications with long operational retention requirements. To satisfy such requirements, digital documents must be retrievable and usable for the entire retention period of a records series. The continued retrievability of digital documents and their associated index data is obviously affected by the stability of media on which such documents and index data are recorded. It also requires the continued availability of compatible hardware and software components for document searching, display, printing, and other retrieval operations. These complications are not unique to digital document implementations; they are encountered in all information management applications that involve electronic records.

As discussed in subsequent chapters, digital documents and their associated index data may be stored on magnetic or optical media. **Stability estimates**, also termed *lifetime estimates* or *life spans*, define the time periods during which such media will support reliable retrieval of recorded information. With computer storage media, reliability is determined by the preservation of signal strength and the absence of permanent read/write errors during recording and playback of information. Stability estimates are principally applicable to storage copies of digital documents and index data recorded on removable media such as optical disks and magnetic tapes. Although hard drives can provide rapid, convenient access to actively referenced documents and index data, they are not stable storage media. Incorporated into computer hardware, hard drives are replaced at relatively short intervals and, while operating, are subject to damage from head crashes or other equipment malfunctions. For secure retention, digital documents and index information recorded on hard drives must be copied onto removable media for offline storage. Such storage copies should be referenced as little as possible. Working copies of any medium can be damaged by use.

The stability of a given information storage medium depends on several factors, including the medium's chemical composition and the conditions under which it is stored and used. Although optical disks and magnetic tapes are sometimes described as *archival media*, they do not offer the permanence implied in that description. On the contrary, optical disks and magnetic tapes are vulnerable to significant time-dependent degradation that eventually will render them unsuitable for accurate retrieval of recorded information. Such changes may be induced by environmental effects or by defects associated with media manufacturing. Further, digital documents and index data recorded on optical disks and magnetic tapes can be damaged by improper media handling. Obvious problems arise where the lifetime estimate for a given medium is shorter than the retention period for digital documents and index data the medium contains.

As an added complication, electronic storage media are designed for use with specific hardware and software components that usually have shorter service lives than the media themselves. To preserve the utility of previously recorded media, new products may offer backward compatibility for reading purposes; that is, they can retrieve information from media recorded by predecessor models in a given manufacturer's product line, but manufacturers do not guarantee that such compatibility will be continued in all future products. Eventually, support for older media and recording formats will be phased out.

Lifetime estimates for specific magnetic and optical storage media and the continued viability of particular recording formats is discussed in subsequent chapters, but their significance for records retention is open to argument. Regardless of the media on which they are stored, digital documents are intended for retrieval by specific application software. Even more than hardware components, software may be updated or otherwise changed in a manner that can render previously recorded information unusable. The latest releases of a given vendor's application programs may not be able to read digital documents produced by earlier versions. This incompatibility can occur within several years of the initial implementation of a given product. The readability of digital documents can be extended indefinitely by periodically converting them to new media or formats—a process termed *data migration*. As discussed in a later chapter, however, the resources required to migrate data can significantly increase the cost of retaining digital documents.

Cost and Justification

Although the costs of hardware and software components discussed in this book have declined steadily and significantly since the 1990s, digital document implementations can involve significant start-up and ongoing costs, which must be accurately identified and incorporated into project and operational budgets. This issue is discussed more fully in Chapter 6 and Appendix B, which presents worksheets for calculating costs for digital document implementations involving electronic document images and character-coded documents.

To be justified, electronic document imaging must ultimately have an impact on an organization's bottom line. Digital document technologies are often presented as economical alternatives to outmoded precomputer approaches to document storage and retrieval, but cost justification is far from certain in every situation. Determination of cost-effectiveness and return-on-investment requires a detailed comparison of digital document costs and benefits in relation to costs and limitations associated with the paper files and micrographic systems that digital documents will supplant. These issues are examined and examples are provided in Chapter 6.

Chapter 2

Creating Digital Documents

Many digital documents are created by word processing programs, e-mail systems, presentation software, spreadsheet programs, computer-aided design software, or other computer applications. Such documents are sometimes described as *born digital.* The indexing, storage, and retrieval concepts described in subsequent chapters can be applied directly to them. More problematic are the many situations in which digital documents must be produced from nondigital sources such as paper documents and microfilm images. These nondigital records include correspondence, memoranda, reports, engineering drawings, and other documents that predate the widespread implementation of word processing and e-mail technology, as well as new records associated with paper-intensive business operations. Although a very high percentage of internal documents may be created in digital form, most organizations continue to receive paper records from external sources. These nondigital records can be scanned for storage and retrieval as digital images. Alternatively, they can be converted to character-coded form by key-entry or optical character recognition. In either case, the creation of digital documents from nondigital sources can be a complicated, time-consuming, and costly undertaking.

This chapter discusses available technologies and procedures for creating digital documents from paper or microfilm records—a process sometimes described as *document conversion.* The chapter begins with a survey of preparation, scanning, and related requirements and methods for digital imaging implementations. In particular, it describes the characteristics and capabilities of document scanners—the most important group of input devices in imaging installations. Later sections examine available options for creating character-coded text from nondigital sources. As its title indicates, this chapter's scope is limited to the creation of digital documents. Indexing and index data-entry, important components of input procedures for digital documents in all formats, are discussed in the next chapter.

Creating Document Images

Electronic document images are produced by scanning paper documents or, less commonly, by scanning microform images. Borrowing terminology utilized in microfilming and data-entry, paper documents to be scanned are described as *source documents*. Image production begins with source document preparation followed by scanner operation and inspection of scanned images with rescanning as necessary. The following sections discuss concepts, equipment, software, and procedures associated with these work steps.

Document Preparation

Document preparation is the essential prelude to creation of electronic document images. Its purpose is to make documents *scanner ready*—that is, to put documents into a condition and sequence appropriate for scanning. Well-prepared source documents are critical to efficient operation of document scanners, effective deployment of scanning labor, and consistent production of usable electronic images.

In most cases, source documents are prepared for scanning in batches. Batch size is determined by application characteristics. In low-volume imaging applications, newly created or received documents may be prepared at a specific time each day or when a sufficient number of pages accumulate. In high-volume imaging installations, document preparation is often a continuous activity. Multiple workers may be dedicated to preparation, while others operate document scanners or perform related production tasks such as image inspection or entry of index data.

All source documents require some preparation, however, specific work steps depend on application requirements, file organization, the physical condition and other attributes of source documents, the type of scanner to be used, and other factors. At a minimum, correspondence, memoranda, project reports, case files, and other office records must be removed from file cabinets, folders, or other containers; unfolded if necessary; and stacked neatly in the correct sequence for scanning. Some document scanners require removal of staples and paper clips from source documents. Even when not required, removal of such fasteners is generally advisable; it improves the productivity of scanner operators and enhances the appearance of electronic document images.

Some source documents are more difficult or time-consuming to prepare than others. Older office records, for example, may be crowded into boxes that must be retrieved from warehouses, basements, closets, or other storage areas and properly identified prior to scanning. Engineering drawings, architectural plans, maps, charts, and other large documents can be awkward to handle. Often rolled for storage, they must be flattened before scanning. Older drawings and maps may be in poor condition from years of repeated reference. Brittle or otherwise fragile documents must be handled carefully. Torn pages must be mended or photocopied prior to scanning.

Post-it™ notes attached to documents may be taped into place or affixed to separate pages. Small sheets of paper, such as message slips, should likewise be taped to larger pages. Very thin pages may need to be photocopied for scanning by the sheetfed devices described later in this chapter. For best image quality and operator productivity, books, reports, catalogs, and other bound documents should be unbound prior to scanning. If unbinding is impractical or impossible (as with rare books, for example), specially designed book scanners are available, but they are expensive. Developed for libraries, some models feature automatic page-turning; even then, scanning bound volumes requires more time and effort than scanning unbound pages.

In certain applications, specially prepared separator sheets must be inserted between documents to identify related groups of scanner-ready pages. Separator sheets are often used with individual patient files in medical records applications, individual student files in educational applications, individual case files in legal applications, and books, reports, or other multipage documents. Sometimes, the separator sheets identify double-sided pages or instruct the scanner operator to treat multiple pages as a unit for indexing or recording on specific media. Alternatively, divider sheets called *targets* may contain identifying information that is scanned before the pages to which they pertain. In a medical records application, for example, a target may indicate the name of the patient whose file is being scanned, the date the scanning was performed, and the number of pages in the file. Depending on the software utilized, separator pages may contain barcodes that change scanner settings or initiate specific scanner actions without operator intervention.

Special requirements and precautions aside, preparation of source documents is one of the most time-consuming and labor-intensive aspects of image production. Unlike other activities described in this chapter, document preparation tasks must be performed manually. Their efficient execution depends on the skill, attentiveness, and motivation of workers to whom they are assigned. Clear procedures and appropriate supervision are consequently essential. Even when preparation is limited to removal of staples and paper clips, sustained operator productivity will rarely exceed 1,000 pages per hour for office records in good condition. At that rate, the contents of one file cabinet drawer (approximately 2,500 pages) will require about 2.5 hours of preparation time, which is equivalent to the throughput rate for certain types of document scanners. Older source documents that may be in more variable condition than newer office records will consequently take longer to prepare—750 to 800 pages per hour are realistic productivity expectations for such documents. Preparation of a one million-page backfile of older records packed in boxes will require at least 1,250 hours of labor.

These estimates of preparation effort are based on the assumption that source documents will be scanned as they are filed without misfile detection, rearrangement, purging of unneeded records, or other evaluation of files or documents for correctness or completeness. If the sequence of pages within a file must be changed or if files must be checked for misplaced or missing pages prior to scanning, preparation time will escalate dramatically. At first glance, purging files of unneeded records prior to scanning may seem advisable. Many files contain multiple copies of documents as well as records with trivial information content. Purging these items can lower image production costs by reducing the number of documents to be scanned. Labor requirements and supply consumption will be correspondingly reduced for image inspection, data-entry, and recording.

Often, however, purging unneeded records increases preparation time without increasing value. To justify purging, any savings that result from the elimination of unneeded records must exceed the labor cost to identify and remove those records. Unfortunately, the required savings may not be attainable. In many applications, knowledgeable persons must examine source documents individually to determine whether they should be scanned or purged. Document content must be evaluated for relevance and future utility, ideally in conformity with predefined retention guidelines. Even the identification of duplicate records can be complicated by the presence of potentially important annotations on one or more copies. This evaluation of individual documents is a time-consuming process. It is also a potentially wasteful activity: If a document is evaluated for purging but retained for scanning rather than discarded, nothing is gained. In such situations, the greater preparation labor associated with document evaluation increases total image production costs. Purging of source documents prior to scanning should consequently be limited to those files that are known to contain a large percentage of readily identifiable, easily removable duplicates or other unneeded records.

Document Scanners

Document scanners are computer peripheral devices that convert paper source documents to electronic images suitable for computer processing and storage. The source documents may be typed, printed, handwritten, or hand drawn. They may contain textual or graphic information in black and white, gray tones, or color. The scanning process, properly termed *document digitization,* was described in Chapter 1. Although characteristics and capabilities of specific devices vary, a document scanner divides each page into a grid of small, scannable units that are variously called *picture elements, pixels,* or simply *dots.* Using optical and photosensitive components, the scanner measures the amount of light reflected by successively encountered pixels within a page. It then generates a corresponding electrical signal that is converted into digital bit patterns. The scanner's light source is usually a cold cathode lamp. The photosensitive component is usually a charge coupled device (CCD) array.

The simplest scanning operations involve office records and engineering drawings that contain dark (usually black) text or line art on a light (usually white) background. Such documents are described as *bitonal.* When digitizing them, document scanners use a zero or one bit to encode each pixel as white or black, depending on the reflectivity. Multibit coding is used to represent gray tones or colors.

As image capture devices, document scanners are the conceptual counterparts of the rotary, planetary, and step-and-repeat cameras employed in microfilm installations. However, unlike microfilm cameras, which record miniaturized document images on photographic film, document scanners do not generate tangible output; nor are they capable of standalone operation. As a computer peripheral device, a document scanner is one component of a scanning workstation that also includes a personal computer, a scanner interface, and software that initiates and controls scanning operations.

As its name implies, an **interface** provides a physical connection between a document scanner and a personal computer, which is usually a Windows-based device.

Depending on the model, a scanner may connect to a personal computer via a USB interface, SCSI interface, or FireWire (IEEE 1394) interface. In any case, a document scanner generates unformatted electronic images that are sometimes described as *raw bit maps*. Image processing programs perform digital coding, compression, enhancement, or other image manipulations required by particular electronic document imaging applications. These programs may reside in read-only memory circuits on a scanner's controller board, or they may be executed by the scanning workstation's personal computer.

In most cases, the scanning workstation's personal computer is equipped with an image-capable monitor suitable for image inspection. Scanning software, which operates on the workstation's personal computer, provides a graphical user interface for scanner set-up and control. It displays information about the status of scanning operations, facilitates image inspection, and formats electronic images for recording on designated computer storage media. The most flexible scanning software will automatically rotate images of documents that were scanned upside down, align images of pages that were skewed during scanning, suppress blemishes and shaded areas within pages, delete blank pages, and adjust scanner settings to accommodate documents of varying color and tonality, thereby improving image quality and minimizing rescanning.

Depending on the system configuration, digitized images may be stored temporarily, pending inspection or other action, on a hard drive within the scanning workstation. In most cases, the scanning workstation ultimately transmits electronic document images to storage devices located elsewhere on a computer network to which the scanning workstation is itself connected.

Document scanners are available in desktop and floor-standing models. During the 1980s, some vendors of electronic document imaging software developed and marketed special scanners for use with their products, but such custom-designed devices are rarely encountered today. Since the 1990s, electronic document imaging vendors have redirected their product research and development activities toward software rather than hardware components. They routinely support and resell scanners developed by peripheral equipment manufacturers. Such scanners are not developed exclusively or even principally for records management applications. To reach the broadest market, scanner manufacturers design their products for a variety of information management activities, including desktop publishing, web page construction, facsimile transmission, form-based data-entry, optical character recognition, and digitization of engineering drawings for processing by CAD software. Although they are outside the scope of this discussion, such applications constitute an important segment of the document scanner market.

Once considered exotic input devices, document scanners are now commonplace peripherals in computer configurations of all types and sizes. Since the early 1990s, document scanners have improved steadily and significantly in product availability, variety, and functionality. Most manufacturers offer a range of models with different cost / performance attributes to address specific customer requirements. Document imaging system vendors typically offer a choice of products, and scanners of different types and manufacturers are often intermingled in a given imaging installation. Thus, an electronic document imaging configuration might include desktop scanners for low-to-medium volume departmental applications, high-speed floor-standing models for production-intensive installations, duplex scanners for applications that involve two-sided pages, flatbed scanners for bound volumes, and large-format scanners for engineering drawings. The following discussion surveys the capabilities and operating characteristics of document scanners employed in electronic document imaging implementations, emphasizing the features and functions most important for records management applications.

Sheetfed vs. Flatbed Scanners

Document scanners are available in sheetfed and flatbed configurations. Sheetfed scanners are sometimes described as *pass-through* or *pull-through scanners*. Pages to be scanned are inserted into a narrow opening from which they are transported individually across a scanning mechanism that includes optical and photosensitive components. Depending on equipment design, the scanned pages are ejected at the back or bottom of the machine. With several models, the ejected pages are conveniently stacked face down in the same sequence in which they were inserted.

A **flatbed scanner**, as its name indicates, features a flat exposure surface on which pages are individually positioned for scanning. (See Figure 2.1.) Most models feature a glass platen on which pages are placed face down, the scanning components being located beneath the glass surface. Much less commonly, flatbed scanners may employ an overhead design in which individual pages are positioned face up for digitization by optical and photosensitive components positioned at the top of a vertical column. Such devices resemble planetary microfilmers in appearance and operation.

Sheetfed scanners, which have dominated electronic document imaging implementations since the industry's inception, are recommended for most records management applications. (See Figure 2.2.) Compared to flatbed scanning, sheetfed operation is faster and yields higher labor productivity; typically, pages can be inserted into a sheetfed scanner's transport mechanism at a much faster rate than they can be positioned on a flatbed scanner's glass platen. (A similar situation prevails in micrographics applications where rotary microfilmers, the counterparts of sheetfed

Flatbed Scanner
(Courtesy: CONTEX)

Figure 2.1

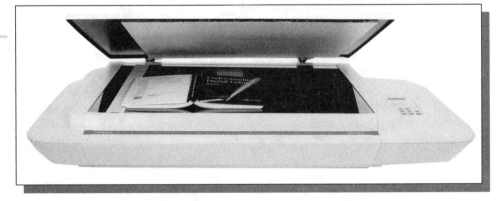

Desktop Sheetfed Scanner

(Courtesy: Eastman Kodak)

Figure 2.2

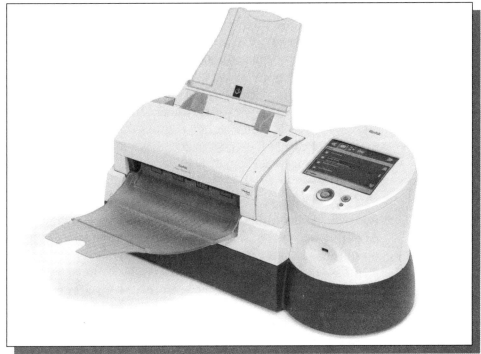

scanners, are much faster than flatbed-style planetary cameras). The productivity advantages of sheetfed scanners vary directly with the volume of pages to be scanned. Flatbed scanners, which tend to be less expensive than sheetfed models, are widely encountered in desktop publishing and web page design where scanning workloads are rarely heavy.

Although seldom preferred to sheetfed devices for digitizing business records, flatbed scanners are employed in some entry-level electronic document imaging configurations intended for low-volume applications. Workload considerations aside, flatbed scanners are necessary for bound volumes or fragile documents. They are consequently used by libraries, manuscript repositories, historical agencies, and other research organizations. Several manufacturers offer special book scanners for such applications. Featuring an overhead design, they incorporate a book cradle with a glass cover that keeps bound pages flat during scanning. For maximum flexibility, some document scanners support both sheetfed and flatbed input methods. An operator can remove or lift the scanner's sheetfeed mechanism to reveal a flat glass surface on which bound volumes or fragile documents can be positioned.

With sheetfed or flatbed devices, individual pages must be individually inserted into a transport mechanism or positioned on a flat surface for scanning. To minimize operator involvement, most document scanners can be equipped with an automatic page feeder as a standard feature or optional accessory. Designed as a multipage stacker, an automatic feeder permits unattended image capture in applications where documents will be scanned in batches. Most often associated with sheetfed scanners, automatic page feeders are supported by some flatbed models as well. Feeder capacities range from 50 pages for inexpensive models to several thousand pages for scanners intended for very high-volume applications; medium-to-high-volume scanners are typically equipped with 100-, 200-, or 500-page feeders.

Depending on the model, an automatic page feeder may restrict the sizes and thickness of input documents. Some automatic page feeders will operate reliably only with letter-size office papers. Others can accept documents in mixed page sizes and thicknesses, but they are not immune to misfeeding, jamming, and skewing. Automatic feeders for check-size documents are available for banking applications. Most automatic feeders can be bypassed for manual insertion of individual pages.

Input Sizes

Automatic feeders aside, all document scanners impose restrictions on the sizes of pages they can accept. Some manufacturers of sheetfed scanners specify a minimum document size for reliable operation, although this restriction may be circumvented by using a transparent document carrier or by affixing a small page to a larger sheet of paper. Some scanners can accept pages as small as two inches square. Others impose a lower limit of A5-size (5.8 by 8.3 inches), A6-size (4.1 by 4.8 inches), or A7-size (2.8 by 4.1 inches) pages. Because pages as small as A7-size are infrequently employed for office documents, these minimum-size restrictions are seldom constraining; for most records management applications, limitations on maximum page sizes are more significant.

Among sheetfed scanners for office applications, most models can accommodate A3-size pages (approximately 11 by 17 inches), the largest paper size routinely employed for business records. With flatbed scanners, the size of the glass platen or other exposure surface determines the maximum page size. The least expensive models limit input documents to 8.5 by 11 inches or smaller. Some flatbed scanners can accommodate A3-size pages, however.

Documents larger than A3-size require a special type of image capture device called a *large-format document scanner*. Such devices are principally intended for engineering drawings, architectural schematics, maps, charts, and other large pages. Depending on the model, a large-format scanner may accept documents up to A0-size (approximately 33 by 44 inches), the equivalent of an E-size engineering drawing. To accommodate oversize drawings, a few models can scan pages that measure up to 50 inches wide by any reasonable length.

Large-format document scanners, such as the one shown in Figure 2.3, are sheetfed devices. The number and variety of available models has increased significantly in recent years. The selection of large-format document scanners is much greater than the selection of microfilm cameras for engineering drawings. In addition to electronic document imaging implementations, large-format scanners are used for conversion of engineering drawings for editing or other processing by CAD programs and geographical information systems (GIS). They can also function as large document copiers, replacing xerographic devices and out-dated diazo printers.

Sheetfed Scanner
for Engineering
Drawings and
Other Large-
Format
Documents

(Courtesy: CONTEX)

Figure 2.3

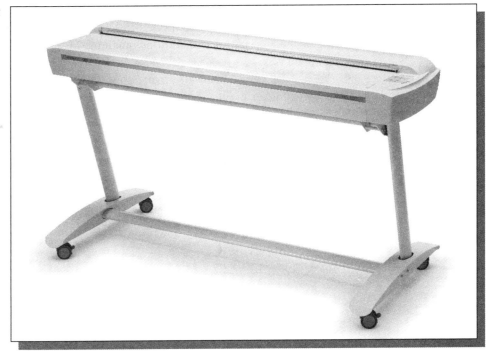

Grayscale and Color

The simplest electronic document imaging applications involve bitonal office records and engineering drawings, which contain dark text or line art on a light background. Scanners that digitize such documents operate in the binary or one-bit mode, so-called because it employs a single bit to encode each pixel. Most document scanners intended for records management applications are binary-mode devices. As their principal limitation, **binary-mode scanners** do not preserve gray tones and colors within source documents. They encode gray tones or colors as either black or white, depending on their relative lightness or darkness. The resulting loss of tonality is rarely significant in business applications, where gray tones and color are absent or merely decorative. In some cases, the omission of color may even be desirable, as when multipart business forms that contain blue text on colored paper are converted to high contrast black-on-white images.

To accommodate photographs and other documents that contain grayscale information, some binary-mode scanners can operate in a half-tone mode. They employ a technique called *dithering* to simulate shades of gray by combining adjacent black and white pixels into blocks. Where a more faithful rendering of gray tones is desired, true **grayscale scanners** employ multiple bits to represent gray pixels. The number of gray shades that a given scanner can reproduce depends on the number of bits used to encode each pixel. Eight-bit scanners, the most popular configuration, can differentiate 256 shades of gray. For maximum flexibility, grayscale scanners can also operate in the binary mode; some models support dithering as well.

Compared to dithering, multibit coding of pixels yields a more accurate representation of photographs, which is advantageous in desktop publishing and computer graphics applications where grayscale images may be edited, resized, or otherwise manipulated. Such image editing is rarely required, and may not be desired, in records management applications, however. Furthermore, grayscale scanning can have an adverse impact on other aspects of system operation. It is slower than binary-mode scanning, and multibit coding of pixels yields images that require significantly more storage space than binary-mode images. All other things being equal, for example, an eight-bit grayscale image of a photograph will require eight times more storage space than a dithered binary-mode representation of the same document.

Binary-mode and grayscale scanners can accept colored documents, but they encode specific colors as black, white, or gray, depending on their tonality and the scanning mode employed. True color scanners are specifically designed to recognize and encode color information within pages. Like grayscale scanners, they utilize multiple bits to encode each pixel. As explained in Chapter 1, most models employ 24 bits per pixel, which can represent almost 16.8 million different colors. Until the mid-1990s, color scanners were limited in availability, intended principally for graphic arts applications, and very expensive. Since that time, however, flatbed, desktop color scanners have become widely available at low prices. In most cases, these devices are bundled with image editing software.

As input devices, inexpensive color scanners are better suited to desktop publishing, web page design, and the preparation of presentation aids than to high-volume creation of digital documents. Because pixels are more extensively encoded, color scanners are usually slower than binary-mode devices, although speeds have improved since the 1990s. In recent years, several manufacturers have introduced production-level models that can scan a letter-size page in several seconds. Some products can differentiate between colored and bitonal documents to automatically activate the appropriate scanning mode. An operator can adjust the color detection threshold to limit color mode scanning to pages with significant color content. As an additional complication, images digitized in the 24-bit color mode require significantly more storage space than binary-mode or grayscale images.

Scanning Resolution

Broadly defined, **resolution** is a measure of the capability to delineate picture detail. As previously described, a scanner divides a source document into a grid of pixels, each of which is sampled for its light reflectance characteristics. The scanning resolution denotes the specific pattern and number of pixels sampled during the scanning process. Scanning resolution is usually measured and expressed as the number of pixels or dots per inch or millimeter within a scanned page—200 dots per inch (dpi) or eight dots per millimeter, for example. For a given page, the horizontal and vertical scanning resolutions are measured and expressed separately. In desktop publishing and computer graphics applications, horizontal and vertical resolutions often differ for a scanned page. In most digital document implementations, however, the scanning resolution is identical for horizontal and vertical dimensions. In such cases, one resolution measurement is stated, and it is assumed to apply to both the horizontal and vertical dimensions of the scanned page.

A few document scanners are limited to a single resolution, but most support more than one. The possibilities range from less than 50 dots per inch to more than 1,200 dots per inch, although not all scanners support that broad range, nor is the entire range appropriate for the digital document applications discussed in this book. Surprisingly, the least expensive desktop scanners, intended for low-volume applications, often support the broadest range of resolutions. Their principal market is desktop or web-based publishing where resolution requirements can vary considerably. Large-format scanners, which convert documents to electronic images for processing by CAD or GIS software, likewise support a varied range of resolutions. Most models can operate at one or more resolutions exceeding 400 dots per inch.

As an increasingly popular approach to document digitization, some scanners support a stated maximum resolution through hardware capabilities while permitting higher resolutions through software-based interpolation, a form of image processing. Resolutions supported by scanning hardware are described as **optical resolutions**. Employing image analysis algorithms, interpolation software adds pixels to electronic document images following scanning, thereby increasing their effective resolution. Thus, a given document scanner may support a maximum optical resolution of 400 dots per inch, but interpolation of digitized images can yield a maximum effective resolution of 800 dots per inch. Interpolated resolution is not necessarily greater than its optical counterpart. Interpolation software can decrease as well as increase resolution. Some newer document scanners support a single optical resolution and rely on interpolation to produce higher or lower **output resolutions**. Thus, an optical scanning resolution of 400 dpi may yield output resolutions ranging from 100 dpi through 800 dpi.

Document characteristics that influence the choice of resolution are described in ANSI/AIIM MS52, *Recommended Practice for the Requirements and Characteristics of Original Documents Intended for Optical Scanning*. Drafting practices that may affect the scanning of engineering drawings are discussed in ISO 3098-0, *Technical Product Documentation—Lettering—Part 0: General Requirements*; ISO 3098-2, *Technical Drawings—Lettering—Part 2: Latin Alphabet, Numerals, and Marks*; and ASME Y14.2M, *Line Conventions and Lettering*. If all documents had black text printed on white paper of uniform opacity in sans serif, 12-point type without italics or hairlines, legible reproduction at high resolutions would pose few problems. Most organizations, however, have no control over the physical characteristics of documents to be scanned. Office files routinely intermingle original documents produced by laser or inkjet printers, older typewritten documents, second- or third-generation photocopies, carbon copies of business forms, faxes, and paper enlargements produced from microforms. New office records pose fewer problems than backfiles, which may contain documents produced by manual typewriters or obsolete photocopying processes. Similarly, older engineering drawings may exist only in poor-quality blueline or sepia copies. Library documents, which may be acquired over many decades from a variety of sources, exhibit the most varied physical and typographic characteristics. Many books and periodicals contain important information printed in small, delicate type fonts. For documents printed in non-Roman alphabets, accent marks and ideographic characters can be particularly difficult to reproduce.

Resolution requirements for document scanning in records management applications have changed little since the early 1980s. Records managers generally agree that 200 dpi is the minimum scanning resolution required for consistently legible reproduction of most office records and engineering drawings. All scanners intended for such documents can consequently operate at 200 dpi. Lower resolutions are seldom appropriate for records management applications because they cannot legibly reproduce information printed in small type sizes. Where supported by a given document scanner they are rarely utilized for storage and retrieval of textual records, although lower resolutions may be acceptable for photographs or illustrations.

Most document scanners can operate at 300 dpi for applications where higher image quality is required or desired; for example, where electronic document images will be processed by OCR software. Most OCR programs require a minimum scanning resolution of 300 dpi for satisfactory performance. Some government regulations specify a minimum scanning resolution of 300 dpi for electronic document imaging implementations that involve certain public records. Several document scanners also support a scanning resolution of 240 dpi, which was employed in some electronic document imaging installations during the 1980s, but it is less commonly encountered today. Where multiple resolutions are supported by a given document scanner, they are operator-selectable through hardware controls, such as switches mounted on the scanner's front panel, or, more commonly, through the scanning workstation's software.

An increasing number of document scanners can operate at 400 dpi (the familiar triad of 200, 300, and 400 dpi is supported by a number of models), 600 dpi, 800 dpi, 1000 dpi, or greater, but such high resolutions are seldom required or desired in records management applications. Appropriateness for display or printing of document images is an important consideration in the choice of scanning resolution. As discussed elsewhere in this book, the resolution of image display devices rarely exceeds 200 dpi and is often considerably lower than that number. Documents scanned at higher resolutions must consequently be adjusted or scaled to lower resolutions for display purposes. In such situations, the greater image detail provided by higher scanning resolutions is lost in display.

By contrast, printers routinely support resolutions of 600 dpi, 1200 dpi, or greater. The increasing availability of such printers at competitive prices may stimulate an interest in high scanning resolutions where printout quality is a critical consideration. To date, however, interest in high scanning resolutions for document storage and retrieval has been confined to certain library and archival applications where digital documents will serve as preservation copies of valuable research materials. Such applications typically distinguish **access resolution**, which is suitable for display or printing, from **preservation resolution**, which provides a very high-quality reproduction of source documents. Preservation resolution typically ranges from 600 dpi to 1,200 dpi, depending on type sizes, page contrast, and other document characteristics. As discussed elsewhere in this book, such high resolutions have potentially adverse impacts on other aspects of system operation. In particular, image storage requirements and transmission times over computer networks vary directly with resolution.

Resolution concepts are not unique to document scanning. They also apply to micrographics technology. As discussed in *ANSI/AIIM TR26, Resolution as It Relates to Photographic and Electronic Imaging*, resolution is an important quality determinant that denotes the sharpness of document images, but the term has different, potentially confusing connotations in scanning and microfilming. Although *scanning resolution* is measured in dots per inch or millimeter, *micrographics resolution* is expressed in lines or line pairs per millimeter (ll/mm) that are discernable within a microfilm image. *Microfilm resolution* is determined by examining a microfilm image of a specially designed test chart and performing specified calculations. For microfilm images reduced 24x, readily attainable resolution measurements range from 70 to 100 lines per millimeter for rotary cameras and 120 to 150 lines per millimeter for planetary cameras. Comparisons of the most common resolutions employed in document scanning and microfilming installations generally favor micrographics technology. To approximately equate scanning resolution with microfilm resolution at 24x reduction, a given scanning resolution, in dots per inch, can be divided by 3 or a given microfilm resolution, in lines per millimeter, can be multiplied by 3. Thus, a scanning resolution of 300 dots per inch is equivalent to a microfilm resolution of 100 lines per millimeter, which is considered good image quality by micrographics specialists. The widely employed scanning resolution of 200 dots per inch equates to a microfilm resolution of just 67 lines per inch, which is considered fair-to-poor image quality by micrographics specialists. To match microfilm resolutions of 120 to 150 lines per millimeter, which are considered excellent image quality by micrographic specialists, scanning resolutions must range from 360 to 450 dots per inch.

Resolution measures the capability to capture fine details in document images. The foregoing numeric comparisons suggest that microfilm images are sharper than their digital counterparts, but image evaluation is a highly subjective activity with little agreement among observers. Although sharpness is important, the legibility of document images is influenced by other factors. In particular, high contrast, which is characteristic of digitized images displayed on computer monitors, can significantly enhance appearance at low resolutions.

Scanning Speed

Since the early 1980s, records managers and others responsible for the implementation of electronic document imaging systems have complained about the time and associated labor required to scan large quantities of documents. Although scanning is a time-consuming, labor-intensive procedure that accounts for a significant component of operating costs in document imaging implementations, the technology continues to evolve and improve. Measured by rated speed, newer document scanners at a given price-point are faster than models available in the 1990s.

A scanner's **rated speed** is the elapsed time required to convert one page to a digitized image from the moment the page is positioned for scanning until digitization is completed. In their technical specification sheets, manufacturers of document scanners indicate rated speeds in seconds per page, pages per minute, or, occasionally, inches per second. The rated speed of a given scanner depends on the device's mechanical characteristics, as well as such application-specific factors as digitization mode, scanning resolution, and page size. In most cases, rated speeds cited by scanner manufacturers are based on letter-size pages digitized in the binary mode at a scanning resolution of 200 dots per inch. Binary-mode scanning is faster than grayscale or color scanning. A device that can scan 20 letter-size pages per minute in the binary mode, for example, may only scan five or six pages per minute in the color mode. Some low-cost color scanners can take a half minute or longer to digitize a letter-size page. They are designed for desktop publishing applications where document digitization is an occasional requirement. When a small quantity of source documents is involved, scanning speed is a minor concern.

Because more pixels must be analyzed, a document scanner's rated speed varies directly with the resolution applied to a given page. Depending on the model, an increase in resolution from 200 dpi to 300 dpi will degrade the scanning time per page by 20 to 35 percent. Because they have greater surface areas, large pages take longer to scan than small ones. A scanner that operates at 5.5 inches per second, for example, can digitize a letter-size page in two seconds but will require 3.1 seconds to digitize an A3-size page. Depending on the resolution employed, a large-format scanner can require several minutes to digitize an engineering drawing, architectural schematic, map, chart, or other large document. As with scanners for office records, newer large-format models in a vendor's product line tend to be faster than their predecessors. Several large-format document scanners can digitize an E-size drawing at 200 dpi in less than 30 seconds.

Document scanners for office records can be divided into three broad groups—low-volume, mid-range, and high-volume—based on rated speed and resulting suitability for particular workloads:

1. Requiring up to 30 seconds to digitize a letter-size page, low-volume scanners are suitable for workloads ranging from 50 to 200 pages per day or a maximum of 50,000 pages per year (the equivalent of approximately 20 file drawers), although they are used occasionally rather than steadily in most installations. The most popular models are flatbed devices. Color mode and grayscale capabilities are standard features. Low-volume scanners are commonplace input peripherals in personal computer configurations. Their principal applications are desktop publishing, web-based publishing, OCR, PC-based facsimile transmission, and digitization of photographs for processing by image-editing software. Low-volume scanners are less useful for records management applications, although some electronic document imaging installations include a low-volume scanner as an auxiliary digitizer for documents that require flatbed operation or color-mode scanning.

2.   Faster scanners are invariably sheetfed, although some models can also operate in the flatbed mode. Mid-range scanners are intended for workgroup or departmental installations. They have rated speeds of two or three seconds per letter-size page (20 to 30 pages per minute) when operating in the binary mode at 200 dpi. Depending on the model, they can support workloads up to 4,000 pages per day, or up one million pages per year (the equivalent of approximately 200 file drawers). Some mid-range scanners operate in the binary mode exclusively, but grayscale and color models are increasingly available.

3.   High-volume document scanners are designed for production-intensive work environments such as document imaging service bureaus and centralized scanning departments within large organizations. Equipped with high-capacity document feeders, their rated speeds from less than one second to 1.5 seconds per letter page (40 pages to more than 80 pages per minute) when operating in the binary mode at 200 dpi. Engineered for reliable operation under heavy workloads, they can digitize 10,000 pages per day or 2.5 million pages per year (the equivalent of approximately 500 to 1,000 file drawers). A high-volume sheetfed scanner is shown in Figure 2.4.

Rated speed, as defined above, measures just one part of the scanning process—the time required to sample pixels within a scanned page. **Scanning throughput**, by contrast, measures the total time required to produce a serviceable digitized image from a scanned page. Scanning throughput is affected by various factors, including the scanning workstation's host computer, the type of scanner interface employed, software characteristics, and operator efficiency. Throughput is also affected by specific image processing routines that follow scanning. Such post-scanning routines—which include image compression, enhancement, and formatting—can require several seconds to

High-Speed Sheetfed Scanner Intended for High-Volume Application

(Courtesy: Eastman Kodak)

Figure 2.4

complete. As a general rule, the attainable and sustainable throughput for a given document scanner will be about one-half the rated speed measured in pages per minute or two to three times the rated speed measured in seconds per page. Therefore, for a scanner with a rated speed of 30 pages per minute or two seconds per page, attainable and sustainable throughput will likely be about 15 pages per minute (900 pages per hour) or four seconds per page. These estimates are based on properly prepared documents, as previously described.

Even when rated speed is adjusted for sustainable throughput, document scanning is usually the fastest work step in image creation. For a given quantity of pages, document preparation usually takes longer than scanning. For any business process, total throughput time is ultimately determined by the slowest work step. As discussed in Chapter 3, image inspection and index data-entry can add minutes of input time per document.

Duplex Scanners

Simplex scanners, the most commonly encountered variety, can digitize one side of a page at a time. Double-sided pages must be turned over and repositioned for scanning. Some electronic document imaging systems employ software-based techniques to minimize the resulting inconvenience. As an example, the top sides in a stack of double-sided pages may be scanned in sequence. The stack is then turned over and the opposite sides are scanned in the reverse direction. Software automatically links the related sides. Single-sided scanners can operate acceptably in electronic document imaging applications that involve occasional double-sided pages. **Duplex scanners,** which digitize both sides of a page at the same time, are preferred for applications in which two-sided pages predominate. Such devices typically feature two sets of optical and photosensitive components located on opposite sides of the scanner's paper path. All duplex scanners are sheetfed in operation.

Duplex scanners are typically designed for high-volume, production-intensive applications. Their rated speeds are measured in pages per minute in the simplex mode and images per minute in the duplex mode. High-volume models can scan 90 letter-size pages per minute in the binary mode at 200 dpi. If all pages are two-sided, they can generate 180 images per minute.

Although duplex scanners can optionally operate in the simplex mode, intermingling of single- and double-sided pages poses obvious problems in records management applications. During document preparation, single- and double-sided pages can be grouped for scanning in batches. The appropriate scanning mode can be activated manually or by specially coded separator sheets inserted between batches. Alternatively, software can detect and automatically delete blank images produced by duplex scanning of single-sided pages.

Image Compression

Most electronic document imaging systems employ computer-based compression algorithms to reduce storage space and network bandwidth requirements for digitized images. Compression algorithms are applied before document images are recorded onto computer storage media. In some electronic document imaging implementations, compression is performed by specially designed circuit boards installed in a document scanner or in a scanning workstation's host computer. Electronic document imaging system vendors acquire such compression boards from manufacturers of specialized imaging components. Alternatively, image compression may be performed by software that operates on the scanning workstation's host computer.

Image compression methods are discussed in ANSI/AIIM TR-33, *Selecting an Appropriate Image Compression Method to Match User Requirements and ISO/TS 12033, Electronic Imaging—Guidance for Selection of Document Image Compression Methods.* The most widely employed image compression algorithms are based on specifications adopted by the International Telecommunications Union (ITU), formerly known as the Consultative Committee on International Telephony and Telegraphy (CCITT). Termed the *Group 3 and Group 4 compression algorithms,* they take their names from the facsimile transmission standards for which they were originally developed. The Group 3 algorithm was popular in the 1980s, but it is not commonly used in new imaging implementations. It employs one-dimensional compression techniques. The Group 4 algorithm uses two-dimensional compression methodologies, which yield higher compression ratios and greater reductions in image storage requirements. Although the availability and cost of adequate computer storage, as discussed in Chapter 3, are of less concern today than they were in the 1990s, high compression ratios are advantageous where large quantities of images are involved. Further, high compression ratios simplify backup operations for document images and reduce bandwidth requirements for transmission of images over computer networks.

The Group 3 and Group 4 compression algorithms employ run-length encoding to reduce the size of document images. With run-length encoding, compression results depend on the tonal characteristics of individual pages. Documents with large amounts of contiguous light or dark space, such as double-spaced, typewritten pages with wide margins or other large blank areas, will yield high compression factors. Densely printed pages, such as single-spaced typewritten pages and business forms with frequent light-to-dark transitions, offer much less compression potential.

Widely cited compression expectations are based on certain test pages with characteristics particularly conducive to run-length encoding. As an example, CCITT Test Image No. 1 is a typewritten, English-language letter printed on business stationery that includes a letterhead with three sizes of type and a graphic logo. The letter itself contains large blank areas. When scanned in the binary mode at 200 dots per inch with Group 4 compression, it requires approximately 12,200 bytes of computer storage. The resulting compression ratio is 38:1. When scanned in the binary mode at 300 dots per inch with Group 4 compression, CCITT Test Image No. 1 requires 18,070 byes of computer storage for a compression ratio of 58:1. Similarly, CCITT Test Image No. 2 is an A4-size business form with static information printed in French in several sizes of sans serif type. Dynamic information is typed into spaces provided for that purpose. With Group 4 compression, the form requires approximately 17,500 bytes of computer storage when scanned in the binary mode at 200 dots per inch and 26,750 bytes of storage when scanned in the binary mode at 300 dots per inch. The resulting compression ratios are 27:1 and 39:1, respectively.

Unfortunately, such impressive compression results cannot be expected in every case. Many office records are densely printed documents with limited compression potential. Business forms, which often contain vertical lines and text printed in small type sizes, can prove particularly troublesome. The Group 4 algorithm yields typical compression ratios of 12:1 to 15:1 across a broad spectrum of office records. In the most favorable circumstances, the average storage requirement per letter-size page is reduced to approximately 33,000 bytes, although 50,000 bytes is a more realistic expectation. Some business forms can require 60,000 to 70,000 bytes per page. Compression ratios for engineering drawings and other large graphic documents, which often have uninterrupted white areas, may be a bit higher, perhaps 20:1 on average.

The Group 3 and Group 4 algorithms are intended for business records, engineering drawings, and other bitonal documents that contain text and/or line art. Other compression methodologies have been developed for continuous-tone photographic images. One of the most widely publicized examples, the JPEG compression method developed by the Joint Photographic Experts Group, is intended for color or grayscale images generated by scanners, digital cameras, and specialized scientific and medical imaging devices. JPEG is actually an interrelated group of algorithms that support various combinations of image quality and compression. The most widely implemented JPEG algorithms employ **lossy compression techniques**, which omit some information from the original image. By contrast, the Group 3 and Group 4 algorithms are **lossless compression techniques**—they reduce image size without omitting any information. For some applications, JPEG compression offers an acceptable sacrifice of image quality to improve the storage capacity of a given medium; for example, with digital cameras, which store compressed photographs on memory cards. JPEG compression is less suitable, however, for archival copies of photographs of high value. JPEG-LS is a lossless implementation of the JPEG compression algorithm. It reduces image size with less of an impact on quality. Ultimately, it may replace lossy JPEG compression for archival applications.

Compared to JPEG, the Group 3 and Group 4 compression algorithms yield relatively low compression ratios, but JPEG is intended for continuous tone images. Other compression algorithms offer comparable reductions in image storage and network bandwidth requirements for bitonal office records. One example is the *JBIG algorithm* developed by the Joint Bi-Level Image Experts Group. It employs lossless techniques that can reduce image sizes by 20 percent or more when compared to Group 4 compression. A new version, called *JBIG2*, can reduce sizes by up to 70 percent when compared to Group 4 compression. To date, however, JBIG and JBIG2 have not been widely adopted by electronic document imaging vendors. To some extent, the increased availability and affordability of high-capacity storage media have made improved compression a less important issue for records management applications than it was in the 1990s. Other image compression methodologies—such as PCX, PackBits, and fractal technology—play little role in electronic document imaging systems for records management applications.

Image Enhancement

Broadly defined, **image enhancement** encompasses technologies and processes that improve the quality of digitized images. Most document scanners incorporate some straightforward enhancement capabilities that improve the quality and consistency of digitized images. Commonly encountered examples include brightness controls, which lighten or darken images, and contrast controls, which establish the threshold that differentiates black and white pixels in binary mode scanning. Activated manually, these features can improve the performance of electronic document imaging systems in applications that involve faded pages or other difficult documents.

Dynamic or adaptive **thresholding**, a sophisticated form of contrast control, automatically adjusts the black-white threshold to compensate for colored forms or other documents that contain text printed on a colored background. In engineering applications, dynamic thresholding is useful for blueline and sepia reproductions of drawings. Several scanners can discriminate between textual and photographic documents or between textual and photographic areas within a page. Dithering is automatically applied to photographs while text is digitized in the conventional binary mode.

Going beyond these convenient features, some electronic document imaging products incorporate computer-based enhancement algorithms to further improve image quality for display, printing, OCR, or other purposes. In addition to electronic document imaging, such enhancement algorithms are employed in photocopying, medical imaging, graphic arts, and other information management applications. They may reside in read-only memory circuits that are built into a document scanner or contained on an interface board to which the scanner is attached; alternatively, enhancement may be performed by image processing software that is executed by the scanning workstation's personal computer. In the latter case, image enhancement may be performed immediately following scanning or at any time prior to image recording.

A useful group of image enhancement algorithms compensates for faulty document positioning during scanning. De-skewing algorithms, for example, rectify image alignment problems caused by the angled movement of pages through sheetfed scanners or improper positioning of pages on flatbed scanners. Rotation algorithms will turn images in 90-degree increments to compensate for pages that were scanned bottom-up or sideways. Cropping algorithms remove dark edges that sometimes border scanned images. They facilitate scanning of mixed-size pages and give images a clean, uniform appearance.

Another group of enhancement algorithms filters digitized images to improve their appearance. Speckle removal algorithms are among the most widely implemented examples. They will delete isolated spots associated with toner flecks, stray pencil marks, and other blemishes. Some image enhancement algorithms will automatically suppress isolated pixels. Background removal algorithms automatically delete patterns, watermarks, shading, or other decorations without affecting any textual information superimposed on them. Line removal algorithms will erase unwanted vertical and horizontal lines and repair partially obliterated characters that intersect unwanted lines. Edge enhancement algorithms will sharpen the edges of characters. Erosion and dilation algorithms reduce or increase line thickness in order to sharpen details. Pixel inversion algorithms change the polarity of document images. They can be used to create positive-appearing images of negative-appearing source documents such as photostats, blueprints, or copies produced by certain microform reader/printers. Pixel inversion is also useful in microfilm scanning, where the source images are usually photographic negatives.

Other image manipulation and editing operations, such as image deletion and resequencing, are selectively supported by scanning software. Some software can merge small pages into a single image or divide large pages into multiple smaller images. Thus, the front and back of a 5" by 8" page might be combined in a single letter-size image, while an A3-size page might be divided into two letter-size images.

Accessories

Some document scanners can be configured with accessories to address specific application requirements. The availability of automatic page feeders in various capacities was noted previously. Some automatic feeders permit the continuous insertion of pages, thereby eliminating interruptions when the input tray is emptied. Some automatic feeders are equipped with sensors that detect double-feeding of pages. An imprinter/endorser can print information on a page before or after scanning. If an endorsement is applied prior to scanning, it appears in the scanned image. Depending on the system, endorsements may be sequentially assigned numbers, operator-specified alphanumerics, or information downloaded from a host computer. In a software-based variant of endorsement, some scanning workstations support image annotation capabilities that add operator-specified text to designated images. Alternatively, images may be annotated with software-generated barcodes.

Multifunctional Scanners

Document scanners described to this point are single-purpose devices designed specifically and exclusively for document imaging applications. Since 1990, manufacturers of computer peripheral equipment have introduced multifunctional equipment that combines scanning with other image management capabilities. *Scanner/printers*, as their name implies, combine scanning and printing functions in a single piece of equipment. They can also function as a photocopier, and, when equipped with a fax modem, as a facsimile transceiver. *Multifunctional scanner/printers* are most often encountered in entry-level electronic document imaging configurations. They are best suited to applications with low-volume scanning and printing requirements. As a characteristic limitation, some multifunctional devices perform one function at a time. In applications with a heavy scanning workload, the machine will be unavailable for printing and vice versa. Multifunctional scanner/printers may further be limited in their operating capabilities. Most models are slower than scanner-only devices and support a narrower range of options.

Another group of multifunctional imaging peripherals combines document scanning with microfilming capabilities. Such devices, which are variously termed *scanner/filmers* or *camera/scanners*, produce both digitized images and photographically reduced microfilm images in a single operation. The earliest models were introduced in the mid-1990s for applications where both micrographic and electronic document images are desired. As discussed elsewhere in this book, some information management applications rely on electronic document imaging systems for rapid retrieval of actively referenced records but prefer microforms to satisfy long-term retention requirements. In such situations, a scanner/filmer offers a labor-saving alternative to microfilming and scanning source documents in separate operations with different equipment. Alternatively, a scanner/filmer can be used as a microfilm camera only or as a document scanner only for applications that do not require both types of images.

Depending on the model, a scanner/filmer may be rotary or planetary in design and operation. *Rotary microfilmers* resemble sheetfed scanners, while *planetary cameras* are flatbed devices. In either case, source documents are microfilmed and digitized in a single exposure. Rotary scanner/filmers, the most common configuration, produce 16mm microfilm, like their camera-only counterparts. Microimage reductions, filming modes, and scanning resolutions vary. When operating in the scanning mode, a scanner/filmer is typically attached to a personal computer equipped with appropriate software.

Most scanner/filmers are high-speed, heavy-duty devices intended for high-volume installations in large-scale imaging projects, centralized document conversion departments, or commercial service bureaus. Their standard and optional features are comparable to those supported by the most expensive microfilm cameras and document scanners. The most capable models support multiple reductions, microimage formats, and scanning resolutions. A variety of optional accessories, including document endorsers and blip encoding units for computer-assisted microfilm retrieval, are available. In some cases, a scanner/filmer can be initially configured as a single-purpose microfilm camera or document scanner that can be upgraded to multifunctional status when required.

Scanner Maintenance

To minimize quality control problems, document scanners must be in proper operating condition. ANSI/AIIM MS44, *Recommended Practice for Quality Control of Image Scanners* discusses quality control concepts and describes a test chart that determines whether a document scanner is appropriate for and properly set up for its intended application. The test chart, which is available from AIIM, reproduces alphanumeric characters in multiple type fonts and sizes. They measure a scanner's ability to capture serifs and other character details. They also determine the smallest type size compatible with legible digitization. Additional isolated alphanumeric characters measure a scanner's ability to digitize very small information areas within a page. Square boxes and accompanying numeric digits printed in each corner of the chart are used to test the dimensions of the scan area and page alignment. Horizontal and vertical line patterns of varying width test a scanner's ability to capture thin lines, while a diagonal line connecting the upper right and lower left corner of the chart tests uniform transport movement. Solid black and white squares in the middle of the chart permit density checking. Other patterns measure the ability to scan halftones.

The chart is designed in such a manner that all document scanners will fail in some respects. The nature of the failure reveals the scanner's characteristics and indicates the types of documents that it cannot scan properly. The chart can also be used to test fax machines, video displays, graphic printers, and other image-capable output devices. The widely publicized *IEEE 167A test chart*, which was developed for fax machines, and the *RIT Process Ink Gamut Chart*, which reproduces the full range of printable colors, are also useful for document scanners. Other potentially useful test charts are described in AIIM TR38, *Compilation of Test Targets for Document Imaging Systems.*

Scanners should be cleaned daily to remove dust, debris, and ink from optical components and the page transport mechanism. With some scanners, the color balance must be adjusted periodically to compensate for reduced luminosity of the scanner's lamp over time. Some scanner manufacturers provide calibration control sheets for this purpose.

Microform Scanners

Scanners described in preceding sections produce electronic images from paper documents. In many records management applications, documents to be included in an imaging implementation were previously microfilmed and then discarded to save space or for other reasons. In such situations, **microform scanners** produce electronic images from microfilm images, which may be recorded on roll microfilm, microfiche, microfilm jackets, or aperture cards.

A microform scanner, such as the one shown in Figure 2.5, combines the attributes of a document scanner and a microfilm densitometer. The scanning component differs from a conventional document scanner in several respects. The page to be scanned is, of course, highly miniaturized, and scannable pixels are microscopically

Personal Computer Workstation that Digitizes Microimages for Display, Storage, Printing, or Distribution

(Courtesy: Eastman Kodak)

Figure 2.5

small. Because the page is a transparent film image rather than an opaque sheet of paper, scanning is based on transmitted rather than reflected light. With the exception of aperture cards, multiple pages are usually recorded on a given microform; page feeding and other document handling tasks are consequently minimized.

Most microform scanning is performed at an effective resolution of 200 or 300 dots per inch, although resolutions as high as 600 dots per inch are encountered in some situations; for example, in digital library implementations involving manuscripts, rare books, or other valuable research materials. Regardless of resolution, a microform scanner's densitometric component measures the amount of light transmitted through successively encountered pixels within a microimage and generates an electrical signal that is converted to digital bit patterns. Most microforms are produced from bitonal documents or engineering drawings that contain dark text or line art on a light background. The resulting microimages, whether negative- or positive-appearing, consist of dark and clear areas. For such bitonal images, microform scanners operate in the binary mode. Pixels that transmit light in excess of a predetermined threshold amount are considered white and are each encoded as a zero bit. Where the amount of transmitted light is lower than the predetermined threshold value, the corresponding pixels are considered black, and each is encoded as a one bit. As previously noted, pixel inversion is typically used to produce positive-appearing electronic images from negative-appearing microforms. To digitize microimages of X-rays or other photographs, grayscale microform scanners use multiple bits to encode gray tones. Eight-bit scanning, the most popular approach, can differentiate 256 shades of gray. Available microform scanners do not support color-mode operation. Color microforms are rarely encountered in records management applications.

Microform scanners have been commercially available since the 1960s. Three broad groups are available as shown in Figure 2.6. The earliest models were intended for facsimile transmission of microimages and for complex retrieval systems that digitized microimages for display by specially designed workstations. Today, microform scanners principally digitize microimages for input to electronic document imaging systems or CAD applications. Secondary applications include digitization of microimages for computer printing, thereby replacing reader/printers and enlarger/printers; computer-input microfilm (CIM), in which digitized microimages are processed by OCR software; and electronic distribution of microimages

Microform Scanners

Figure 2.6

Microform Scanners

1. Production-level devices that can digitize large quantities of microimages at relatively high speed with little or no operator intervention.

2. Reader/scanners that require operator involvement to select document images to be scanned within a given microform.

3. Microfilm drives that digitize microimages for display by personal computers.

through facsimile transmission or over computer networks. Product variety and functionality have improved considerably since the early 1990s.

The following sections describe and discuss the most important characteristics and capabilities of each group of microform scanners.

Production-Level Models

The principal application for production-level microform scanners is digitization of microform backfiles for input into electronic document imaging systems. They can also be incorporated into hybrid information management implementations that combine electronic document imaging for active retrieval with microforms for long-term retention of recorded information. In such implementations, documents are initially microfilmed, and the resulting microimages are digitized to create electronic document images. The market for production-level microform scanners is necessarily limited by the applications they serve. For most organizations, microform backfile conversions are one-time or occasional occurrences of limited scope. Such projects do not warrant the purchase of specialized equipment that is not needed on a continuing basis. Consequently, many corporations, government agencies, and other organizations rely on outsourcing arrangements for their high-volume scanning requirements. Since the mid-1990s, many micrographics service bureaus have added microform scanning capabilities to their offerings.

Depending on the model, a production-level microform scanner may be able to digitize microimages recorded on 16mm or 35mm microfilm reels, 16mm microfilm cartridges, microfiche in various formats, or aperture cards. Some production-level scanners are single-purpose devices intended for one type of microform. Others employ interchangeable media transports to accommodate multiple microforms, but not necessarily all types. Roll microforms may be recorded in the cine or comic mode. Best results are obtained when images are uniformly aligned and evenly spaced within a microform. Blipped 16mm microfilm and standard microfiche are the preferred formats. Microfilm jackets, with their characteristically variable image spacing, can pose problems. Some restrictions may be imposed on original document sizes and reductions. Available production-level scanners can accept silver gelatin, diazo, and vesicular films in positive or negative polarity.

Like scanners for paper documents, production-level microform scanners are computer peripheral devices. A production-level microform scanner is one component in a scanning workstation that includes a host computer, an image processing board, and software that controls the scanner's operation. The host computer may be a personal computer or a more powerful server-class device. As previously noted, production-level microform scanners are designed for unattended digitization of microimages, but an operator usually previews microforms to determine optimal scanner setting and identify special problems such as overlapping frames, skewed microimages, or low contrast. Scanning time depends on the resolution selected for a particular application as well as such microform characteristics as reduction, image size, and interframe spacing. A typical production-level scanner, operating at 200 dots per inch, requires one or two seconds to digitize an image recorded on 16mm microfilm or microfiche. An aperture card containing a microimage of one E-size drawing (36 by 48 inches) will require 30 seconds to two minutes of scanning time.

Among their special features, production-level scanners will clean microforms to remove dust and oils prior to scanning. To minimize microform handling, micro-fiche and aperture card scanners may be optionally equipped with stacker-feeders. Edge-detection capabilities can locate variably spaced images within a microform. The polarity of microimages can be maintained or reversed during digitization. Under software control, microimages can be aligned, rotated, cropped, or erased. Blank areas and splices can be skipped. Microimages of continuous forms, oil well logs, EKG printouts, and other long documents can be scanned in their entirety or segmented. Automatic thresholding can adjust the black/white scanning threshold to compensate for variations in microform density. It facilitates digitization of microimages produced from colored business forms or blueline copies of engineer-ing drawings. Image enhancement algorithms can delete isolated spots, sharpen edges, and reduce or increase line widths. Image enhancement may be performed by the scanner itself, by an image processing board to which the scanner is attached, or by software operating on the scanning workstation's computer.

Reader/Scanners

A *reader/scanner*, sometimes described as a *digital microimage workstation*, combines the capabilities of a microform reader and an image digitizer. It produces electronic document images from magnified microimages that are projected on a microform reader's screen. Square screens, measuring 11 to 12 inches per side, are typical. Available magnifications correspond to popular reductions employed in microfilm applications. Some models support zoom lenses.

Reader/scanners resemble microform reader/printers in appearance and opera-tion, but they produce electronic images rather than paper copies. Microimages must be individually located, displayed, focused, and positioned for scanning. Some reader/scanners will automatically rotate and center microimages. Dark borders can be removed, and specific portions of a microimage can be masked to prevent scanning of sensitive information. With scanning times ranging from 5 to 10 seconds per microim-age, reader/scanners are much slower than production-level microform scanners. Most reader/scanners operate in the binary mode and support Group 4 compression. A typ-ical scanning resolution is 200 dots per inch for microimages reduced 24x.

Although the production-level scanners described previously digitize all or most images from within a given microform, reader/scanners are best suited to selective scanning of microimages for input to an electronic document imaging sys-tem. Alternatively, a reader/scanner can operate as a digital reader/printer. Digitized versions of magnified microimages are transmitted to a laser printer for hard-copy production. Copies can be printed individually or in batches. In network installa-tions, a single laser printer can serve multiple reader/scanners. Reader/scanners can also digitize microimages for attachment to e-mail messages, OCR, input to desk-top publishing programs, facsimile transmission, or other purposes.

Microfilm Drives

A *microfilm drive* is a computer peripheral device that retrieves and digitizes microim-ages for display by a Windows-based computer, to which it is connected. Microfilm drives accept 16mm microfilm cartridges and incorporate film transport and scanning components. Although reader/scanners are modeled after microform reader/printers, microfilm drives are modeled after computer storage devices. They operate much like magnetic tape drives, floppy disk drives, CD drives, DVD drives, and other storage peripherals that employ removable media. At retrieval time, a 16mm cartridge containing a desired microimage is manually loaded into the microfilm drive, which operates online to a personal computer. On instructions from the personal computer, the drive's transport mechanism advances the microfilm to the desired frame, which may be identified by a computer-maintained index or in some other way. The microfilm drive scans the retrieved microimage, producing a digitized version that is displayed in a window on a personal computer's monitor. The digitized image can be input into an electronic document imaging system, processed by OCR programs, printed, transferred to another storage medium, or distributed electronically via fax, e-mail, or other methods. The typical scanning time is less than five seconds per microimage.

Image Inspection

Following scanning, electronic document images are typically routed to a temporary file, pending inspection and, if necessary, rescanning. The purpose of inspection is to ensure that document images are sufficiently legible and usable for their intended purposes, which may include display, printing, facsimile transmission, or OCR. Obvious mechanical and legibility problems that necessitate rescanning include excessive page skewing, double-feeding or other misfeeding of pages, pages scanned upside down or backwards, pages with folded corners, obliteration of information within pages, insufficient clarity or contrast, blotches or other blemishes, and curved or jagged lines within images. Depending on the application, inspection may encompass all electronic document images or be limited to a predetermined sample. Careful inspection of all images is critical if paper documents will be discarded following scanning. Sample-based image inspection is discussed in ANSI/AIIM TR34, *Sampling Procedures for Inspection by Attributes of Images in Electronic Image Management (EIM) & Micrographics Systems.*

Inspection is a labor-intensive, time-consuming work step that involves visual examination of document images displayed on a high-resolution computer monitor. Printed copies may be produced as well. Inspection may be performed at a dedicated workstation or integrated with data-entry operations. Because inspection may be two to three times slower than scanning, inspection at the scanning workstation is not recommended. Individual images may be inspected at full-size or in a magnified view for operator examination. Alternatively, special inspection software can display multiple images in a *thumbnail format* that facilitates detection of skewing, double-feeding, or other page-alignment defects. Any thumbnail image can be selected for full display.

Imaging Service Bureaus

Any of the image production steps discussed in this chapter can be performed in-house or outsourced to a service bureau. A document imaging service bureau is a business that performs one or more imaging operations to customer specifications using the customer's own source documents. The customer may be a corporation, government agency, not-for-profit institution, or other organization. A service bureau may offer any combination of image production and support services, including consulting for application selection and systems design, document preparation, source document scanning, image inspection, index planning and data-entry, and media duplication. Some imaging service bureaus also offer microfilming, microform scanning, and related services for integration of electronic document imaging and micrographics technologies. Depending on the service bureau and customer requirements, imaging operations may be performed at the service bureau's facilities or at the customer's location, although onsite implementations are more costly and may limit the types of services to be offered. Some service bureaus also sell electronic document imaging hardware and software. Occasionally, imaging service bureaus provide other types of information management or reprographic services such as photocopying, desktop publishing, high-volume computer printing, web site design, or intranet development.

Outsourcing arrangements are increasingly popular in information management operations. Many organizations contract with service bureaus for at least one phase of image production. Service bureaus can, for example, scan documents that were prepared in-house. They can likewise inspect and index images produced by an in-house scanning department. Even organizations with extensive in-house image production facilities use service bureaus to supplement or enhance their own capabilities in unusual situations. Imaging service bureaus are particularly useful for high-volume work that must be completed in a short time or for tasks, such as image reformatting or microform scanning, that require special equipment, software, or technical expertise that are unavailable in house.

Service bureau capabilities and rates vary. Most charge by the hour for document preparation and by the page for document scanning, including image inspection and recording media. The nature and acceptability of services to be rendered must be negotiated between the customer and the service bureau's management. A tour of the service bureau's facilities prior to contract award is strongly recommended. Critical criteria for service bureau selection are listed in Figure 2.7.

Service Bureau Selection Criteria

Figure 2.7

Service Bureau Selection Criteria

- A demonstrated understanding of the customer's requirements

- Imaging equipment, software, and technical expertise appropriate to the tasks to be performed

- The ability to provide high-quality service within customer-specified deadlines

- A record of satisfactory performance in similar applications

- Assurance that the service bureau will safeguard source documents in its possession

Creating Character-Coded Documents

As previously defined, character-coded digital documents contain alphabetic characters, numeric digits, punctuation marks, and other symbols that are represented by predetermined bit sequences. Many, if not most, character-coded documents originate in digital form. These documents are born digital. Word processing documents and e-mail messages, for example, are created by typing textual information into programs suitable for that purpose and/or by cutting and pasting textual information from other digital sources.

In many situations, however, character-coded digital documents must be created from existing paper records. They may be created by key-entry—that is, by typing the content of the records into a text file—or by OCR, a partially automated procedure that combines scanning and image processing with manual verification and error correction procedures. The following sections explain these methods. Compared to scanning an equivalent quantity of source documents, the creation of character-coded digital text from paper records by key-entry or OCR will be more complicated, time-consuming, and expensive. Character-coded digital documents are required, however, for full-text indexing, as discussed in Chapter 3.

Key-Entry Methods

Since the inception of computer technology, key-entry (typing) has been the most common method of converting human-readable information into machine-readable form. As alphabetic characters, numeric digits, punctuation marks, and other symbols are typed, the bit patterns that encode them are generated. Key-entry's principal advantages are confirmed by decades of experience: it is suitable for any information that can be typed and, when appropriate verification measures are implemented, it is highly reliable. As a method of converting the contents of paper documents to computer-processible form, however, key-entry is labor-intensive and time-consuming. These limitations are particularly significant where large numbers of documents are involved.

The formula in Figure 2.8 may be used to calculate the labor requirement for creating character-coded digital documents by typing the contents of a given quantity of paper documents.

Labor requirements are determined by the amount of work to be performed and the productivity rate. For a given document collection, the key-entry workload—which is based on the number of documents (D), the number of pages (P), and the number of characters per page (C)—can be reasonably estimated by examining a sample of the documents. The typing rate (R) depends on operator skill, which may vary considerably. Surveys of data-entry installations conducted during the 1970s and 1980s by the Data Entry Management Association (DEMA)—now known as The Association for Work Process Improvement (TAWPI)—indicate that input rates for full-time data-entry operators range broadly from 6,000 keystrokes per hour to 15,000 keystrokes per hour. Since the early 1980s, rates for full-time, experienced data-entry personnel have averaged 10,000 to 11,000 keystrokes per hour sustained throughout an eight-hour workday. These average rates are equivalent to typing speeds of 28 to 31 words per minute, based on the long-standing measure of six characters per word (five characters plus the adjacent space) used in typing textbooks. Table 2.1 presents equivalent typing speeds and key-entry times per 1,000 characters for various keystroking rates. Table 2.2 calculates the key-entry cost per 1,000 characters at various combinations of keystroking speed and hourly compensation.

Labor
Requirement
Formula for
Character-Coded
Digital Document
Creation

Figure 2.8

Labor Requirement Formula Character-Coded Digital Document Creation
$T = ((D \times P \times C) / R) * V$
Where:

T	=	the key-entry time in person-hours
D	=	the number of documents to be converted
P	=	the average number of pages per document
C	=	the average number of characters per page, including blank spaces, carriage returns, and other control characters that must be typed but are invisible
R	=	the typing rate in keystrokes per hour
V	=	a verification factor

Key-Entry Time
at Various
Keystroking
Rates

Table 2.1

Keystrokes per Hour	Typing Speed (Words/Minute)	Data-Entry Time (Hours)	Data-Entry Time (Minutes)
6,000	16.7	0.167	10.0
7,000	19.4	0.143	8.6
8,000	22.2	0.125	7.5
9,000	25.0	0.111	6.7
10,000	27.8	0.100	6.0
11,000	30.6	0.091	5.5
12,000	33.3	0.083	5.0
13,000	36.1	0.077	4.6
14,000	38.9	0.071	4.3
15,000	41.7	0.067	4.0

Key-Entry Cost
Without
Verification and
Error Correction

Table 2.2

Keystrokes	Hourly Compensation							
per Hour	$8	$9	$10	$11	$12	$13	$14	$15
6,000	$1.33	$1.50	$1.67	$1.83	$2.00	$2.17	$2.33	$2.50
6,500	$1.23	$1.38	$1.54	$1.69	$1.85	$2.00	$2.15	$2.31
7,000	$1.14	$1.29	$1.43	$1.57	$1.71	$1.86	$2.00	$2.14
7,500	$1.07	$1.20	$1.33	$1.47	$1.60	$1.73	$1.87	$2.00
8,000	$1.00	$1.13	$1.25	$1.38	$1.50	$1.63	$1.75	$1.88
8,500	$0.94	$1.06	$1.18	$1.29	$1.41	$1.53	$1.65	$1.76
9,000	$0.89	$1.00	$1.11	$1.22	$1.33	$1.44	$1.56	$1.67
9,500	$0.84	$0.95	$1.05	$1.16	$1.26	$1.37	$1.47	$1.58
10,000	$0.80	$0.90	$1.00	$1.10	$1.20	$1.30	$1.40	$1.50
10,500	$0.76	$0.86	$0.95	$1.05	$1.14	$1.24	$1.33	$1.43
11,000	$0.73	$0.82	$0.91	$1.00	$1.09	$1.18	$1.27	$1.36
11,500	$0.70	$0.78	$0.87	$0.96	$1.04	$1.13	$1.22	$1.30
12,000	$0.67	$0.75	$0.83	$0.92	$1.00	$1.08	$1.17	$1.25
12,500	$0.64	$0.72	$0.80	$0.88	$0.96	$1.04	$1.12	$1.20
13,000	$0.62	$0.69	$0.77	$0.85	$0.92	$1.00	$1.08	$1.15
13,500	$0.59	$0.67	$0.74	$0.81	$0.89	$0.96	$1.04	$1.11
14,000	$0.57	$0.64	$0.71	$0.79	$0.86	$0.93	$1.00	$1.07
14,500	$0.55	$0.62	$0.69	$0.76	$0.83	$0.90	$0.97	$1.03
15,000	$0.53	$0.60	$0.67	$0.73	$0.80	$0.87	$0.93	$1.00

The purpose of verification is to detect data-entry errors. Where key-entry is used, the most accurate approach to verification is *double-keying*, also known as *keystroke verification*. Documents to be converted to character-coded text are typed twice. The second typing may be performed immediately after initial key-entry or at a later time. It may be performed by the key-entry operator or by a different person. Under software control, the second typing is compared to the first, and the verifying operator is alerted to any discrepancies. An error may have occurred in the initial typing, in the second typing, or in both sets of keystrokes. The suspect characters are examined to determine the errors, and corrective action is taken, usually by overtyp-

ing errors with correct characters. Double-keying can be used with any type of information, including the complete text of documents, but it is rarely done for reasons
discussed next. In digital document implementations, double-keying is most often
applied to entry of index data, as explained in Chapter 3.

Taken together, double-keying and error correction yield a verification factor
(V) of 2.25 for the labor requirement formula presented in Figure 2.3.
Consequently, if initial key-entry for a given quantity of documents requires 100
person-hours, the total key-entry time (T) will be 225 hours. Table 2.3 calculates the
key-entry cost per 1,000 characters, including double-keying and error correction

Key-Entry Cost,
Including
Double-Keying
and Error
Correction

Table 2.3

Keystrokes	Hourly Compensation							
per Hour	$8	$9	$10	$11	$12	$13	$14	$15
6,000	$3.00	$3.38	$3.75	$4.13	$4.50	$4.88	$5.25	$5.63
6,500	$2.77	$3.12	$3.46	$3.81	$4.15	$4.50	$4.85	$5.19
7,000	$2.57	$2.89	$3.21	$3.54	$3.86	$4.18	$4.50	$4.82
7,500	$2.40	$2.70	$3.00	$3.30	$3.60	$3.90	$4.20	$4.50
8,000	$2.25	$2.53	$2.81	$3.09	$3.38	$3.66	$3.94	$4.22
8,500	$2.12	$2.38	$2.65	$2.91	$3.18	$3.44	$3.71	$3.97
9,000	$2.00	$2.25	$2.50	$2.75	$3.00	$3.25	$3.50	$3.75
9,500	$1.89	$2.13	$2.37	$2.61	$2.84	$3.08	$3.32	$3.55
10,000	$1.80	$2.03	$2.25	$2.48	$2.70	$2.93	$3.15	$3.38
10,500	$1.71	$1.93	$2.14	$2.36	$2.57	$2.79	$3.00	$3.21
11,000	$1.64	$1.84	$2.05	$2.25	$2.45	$2.66	$2.86	$3.07
11,500	$1.57	$1.76	$1.96	$2.15	$2.35	$2.54	$2.74	$2.93
12,000	$1.50	$1.69	$1.88	$2.06	$2.25	$2.44	$2.63	$2.81
12,500	$1.44	$1.62	$1.80	$1.98	$2.16	$2.34	$2.52	$2.70
13,000	$1.38	$1.56	$1.73	$1.90	$2.08	$2.25	$2.42	$2.60
13,500	$1.33	$1.50	$1.67	$1.83	$2.00	$2.17	$2.33	$2.50
14,000	$1.29	$1.45	$1.61	$1.77	$1.93	$2.09	$2.25	$2.41
14,500	$1.24	$1.40	$1.55	$1.71	$1.86	$2.02	$2.17	$2.33
15,000	$1.20	$1.35	$1.50	$1.65	$1.80	$1.95	$2.10	$2.25

at various combinations of keystroking speed and hourly compensation. As its principal advantage, double-keying is a highly reliable method of error detection. Its failure rate is limited to those cases where exactly the same mistake is made during both the initial and second typing. Presumably, the failure rate will be a very small percentage of the entered data. Double-keying is consequently the preferred verification method where errors are intolerable.

The alternative to keystroke verification is *sight verification* (proofreading). An operator examines key-entered information on a computer monitor or in a printed listing, comparing it to source documents as necessary. As its principal advantage, proofreading requires less time and labor than double-keying. Assuming a throughput rate of 600 characters per hour (100 words per minute), a typewritten page containing 1,000 characters will require approximately 1.7 minutes to proofread. Additional time must be allocated for correction of detected errors. Even then, however, proofreading will be 2.5 to 6 times faster than double-keying for key-entry rates ranging from 6,000 to 15,000 keystrokes per hour. The resulting verification factor (V) will range from 1.35 at 6,000 keystrokes per hour to 1.75 at 15,000 keystrokes per hour. At 9,000 keystrokes per hour, a reasonable expectation in many work environments, the verification factor will be 1.6.

Table 2.4 calculates the key-entry cost per 1,000 characters, including proofreading and error correction time at various combinations of keystroking speed and hourly compensation. Because proofreading time does not vary with a key-entry operator's typing skill, it offers the greatest advantage over double-keying at slow typing rates. At a data-entry rate of 6,000 keystrokes per hour, proofreading will reduce data-entry costs by about 48 percent when compared to double-keying. At 15,000 keystrokes per hour, however, the reduction is 37 percent.

Although it can reduce labor requirements and costs, proofreading demands a high level of operator attentiveness, which is difficult to sustain. As a result, proofreading may fail to detect all incorrect characters in entered data; the presence of typographical errors in books and other publications attests to the unreliability of proofreading. In digital document applications, proofreading is significant because undetected keystroking errors can lead to retrieval failures.

To improve error detection, proofreading might be augmented by spell-checking software, but such programs have notable limitations as data verification tools. They cannot detect keystroking errors in personal names, numeric values, or nonalphabetic symbols such as punctuation marks. Their effectiveness is further limited by the contents of their spelling dictionaries, which may not include specialized terminology associated with certain business activities or subjects. Although spelling dictionaries can usually be customized to include such terminology, the process is time-consuming. Finally, spell-checking programs will not detect typing errors that result in a correctly spelled but inappropriate word.

Regardless of the verification method employed, the effort and cost to convert the contents of paper documents to computer-processable form are the most formidable obstacles to digital document implementations based on character-coded text. As an example, a collection of 100,000 pages, which would occupy nine 4-drawer filing cabinets in paper form, will contain about 200 million characters, assuming an

Key-Entry Cost,
Including
Proofreading and
Error Correction

Table 2.4

Keystrokes	Hourly Compensation							
per Hour	$8	$9	$10	$11	$12	$13	$14	$15
6,000	$1.56	$1.75	$1.95	$2.14	$2.34	$2.53	$2.73	$2.92
6,500	$1.45	$1.64	$1.82	$2.00	$2.18	$2.36	$2.55	$2.73
7,000	$1.37	$1.54	$1.71	$1.88	$2.05	$2.22	$2.39	$2.56
7,500	$1.29	$1.45	$1.61	$1.77	$1.94	$2.10	$2.26	$2.42
8,000	$1.22	$1.38	$1.53	$1.68	$1.84	$1.99	$2.14	$2.30
8,500	$1.17	$1.31	$1.46	$1.60	$1.75	$1.89	$2.04	$2.18
9,000	$1.11	$1.25	$1.39	$1.53	$1.67	$1.81	$1.95	$2.09
9,500	$1.07	$1.20	$1.33	$1.47	$1.60	$1.73	$1.87	$2.00
10,000	$1.02	$1.15	$1.28	$1.41	$1.54	$1.66	$1.79	$1.92
10,500	$0.99	$1.11	$1.23	$1.36	$1.48	$1.60	$1.73	$1.85
11,000	$0.95	$1.07	$1.19	$1.31	$1.43	$1.55	$1.66	$1.78
11,500	$0.92	$1.03	$1.15	$1.26	$1.38	$1.49	$1.61	$1.72
12,000	$0.89	$1.00	$1.11	$1.22	$1.34	$1.45	$1.56	$1.67
12,500	$0.86	$0.97	$1.08	$1.19	$1.30	$1.40	$1.51	$1.62
13,000	$0.84	$0.94	$1.05	$1.15	$1.26	$1.36	$1.47	$1.57
13,500	$0.82	$0.92	$1.02	$1.12	$1.22	$1.33	$1.43	$1.53
14,000	$0.80	$0.89	$0.99	$1.09	$1.19	$1.29	$1.39	$1.49
14,500	$0.78	$0.87	$0.97	$1.07	$1.16	$1.26	$1.36	$1.45
15,000	$0.76	$0.85	$0.95	$1.04	$1.14	$1.23	$1.33	$1.42

average of 2,000 characters per page. At an input rate of 10,000 keystrokes per hour, which may be optimistic in some circumstances, initial key-entry will require 20,000 person-hours of labor. Proofreading and error correction will yield a total effort of 32,000 person-hours. By contrast, the creation of digital images from 100,000 pages will require less than 1,000 hours, including document preparation, scanning, and image inspection, with rescanning as necessary. Compared to digital images, character-coded documents require less storage space and network bandwidth, but the resulting cost savings are rarely sufficient to offset the higher cost of creating character-coded digital documents.

As previously mentioned, key-entry is a time-consuming, labor-intensive input method. It is not affected by technical innovations. Computer keyboards have not changed significantly since the 1970s. Efficiency depends entirely on operator skill, which can be improved by training. Ultimately, however, key-entry speeds are limited by physiological factors. At a given skill level, only lower wages will reduce costs.

To achieve the skill level and lower wages, some organizations have outsourced document conversion to offshore data-entry companies, which operate in countries where key-entry skills are high but wages are low. Depending on the nature and quantity of documents to be converted to character-coded text, offshore key-entry rates typically range from $1 to $3 per 1,000 characters, including verification by double-keying and error correction.* By contrast, in-house key-entry at an optimistic rate of 10,000 keystrokes per hour by a full-time employee who is paid $15 per hour, including benefits, will cost about $3.40 per 1,000 characters, including verification by double-keying and error correction. Although outsourcing adds some logistic complications—in most cases, source documents must be photocopied for shipment to the offshore location and a sample of the completed work must be inspected by the customer—favorable labor rates can reduce costs by 25 percent or more when compared to in-house key-entry using full-time, experienced employees. As additional advantages, outsourcing will reduce supervisory and equipment requirements for key-entry projects.

Criteria for selecting a data-entry service company are similar to those associated with other outsourcing arrangements. They include a demonstrated understanding of the customer's requirements; labor, equipment, software, and technical expertise appropriate to the work to be performed; the ability to perform high-quality work within customer-specified deadlines; a record of satisfactory completion in similar applications; and assurance that the data-entry company will safeguard source documents and digital documents in its possession.

Optical Character Recognition

Optical character recognition (OCR) is a potentially economical alternative to key-entry for creation of character-coded digital documents. Broadly defined, OCR is a computer input method that combines scanning technology with image analysis to identify or read characters contained in typewritten or printed documents. In a typical OCR implementation, a scanner produces electronic images from textual documents. The imaging work steps discussed in preceding sections—document preparation, page scanning, and image inspection—are performed and their associated costs incurred. An OCR program then processes the images to recognize the

---

*   These rates do not include shipping charges and the cost of recording media. A data-entry company may record digital documents on magnetic tapes, diskettes, or other media specified by the customer. Alternatively, the data-entry company may transmit completed work to the customer electronically. To obtain a price quote, an application planner can mail or fax a statement of requirements with copies of typical source documents to one or more data-entry companies. Accuracy requirements, including corrective actions or penalties to be invoked for noncompliance, must be clearly defined in contractual arrangements.

alphabetic characters, numeric digits, punctuation marks, or other textual symbols they contain. To accomplish this recognition process, it analyzes the light and dark pixels within images. When a character is recognized, the OCR program generates a predetermined bit pattern that encodes the character digitally, just as if it had been typed. The recognized text is then displayed for proofreading and error correction, which is accomplished by overtyping the incorrect characters with correct ones. Depending on the OCR program, the resulting character-coded document may be saved in any of several formats: Some possibilities include unformatted ASCII (text-only); the rich text format (RTF), which preserves page layouts and character attributes for compatibility with popular word processing programs; and the portable document format (PDF).

OCR's effectiveness depends on its ability to accurately recognize characters contained in source documents. Driven by two decades of research and innovation, the accuracy of OCR software has improved steadily and significantly since the 1970s. The earliest OCR products employed matrix-matching technologies that limited recognition to specific fonts and type sizes. These products matched the characters in scanned pages against a database of character bitmaps (patterns of light and dark pixels) for each of the supported fonts and type sizes. A character was recognized when (and if) it matched one of the bitmaps. The simplest OCR programs operated on fonts such as OCR-A and OCR-B that were designed specifically for machine recognition. Others could recognize the most common typewriter fonts, such as Courier and Prestige Elite, with reasonable accuracy. With some products, accuracy could be improved by training based on preselected samples of text, but, even then, matrix-matching technology could not reliably recognize the varied array of documents encountered in records management applications.

During the 1990s, matrix matching was supplanted by omnifont OCR products based on *feature extraction technology*, which recognizes characters by their most important features. An uppercase letter "A," for example, is recognized as a character with two diagonal lines joined at the top and bisected by a horizontal crossbar. Similarly, an uppercase "D" is recognized as having one vertical line joined at the ends by a loop. As its principal advantage, feature extraction transcends ornamental differences associated with particular type fonts, sizes, and styles; presumably, the letter "O" will be recognizable as a continuous loop whether it is printed in the Courier or Times Roman font, boldface or italicized, large or small.

Building on research in cognitive science, probability theory, and other disciplines, newer omnifont OCR programs incorporate enhanced feature extraction capabilities, along with enhancements that improve accuracy. When a character cannot be conclusively identified, grammatical rules and contextual clues narrow the possibilities. Evaluation of surrounding characters, for example, can determine the likelihood that a given character forms a word. If the surrounding characters are "b" and "t", for example, contextual clues will confirm that an ambiguous character is a lowercase "u" rather than a lower-case "v." Grammatical rules can determine whether a character is upper- or lowercase or enable an OCR program to differentiate similar characters such as the uppercase "I," the lowercase "l," and the numeral "1."

With the most powerful OCR programs, sometimes described as *intelligent character recognition (ICR)* products, recognition algorithms are based on complex mathematical models. They can accurately identify characters in all languages that use the Latin alphabet, including French, Spanish, Italian, Portuguese, Dutch, Swedish, Norwegian, and Danish. Some products recognize characters in non-Latin alphabets, such as Cyrillic and Greek, and in Asian languages such as Chinese, Japanese, and Korean. To improve accuracy, some OCR programs use multiple recognition algorithms, which vote to resolve the identity of ambiguous characters. Each algorithm identifies the character and reports its confidence level. The program then determines the most likely choice. Because available OCR algorithms were developed independently and utilize different methods, they can operate effectively in tandem; characters that cannot be accurately recognized by one algorithm may be correctly identified by a different one.

Although the technical sophistication of OCR products has increased steadily and significantly since the 1980s, a source document's physical, typographic, and formatting attributes remain key determinants of OCR accuracy. OCR programs work best with typewritten or printed text. Despite decades of research, accurate recognition of handprinted characters or cursive writing remains difficult to achieve. Original documents with black characters clearly printed on a white background are preferable to colored pages, faded documents, or photocopies with toner flecks or other blemishes. Numeric characters are easier to recognize than alphabetic characters. However, fewer numeric characters are usually in typical textual documents. Uppercase characters are easier to recognize than lowercase characters, which are often smaller. Typewritten or laser-printed text is easier to recognize than dot-matrix characters. Large type sizes are easier to recognize than smaller ones. Monospaced type fonts, such as Prestige Elite and Courier, are easier to recognize than proportionally spaced fonts such as Times Roman. Characters that touch are difficult to differentiate. Text in footnotes, captions, tables, columns, and marginal notations poses special problems; often, page areas that contain such text must be zoned or delineated for separate processing. Recognition accuracy is also affected by the resolution of digitized images that OCR software must process. Most OCR products require a minimum scanning resolution of 300 dpi. Lower resolutions can break lines and fill gaps within characters, rendering them unrecognizable. Some OCR programs can accommodate document images scanned at 400 dots per inch or greater resolution, which may improve recognition accuracy for contract clauses, footnotes, and other information printed in very small type sizes.

OCR programs increasingly incorporate pre- and post-recognition features to improve accuracy and compensate for variations in the legibility of source documents. Prerecognition capabilities include enhancement algorithms that straighten skewed pages, lighten or darken images; remove speckles, streaks, and background shading; and sharpen characters to make them clearer and more recognizable. When processing business forms, some OCR programs can remove horizontal and vertical lines that overlap textual information. They can also detect areas within pages that contain charts, illustrations, or other graphic information and will automatically exclude those areas from recognition processing.

Despite these innovations, OCR is far from a perfect technology. Errors, which are inevitable, must be detected and corrected by proofreading. Unrecognized or suspicious characters are highlighted for operator verification and, where appropriate, typing of correct replacements, which may require examination of source documents. Wherever possible, OCR programs provide word suggestions, which are derived from spelling dictionaries. Some programs use voice synthesis to read recognized text aloud. Even then, some errors may be missed. In any case, the proofreading requirement must not be underestimated: an OCR accuracy rate of 98 percent yields 40 errors in a 2,000-character, double-spaced typewritten page. At 10 seconds per error, correction will require approximately 7 minutes. Depending on document characteristics and other factors, some characters may be marked as suspicious. These characters must be individually examined even though no correction is required. More ominously, because it can adversely impact retrieval operations based on full-text searching of digital documents, some recognition errors may not be flagged for operator examination.

Chapter 3

Indexing Digital Documents

Whether they are born digital or created from paper or microfilm records, digital documents must be indexed for retrieval when needed. When describing and demonstrating their products, digital document technology vendors typically emphasize the distinctive performance characteristics and capabilities of specific hardware and software components. Hardware demonstrations highlight the most impressive features of specific devices such as the operating speeds of document scanners and the display qualities of high-resolution monitors. Software demonstrations emphasize powerful retrieval functionality and compatibility with popular third-party applications, as well as graphical interface characteristics that facilitate learning and use. Document indexing is usually demonstrated in the context of hypothetical, rudimentary business applications that can be easily presented with a minimum of explanation to a broad spectrum of prospective customers. Documents utilized in such demonstrations are pre-indexed, and application analysis is presented as a *fait accompli*. Indexing concepts, the rationale for utilizing particular indexing methodologies, and the complexities of indexing theory and practice are rarely discussed.

Although hardware and software components are undeniably important, the successful implementation and distinctive retrieval capabilities of digital document technology ultimately depend on the characteristics and effectiveness of indexing concepts and procedures employed in particular applications. Index information is a significant carrier of value in digital document implementations. If document indexing is not carefully planned and properly executed, retrieval failures can be expected. The critical relationship between indexing methods and retrieval effectiveness is well established in information science. Research studies spanning four decades confirm that indexing errors, particularly the omission or inappropriate use of subject terms, are a leading cause of retrieval failures in computer-based information systems. If a document is not properly indexed, it is, in effect, lost. Inadequate indexing compromises reliable retrieval, a principal objective of many digital document implementations.

Despite its importance, indexing is a neglected aspect of digital document implementations. Although many publications describe the capabilities of digital imaging, text retrieval, and document management technologies and products, very little discussion of the systems analysis principles associated with indexing digital documents is published. The published literature on indexing theory and practice emphasizes content analysis of journal articles, technical monographs, scientific reports, newspapers, and other publications. Intended principally for library applications, indexing studies rarely deal specifically with organization and retrieval of business records, but they do present many ideas that are broadly applicable to records management problems. This chapter surveys document indexing concepts and procedures, emphasizing analytical and application development principles that are most significant for digital document implementations. It also examines technologies and methodologies for entry of index information into systems that manage digital documents.

Document Indexing Concepts

Although collections of digital images and character-coded text are often described as *databases*, systems that store and retrieve digital documents actually employ two interrelated databases: a document collection and an index to it. Most digital document systems incorporate database management software that can accommodate a broad range of application requirements. Software developers, value-added resellers, system integrators, and other vendors provide the necessary database management components. However, planning and implementation of indexing concepts and procedures for specific document collections are typically the customer's responsibility. Some vendors will help customers perform these tasks; but apart from a general familiarity and experience with information management and systems analysis concepts, vendors have little, if any, formal training in document indexing. Unless paid consulting services are involved, vendors rarely have the time to conduct a rigorous examination of customers' indexing requirements.

The following sections review basic indexing concepts, emphasizing the identification of indexing parameters and selection of index values. The discussion is limited to conventional, parameter-based indexing methods that utilize words, phrases, numbers, or other information as document descriptors. Parameter-based indexing is applicable to digital documents in image and character-coded formats. Full-text indexing, an alternative to parameter-based indexing for character-coded documents, is discussed later in this chapter.

Indexing Parameters

An **indexing parameter** is a category of information by which documents will be indexed for retrieval; also referred to as a *field*. Depending on application requirements, digital documents must be indexed by one or more parameters (fields). Some software products organize digital documents into folders according to customer-defined file plans. Sometimes described as a *file taxonomy*, a **file plan** is a systematic categorization scheme that groups documents pertaining to a given matter. A file plan defines topical or other categories into which documents will be grouped, and a folder is established for each category. Within a given folder, digital documents are stored as individually labeled computer files. Authorized persons can drag and drop digital documents into appropriate folders in the manner of conventional filing. With the Windows operating system, for example, this transfer can be done from the desktop or by using Windows Explorer. Alternatively, batches of digital documents can be transferred from designated file directories into specific folders.

This approach, which emulates conventional filing practices for paper documents, is essentially indexing with a *single parameter*, which may be a personal name, subject heading, project number, case file number, or other designator. It is suitable for medical records, legal cases, student records, personnel records, and other straightforward applications where multiple related documents are retrieved as a group without differentiation by document type or other parameters. Thus, digital documents for a given patient will simply be grouped in a folder labeled with the patient's name. Individual digital documents are identified by file labels, which may include a date, document type, or other information—for example, "Smith, Mary, pathology report, 05-05."

Employing a more complex organization, folders may be nested within folders. In a medical records application, for example, a master folder may be created for each patient. Within the master folder, subfolders may be created for specific types of documents, such as patient histories, test results, clinician's notes, radiological records, insurance claims, and so on. Similarly, an engineering organization's project file plan may provide a master folder for each project. Each master folder will be divided into subfolders for specific types of project records, including statements of work, contract documents, correspondence, project budgets, project reports, and other work products. Subfolders may be further subdivided to organize large quantities of digital documents. A project reports subfolder, for example, may contain nested subfolders that group reports by date or type. A contracts subfolder may contain nested subfolders for specific types of contract documents such as proposals, agreements, and amendments. A correspondence subfolder may contain nested subfolders that categorize correspondence by subject, date, names of correspondents, or other parameters.*

The file plan approach described above is flexible. Software imposes no practical limits on hierarchical levels of folders and subfolders. Authorized persons can create, delete, rename, or move folders and subfolders to accommodate changes in application requirements. However, measured by their ability to retrieve digital documents when needed, folder-oriented file plans suffer the same limitations as the paper filing systems

---

* The terminology used in this discussion requires clarification. Since its inception, the field of computing has borrowed terms from records management, but computer files and folders are not exactly analogous to their paper counterparts. In the examples cited here, digital documents are stored as individual computer files within folders, each document being treated as a separate computer file. In paper filing systems, by contrast, the term *file* variously refers to a single folder, to a collection of related folders, or to a cabinet that contains multiple folders and documents. It never denotes a single document within a folder.

on which they are typically modeled. With its orderly arrangement of categories and subcategories, a well-designed file plan embodies an appealing principle: a place for everything and everything in its place. Problems arise, however, when a document should properly be filed into more than one category.** Further, time-consuming browsing through folder contents is often necessary to identify pertinent documents within a folder or subfolder. A list of folder contents is displayed for operator perusal. Depending on the application, this list may contain many entries. Descriptive labels, which are necessarily brief, may not conclusively identify the documents needed for a given purpose. In such situations, the digital documents themselves must be individually examined by opening them, either by launching their originating applications or by using a viewer program that can display documents in various formats. *Multiparameter indexing*, as discussed next, addresses these problems. Documents are not limited to a single folder, and searches can be narrowed to specific documents within folders.

The identification of appropriate indexing parameters or categories is an essential first step in planning a digital document implementation. If a document is not indexed by a given parameter, it cannot be retrieved by that parameter. The identification of indexing parameters often precedes the selection of hardware and software components. It may occur at an early stage of systems analysis when application requirements are initially delineated. Thus, when preparing a proposal to replace paper records with digital documents, a records manager or other information specialist will usually include a suggested list of indexing parameters or an equivalent discussion of the proposed system's indexing characteristics, although such preliminary indexing decisions may be modified or refined in later stages of system planning and implementation.

A digital document implementation creates and maintains a computer database that serves as an index to a document collection, which may include digital images, character-coded text, CAD files, spreadsheets, or other types of computer-processible documents. The index database contains one record for each digital document included in a given collection. These index records contain pointers to the digital documents to which they pertain. Multipage documents are typically treated as a unit for indexing purposes.

Records in the index database are divided into fields that correspond to indexing parameters selected for the corresponding document collection. These fields are customarily divided into two groups: key fields and nonkey fields. **Key fields,** the most important type in digital document implementations, correspond to the indexing parameters identified for a particular application. They contain names, subject

---

**   Dual categories are a long-recognized problem in library-developed file plans, such as the Dewey Decimal System and the Library of Congress Classification system, which arrange books on shelves by subject. Each book is assigned a single classification code that corresponds to its subject-oriented shelf location. These library file plans are remarkable achievements, but many books might be appropriately shelved in two or more categories. Further, some books, such as works of fiction, are not well served by subject indexing. Addressing these inadequacies, a library's author, title, and subject catalogs provide additional methods of identifying books needed for specific purposes. If a well-organized file plan is sufficient for reliable retrieval, those supplementary mechanisms would not be necessary.

terms, dates, or information by which digital documents will be retrieved. **Nonkey fields**, by contrast, contain descriptive information that is important but will not be used for retrieval. Instead, information contained in nonkey fields is displayed when index records are retrieved through searches involving key fields.

Nonkey fields are especially useful where digital document technologies are integrated into broader database management applications. In such situations, information contained in the nonkey fields within database records may satisfy many retrieval requirements. In an application involving human resources documents, for example, database records may include nonkey fields for employee addresses and telephone numbers, thereby eliminating the need to view digital documents to obtain such information. As an additional advantage, information contained in nonkey fields can facilitate relevance judgments where many digital documents are retrieved by a given search. In an application involving technical reports, for example, database records may include abstracts, tables of contents, annotations, or other document summaries in nonkey fields. That information can help searchers determine which digital documents should be viewed.

When developing indexing procedures for a given digital document implementation, a records manager or other information specialist studies the target application and prepares a database plan for consideration by prospective users and others involved in system installation, configuration, and operation. The plan includes a proposed list of key and nonkey fields that will be reviewed, revised as necessary, and ultimately approved by interested parties. Key fields are typically identified by interviewing users to determine their retrieval requirements and, where digital documents will replace paper files or micrographic systems, by observing existing filing practices and retrieval methodologies. For nonkey fields, the application planner must consult with users to determine additional descriptive information to be displayed when index records are retrieved. These methods are not unique to digital document implementations. They also apply to other technologies, such as computer-assisted microfilm retrieval, that employ document indexing.

Although conclusive determination of indexing parameters requires a careful analysis of specific retrieval requirements, some obvious possibilities can be identified for commonly encountered records management applications. As an example, the following list presents key and nonkey fields for indexing office documents:

☐ Date	key field
☐ Date entered	nonkey field
☐ Document type	key field
☐ Author	key field
☐ Author Affiliation	key field
☐ Recipient	key field
☐ Recipient Affiliation	key field
☐ Subject(s)	key field
☐ Notes	nonkey field

In digital document implementations, an index database is sometimes characterized as metadata because it contains information about information. The examples of key and nonkey fields presented above are similar to those delineated in ISO 15836, *Information and Documentation—The Dublin Core Metadata Element Set*. All suggested fields are key fields except "notes" and "date entered." The "notes" field may contain a document summary, evaluative comments, instructions for further action, or other descriptive information. The "date entered" field indicates the date a digital document was accessioned (by scanning, key-entry, OCR, or transfer from an originating application) and indexed. The "date" field, a key field, stores the date on which a given document was written, assuming that the document is dated. Date information is frequently used to narrow retrieval operations to specific time frames. The "document type" field identifies particular types of office records such as correspondence, memoranda, e-mail messages, budgets, or reports. With this key field, retrieval can be limited to a particular type of document.

The "author" and "recipient" fields contain personal names. The "recipient" field is typically associated with correspondence, memoranda, e-mail messages, and other documents received from external sources. Although personal names are important, authors and recipients may be more meaningfully identified by the internal departments or external organizations with which they are affiliated. A manager evaluating the performance of a given contractor, for example, may need to retrieve all correspondence to and from that contractor, regardless of the specific author or recipient of the correspondence. The "subject(s)" field contains words or phrases that represent the subject content of a document, one of the most important retrieval parameters for business records. This field is typically a multivalue field because office documents may treat multiple subjects. Usually, limits are placed on the number of subject words or the length of the subject field. Concepts and complications of subject indexing are discussed later in this chapter.

Taking another example, the following list presents possible key and nonkey fields for indexing technical reports created by engineering organizations, pharmaceutical companies, government laboratories, and other research and development organizations:

- [ ] Date   key field
- [ ] Report number   key field
- [ ] Project number   key field
- [ ] Author(s)   key field
- [ ] Title   key field
- [ ] Originating department   key field
- [ ] Subject(s)   key field
- [ ] Abstract   nonkey field
- [ ] Page length   nonkey field

Computer-based indexing systems for technical reports predate digital document technology by several decades. These applications are consequently well understood. Most of the field designations are self-explanatory. Assuming that index values are accurately selected, the key fields presented in this example will permit searches for technical reports written by a specified person, produced by a specified department, associated with a specified project, or dealing with a specified subject. "Author" and "subject" are multivalue fields. Many technical reports have multiple authors and require multiple subject terms for adequate indexing. The "abstract" and "page length" fields contain useful descriptive information. Abstracts, as previously noted, can facilitate relevance decisions, thereby minimizing the viewing of irrelevant documents. For lengthy documents, a searcher may elect to print them for later study rather than display them for online examination. Depending on software capabilities, the abstract may be designated a key field, in which case searches could be performed for specific words within the abstract. Similar full-text retrieval functionality is useful for document titles. Full-text indexing and retrieval concepts are discussed later in this chapter.

Addressing a common document retrieval application in architectural firms, engineering organizations, construction contractors, manufacturing companies, utility plants, transportation agencies, military installations, and many other organizations, the following list presents possible key and nonkey fields for indexing engineering drawings associated with design, manufacturing, and construction activities:

☐ Date	key field
☐ Project number/name	key field
☐ Drawing number	key field
☐ Revision number	key field
☐ Title	key field
☐ Drawing type	key field
☐ Object depicted	key field
☐ Producer	key field
☐ Original size	nonkey field
☐ Original material	nonkey field
☐ Number of sheets	nonkey field
☐ Notes	nonkey field

Again assuming that accurate index values are selected and appropriate software capabilities provided, the indicated fields will permit retrieval of drawings by various combinations of date, project number or name, drawing number, revision number, title, drawing type, object depicted, and producer. Title information will presumably be taken from the title block. The "object depicted" field contains descriptive information, such as a product, component, or building name, not included in the drawing's title. For digital documents produced by scanning preexisting drawings rather than by CAD technology, nonkey fields contain information about an original drawing's size, represented by code letters or international paper designations, and its medium such as paper or transparencies. The notes field may contain comments, instructions, or other information about a drawing.

As a final example, the following list presents possible key and nonkey fields for indexing order files in a customer service department:

☐	Date	key field
☐	Document type	key field
☐	Customer name	key field
☐	Internal order number	key field
☐	Customer order number	key field
☐	Invoice number	key field
☐	Description of order	nonkey field
☐	Notes	nonkey field

In paper form, such files are typically arranged by customer name or order number. They may contain purchase orders, invoices, correspondence, or other documents necessary to answer customers' questions and resolve problems pertaining to particular orders. With the key fields outlined above, customer service representatives will be able to retrieve digital documents by various combinations of document type, date, and identifying numbers, assuming accurate selection of index values and appropriate software capabilities. The nonkey fields can contain descriptive information, comments, or instructions.

Index Values

Indexing is based on the premise that the contents of documents can be adequately represented by descriptive labels that serve as document surrogates. Indexing involves an analysis of the content or other characteristics of documents and the determination of appropriate labels for designated indexing parameters. For purposes of this discussion, the descriptive labels associated with specific indexing parameters are termed *index values*. Indexing parameters, as discussed above, are defined for an application as a whole; index values describe specific documents in a manner determined by those parameters. Index characteristics and indexing methods are presented in several standards and related publications, including ISO 5963, *Documentation—Methods for Examining Documents, Determining their Subjects, and Selecting Indexing Terms*, ISO 999, *Information and Documentation—Guidelines for the Content, Organization, and Presentation of Indexes*, NISO TR-02, *Guidelines for Indexes and Related Information Retrieval Devices*, and AIIM TR40, *Information and Image Management—Suggested Index Fields for Document in Electronic Image Management (EIM) Environments*.

Often, the values appropriate to specific indexing parameters can be determined by a cursory examination of documents; for example, documents with dates, author names, and recipient names used to index office correspondence and memoranda. Such documents are usually formatted in a manner that highlights the indicated information. Interdepartmental memoranda, for example, are often created on special stationery that includes labeled heading areas for dates and names. That information is also prominently featured in printed copies of e-mail messages. Similarly, purchase orders and other standardized business forms contain labeled sections for dates, purchase order numbers, vendor names, and other information. The date, author(s), title, and originating department usually appear on the cover of a technical report. The title block of an engineering drawing typically contains the drawing number, date, project number, producer, and revision number in labeled boxes. The drawing's size, material, and number of pages can usually be determined by physical examination.

In such straightforward situations, appropriate index values can be quickly and easily extracted from documents by administrative or data-entry personnel. Identifying index values is not so easy with subject indexing, which requires content analysis—the determination of "aboutness"—and the expression of that determination in words or phrases that are variously called *subject terms, subject headings, subject descriptors, subject identifiers,* or *subject keywords.* Because subject indexing is an intellectually demanding and potentially time-consuming task, simpler indexing parameters—such as names, dates, and numeric identifiers—are preferable. In many records management applications, however, subject indexing is unavoidable; for example, with office correspondence, technical reports, and management reports. In such situations, application planners must develop and implement indexing procedures that will facilitate document analysis and promote effective retrieval. The following discussion outlines major issues in subject analysis of documents and reviews the distinctive characteristics and limitations of particular subject indexing methodologies.

Subject Term Selection

Subject indexing can be based on assigned or derived terms. In the former approach, an indexer selects descriptive words or phrases based on a reading and analysis of all or part of a document. The selected words or phrases may or may not appear in the document itself. In either case, the assigned subject terms represent the indexer's understanding of concepts treated in the document. As a result, this approach to subject indexing is sometimes called **concept indexing**.

In **derived term indexing**, subject descriptors are extracted from all or selected portions of a document. The index terms must appear in the document itself; no other words are permitted. This approach is based on a simple, though admittedly arguable, premise: Presumably, an author's own words accurately represent a document's subject content. In manual indexing systems, some analysis of document content is required to identify subject descriptors. Even so, proponents of derived term indexing argue that it is faster than the assigned term approach; indexers can simply underline product names, trade names, specialized terminology, or other words that appear in documents rather than thinking up terms that reflect specific concepts.

The derived term approach to document indexing is also compatible with software extraction of subject words from titles, abstracts or other document segments—assuming, of course, that the indicated segments are in character-coded form. A widely encountered form of automated indexing, first implemented in the 1960s, derives subject terms from the titles of technical reports, journal articles, or other documents. It can also be applied to engineering drawings, memoranda, and other business records that have titles or pseudo-titles such as subject lines. As discussed later in this chapter, **full-text indexing** carries derived term indexing to its extreme by using every word in a document as an index term.

Research studies that compare assigned and derived term indexing do not demonstrate a conclusive advantage for either approach. Each method has its proponents, but, given the complexities of subject indexing, both approaches leave many documents unretrievable. Assigned term indexing, however, can employ vocabulary control to improve retrieval performance in some situations. In this context, *indexing vocabulary* denotes the subject terms utilized to index a given collection of documents. As defined above, derived term indexing uses the vocabulary of the document itself—the author's own language—to represent subject concepts. It is consequently considered an uncontrolled indexing methodology. Except for the requirement that they appear in the document itself, no restrictions are placed on the words that can be used as subject terms. Synonymous terms, related words, and singular or plural forms of nouns can be used indiscriminately, although some indexers recommend the consistent use of *singular noun forms*—a practice employed by most dictionaries—as a rudimentary concession to vocabulary control.

In assigned term indexing, by contrast, a list of authorized words or phrases can facilitate the selection of subject terms. Such an indexing aid is variously called a *thesaurus* (plural form: thesauri) or a *subject authority list.* Thesaurus characteristics are presented in ISO 2788, *Documentation—Guidelines for the Establishment and Development of Monolingual Thesauri,* ISO 5964, *Documentation—Guidelines for the Establishment and Development of Multilingual Thesauri,* and ANSI/NISO Z39.19, *Guidelines for the Construction, Format, and Management of Monolingual Thesauri.* An effectively designed thesaurus presents a structured view of a particular activity or field of knowledge as reflected in subject words or phrases. In addition to providing a codified, standardized list of authorized index terms, a thesaurus typically includes cross-references from unauthorized synonyms to approved terms and from authorized terms to broader, narrower, or otherwise related terms. It may also contain scope notes that define the ways in which authorized terms can be used for indexing purposes.

Some research studies suggest that the availability of a thesaurus promotes consistency where subject indexing is performed by multiple persons. A thesaurus can also facilitate selection of search terms and formulation of retrieval strategies. The time and cost associated with thesaurus creation and maintenance, however, are major impediments to their implementation in business applications. A thesaurus developer must collect potential subject terms from various sources, including other thesauri where available; consolidate the terms into a single listing; review the terms for suitability; prepare scope notes for authorized terms; eliminate synonyms and plural noun forms; and construct cross-references to link related terms and to direct indexers from unauthorized terms to approved entries. Once the initial edition of a thesaurus is prepared, a formal maintenance procedure must be established to deal with new terms and the modification of existing entries.

Requiring months or even years to prepare, thesauri are impractical in business-oriented records management applications, where rapid implementation is a paramount consideration. As a possible exception, digital document implementations in specialized subject areas—such as aeronautics, medicine, petroleum engineering, education, or pharmaceuticals—may be able to adapt existing thesauri or lists of subject headings created for use with published indexes or online databases.

Although discussions of vocabulary control most often deal with subject terms, personal and corporate names—including names of companies, government agencies, educational institutions, and not-for-profit organizations, as well as departmental names within a given organization—can pose problems for both indexers and searchers in digital document implementations. Index values for personal name fields may variously, inconsistently, and unpredictably contain complete forenames and middle names, or simply one or more initials. Corporate names may be entered in complete or abbreviated forms—International Business Machines, International Business Machines Corporation, IBM, or IBM Corporation, for example. Government agency names may be subject to even greater variation—for instance: Department of Defense, DoD, U.S. Department of Defense, U.S. DoD, United States DoD, and United States Department of Defense. Full names, abbreviations, and acronyms may be used interchangeably and indiscriminately.

A **name authority list** can address these problems. A variant form of thesaurus, it establishes approved forms for personal and corporate names to be used as index values. It also provides cross-references from unauthorized forms, such as abbreviations and acronyms, to approved forms. Compared to thesauri, name authority lists are easier to construct and maintain. Employee names and departmental names can be taken from organizational directories. Published reference sources, such as business and government directories, can establish authorized forms for names of external organizations. Indexing rules can specify whether full corporate names or acronyms are to be used, as well as procedures for cross-references.

Indexing Consistency

Among other issues that can affect retrieval performance in digital document implementations, indexing consistency denotes agreement in the type and number of index values selected for documents of similar content. Consistency is principally an issue in the assigned-term approach to subject indexing. Inconsistency is limited when selecting index values for authors' names, dates, project numbers, order numbers, or other non-subject fields listed in previous examples, although format inconsistencies are possible in the absence of a name authority list. Derived-term subject indexing, as previously defined, depends entirely on the words contained in documents. Consistency considerations are less significant, but not necessarily irrelevant, in such situations.

Indexing consistency has two aspects: **inter-indexer consistency** denotes agreement in the selection of subject terms when documents of similar content are indexed by different persons, while **intra-indexer consistency** denotes agreement in the selection of subject terms for similar documents indexed by the same person. In either case, indexing consistency is closely linked to indexing quality. Consistent selection of subject terms promotes effective retrieval. However, information science research spanning four decades suggests that indexing consistency is difficult to achieve. Subject indexing is a complex intellectual task. The selection of subject terms is influenced by various factors, including the semantic characteristics and readability of documents, as well as an indexer's ability to recognize and express subject concepts. Research studies of identical documents indexed by different persons have found significant variations in the number of subject terms assigned and in the use of synonymous terms. Agreement about the subject content of a given document does not guarantee consistent selection of index terms to represent that content.

Published studies of intra-indexer consistency, involving documents that were accidentally indexed twice by the same person, likewise report significant variations in the selection of subject terms.

Several studies have found that the availability of thesauri, lists of subject headings, lists of previously used index terms, or other indexing aids can improve consistency. Experiments likewise indicate that subject indexing based on titles or abstracts yields higher consistency than indexing from complete documents. That observation is more applicable to technical reports than to business records, which may lack abstracts or meaningful titles. Research also suggests that experienced indexers are more consistent in their selection of subject terms than inexperienced indexers.

Indexing Depth

Indexing depth refers to the number of indexing parameters and the number of index values per parameter to be applied to individual documents. The database management software employed in most digital document implementations imposes few restrictions on the number of indexing parameters (fields) or index values in a given application. As the previously cited examples indicate, digital documents are commonly indexed by multiple parameters, thereby permitting flexible retrieval approaches. Many records management applications are adequately served by 10 or fewer key fields. Where subject indexing is involved, multiple subject terms are customarily allowed. If desired, document images can be indexed with dozens of subject terms at varying levels of specificity, but given the time and cost associated with extensive document analysis such exhaustive indexing is seldom practical or justifiable.

Indexing depth is closely related to retrieval performance. In particular, it affects two widely discussed measures of retrieval effectiveness: *recall* and *precision*. **Recall** measures the number of relevant documents retrieved by a given search as a percentage of the total number of relevant documents in a given collection. If a search retrieves 16 of 20 relevant documents, for example, the recall is 80 percent. **Precision**, by contrast, measures the number of relevant documents retrieved by a given search as a percentage of the total number of documents, relevant and irrelevant, retrieved. If a search retrieves 20 documents of which 12 are judged to be relevant, the precision is 60 percent. As a practical matter, precision can be calculated by sorting through search results to distinguish relevant from irrelevant documents. Recall, by contrast, has conceptual rather than practical significance. It can only be tested under artificial circumstances where the number of documents relevant to a given search is predetermined.

Ideally, a digital document implementation will provide full recall of relevant documents without retrieving any irrelevant ones, but that objective is unattainable. In practice, an inverse relationship exists between recall and precision. Indexing methods that improve recall tend to degrade precision, and vice versa. Indexing depth promotes recall; the greater the number of subject terms assigned to a given document, the greater the likelihood that all documents about a particular subject will be retrieved. On the other hand, indexing depth degrades precision; the greater the number of subject terms assigned to a given document, the greater the likelihood that some terms will reflect minor aspects of the document's content. On examination by a searcher, such documents are often judged to be irrelevant for a particular information requirement such as with full-text indexing where all words in documents become index terms. As discussed later in this chapter, full-text indexing provides high recall but characteristically retrieves many irrelevant documents. Precision is enhanced by limiting indexing to a few, well-selected subject terms that represent a document's primary content.

These effects are well documented in information science publications, but the decision to emphasize high recall or high precision is determined by application requirements. Where searchers are willing to tolerate irrelevant results to ensure maximum retrieval of relevant documents, indexing depth is encouraged. In other situations, searchers may find irrelevant documents annoying. They want a few highly relevant documents that can be quickly identified without having to sort through irrelevant documents. To accomplish quick identification of highly relevant documents, the application planner should limit the number of subject terms per document. As a compromise, separate index fields can be allocated for major and minor subject terms. Where high recall is desired, both fields can be searched. To increase precision, searches can be limited to major subject terms. This approach is utilized by some bibliographic databases and their printed index counterparts, including MEDLINE (*Index Medicus*) and ERIC (*Current Index to Journals in Education*).

Indexing Personnel

Publishing companies, scholarly associations, and other organizations that produce bibliographic databases and printed indexes typically hire subject specialists and/or persons with indexing training or experience. Such expertise is rarely used in business-oriented applications, where index terms are selected by the creators or recipients of documents. In such situations, indexers receive little or no training, and their subject knowledge, experience, and motivation may vary considerably.

Fortunately, research studies have found no significant differences in retrieval effectiveness for documents indexed by persons with diverse subject knowledge and indexing experience. Several studies suggest that authors, can effectively index their own documents; after all, they wrote them and are presumably most knowledgeable about their contents. Most publishers of bibliographic databases and printed indexes consider author-supplied subject terms a useful adjunct to their own indexing operations. Given the varied indexing arrangements encountered in digital imaging installations, these findings are encouraging. Motivation is another matter, however; document creators and recipients may not appreciate the importance of indexing and are often reluctant to give it their full attention.

Full-Text Indexing

Full-text indexing is a computerized indexing method for character-coded documents or document surrogates such as abstracts, summaries, and annotations. The subject of much research over the past four decades, full-text indexing is based on derived-term indexing concepts. Full-text indexing software processes character-coded documents, identifies the words they contain, and extracts them for inclusion in an

inverted index, a computer file that lists words with pointers to the digital documents in which they appear. To simplify lookups, the inverted index is typically an alphabetic list of words extracted from digital documents. Some inverted indexes merely list the documents that contain specific words; others indicate the exact location(s) of a word within a document. In either case, the indexing process is automatic: Words are typically identified as strings of characters delimited by punctuation marks or spaces. This parsing of character-coded text is performed by utility programs that are described as *word breakers*. Some full-text indexing programs employ multiple word breakers for applications that involve multilingual documents.

In theory, a full-text indexing program generates an entry in an inverted index for every word in a digital document. In practice, however, some words are usually excluded. These words include prepositions, conjunctions, interjections, adverbs, and certain adjectives that rarely convey subject content. The excluded words, known as *stop words* or *noise words*, are stored in a file called a *stop list*, which the indexing program matches against the words encountered in a digital document. Single-letter words, such as "I" and "a," and possibly two-letter words, such as "an" and "if," may be automatically excluded without checking the stop list. For applications that involve multilingual documents, the full-text indexing program may store multiple stop lists or a single list that contains stop words in multiple languages. To address special application requirements, some full-text indexing programs allow users to add words to or delete words from a stop list, but some application planners argue against this practice, noting that the inclusion of irrelevant nouns, verbs, or adjectives as index terms increases the size of the index but has no negative impact on retrieval performance.

Once reserved for special situations, full-text indexing is now commonplace. It is used, for example, by web search engines, and full-text indexing capability is supported as a standard or optional feature by document imaging, content management, and records management application software. Full-text indexing is intended for character-coded digital documents, but full-text indexing programs differ in the document formats they can process. Some programs require character-coded documents in the plain text format. Others can index various combinations of word processing files, PDF files, e-mail messages, spreadsheet files, and web pages. Full-text indexing is not applicable to CAD files, audio files, video files, or other nontextual information. Full-text indexing is not applicable to document images unless OCR technology is used to convert their contents to character-coded text. A number of imaging systems use this approach to permit full-text searching of document images.

Although full-text indexing functionality is enthusiastically promoted by software vendors, information science research indicates limitations as well as advantages. As discussed in Chapter 4, full-text indexing permits searches for documents that contain specific words, including personal and organizational names, product names, project names, chemical names, and other words that may not be included in the field-based indexing, assigned-term indexing methods previously described. Studies of specific applications confirm that full-text indexing permits retrieval of documents that could not be retrieved by field-based indexing. Compared to field based-indexing, full-text indexing provides great indexing depth. Where the number of subject terms is limited, assigned-term indexing necessarily emphasizes major concepts. With full-text indexing, by contrast, most nouns and verbs become searchable index terms. These searchable index terms yield high recall but characteristically low precision. Full-text searches can locate documents that treat specific topics peripherally, but they often retrieve many irrelevant documents. Several studies have demonstrated that precision is improved if full-text indexing is limited to abstracts or document summaries. Compared to full-text indexing of abstracts, full-text indexing of complete documents in technical libraries appears to offer little improvement in retrieval performance, but these findings have limited significance for records management applications. Unlike technical reports and other library materials, few business records have abstracts. Because full-text indexing relies on derived-term methods, it does not employ vocabulary control. For comprehensiveness, synonymous subject terms and variant forms of names must be individually searched.

Retrieval performance aside, automatic derivation of index terms from digital documents offers economic advantages over field-based, assigned-term indexing. Manual indexing is an intellectually demanding, time-consuming, and labor-intensive activity. In applications where long, complex documents must be analyzed by multiple parameters, indexers may spend 10 minutes or longer on a single document. As an example, a medium-size pharmaceutical laboratory that performs drug discovery, development, and testing may produce 10,000 to 15,000 chemical compound analyses, safety assessments, microbiology reports, clinical protocols, technical memoranda, and other research documents per year. Optimistically, assuming that an entry-level information scientist with undergraduate training in biology or chemistry can index six such documents per hour, 1,670 to 2,500 hours of indexing labor will be required to analyze the laboratory's report output for a single year. If indexers are paid $50,000 per year plus 30 percent fringe benefits (effectively $32.50 per hour), the annual cost to index 10,000 to 15,000 reports will range from $54,375 to $81,250.

Given their time-consuming nature, assigned-term indexing methods are poorly suited to applications, such as litigation support, where large numbers of documents must be indexed in a short period of time. Even where rapid turnaround is not a paramount consideration, high-volume indexing operations will require a large staff and strict supervision to make indexing information available to interested parties in a reasonable time frame. Although assigned-term indexing based on intellectual analysis of documents may be successfully applied to a small quantity of newly created documents, subject indexing of large backfiles often proves prohibitively expensive.

Full-text and field-based indexing are not mutually exclusive methodologies. Full-text and field-based indexing can be effectively combined in a given application. In a pharmaceutical company, for example, a collection of character-coded technical reports might be indexed by the author's name, title, date, and subject terms, with full-text indexing being applied to the contents of the reports or to abstracts where available.

Automatic Categorization

As the name implies, **automatic categorization** is a form of automatic indexing in which software analyzes digital documents and assigns them to categories in a predefined file plan or indexing scheme. As with full-text indexing, the documents to be categorized must be character-coded. Depending on its content, a given digital document may be assigned to one or more index categories.

Categorization software products, sometimes described as *categorization engines*, employ synonym lists, pattern-matching algorithms, word clustering, word frequencies, word proximities, and other lexical and statistical concepts and tools to analyze a document's content and identify key words or phrases for indexing purposes. Unlike full-text indexing programs, which create index entries for all words except those on a stop list, categorization software evaluates rather than extracts words. Some categorization engines employ rule-based approaches in which certain words or phrases are associated with specific file plan categories. The categorization rules must be developed by persons familiar with the application served by the file plan. Other categorization engines use an example-based approach, in which documents are compared to a training set of documents previously categorized by a knowledgeable person. The larger the training set, the more accurate the results. To obtain best results, some categorization engines employ a combination of these methods. With most programs, automatic categorization can be supplemented by human intervention where the analysis of document content falls below a predetermined confidence threshold.

The subject of several decades of information science research, categorization engines are still evolving. Although a growing number of companies offer categorization products, their ability to accurately categorize digital documents depends on several factors, including document content and the nature and complexity of file plans associated with specific applications. With some document collections, file plans can include hundreds or even thousands of categories. To improve accuracy, some software developers offer predefined file plans for specific industries, such as law firms and investment banking, or commonly encountered business functions such as human resources or marketing.

Advocates of automatic categorization contend that it offers a favorable trade-off of accuracy for speed when compared to human indexing in applications that involve large backfiles of uncategorized documents. Although human indexing is time-consuming and labor-intensive, categorization engines can process thousands of documents per hour. However, an incorrectly categorized document cannot be retrieved when needed, regardless of how quickly it was analyzed. In its defense, automatic categorization is a relatively new technology. As it develops, categorization accuracy is likely to improve. As discussed elsewhere in this book, accuracy was once a significant problem for OCR, but reliability increased as the technology matured.

Index Data-Entry

After subject terms or other index values are selected, they must be converted to computer-processible form for inclusion in the database that serves as an index to digital documents. This task is the index data-entry. In digital document implementations, as in other computer applications, two methods account for the majority of data-entry activity: key-entry and auto-indexing, which includes barcoding and OCR. Other, more specialized data-entry methods, such as speech recognition, are currently limited in their capabilities and consequently in their suitability for digital document implementations, although that situation may change as the technology improves.

The following discussion applies to field-based indexing only. As previously defined, a full-text indexing program extracts index terms from digital documents. Manual intervention is limited to periodic initiation of indexing operations by transferring digital documents from their native applications to the full-text indexing program. This process is usually done in batches at predetermined intervals. Index data-entry is not required. Term extraction can require considerable computing power, however. A fast processor with large amounts of random-access memory and hard disk space is consequently recommended. In most installations, full-text indexing software operates on a dedicated server. When it is working reliably, automatic categorization likewise eliminates the need for manual entry of index information.

Key-Entry Methods

In digital document implementations, as in computer applications generally, key-entry (typing) of field values is the most prevalent data-entry methodology. For that purpose, digital document installations include one or more data-entry stations equipped with a keyboard and video display device. In low-volume implementations, key-entry of index data may be performed by the same workstation that creates electronic images or character-coded text. As described in Chapter 2, a source document is scanned or its contents are converted to character-coded form by key-entry or OCR. The resulting digital document is displayed on a computer monitor for inspection, followed by rescanning or other error correction as necessary. When scanning is completed, field values for the digital document are typed in a manner prescribed by the database management software used to index the images. This sequence of work steps is then repeated for the next source document.

In most digital document implementations, however, creation of digital documents and index data-entry are performed at different times by different workstations. Documents are scanned in batches, for example, for later inspection, OCR, and index data-entry. This approach is well suited to imaging applications where a single scanner can handle the image capture workload, but lengthy database records necessitate multiple data-entry stations to achieve an acceptable level of work throughput. Alternatively, document input and data-entry responsibilities may be assigned to separate units within an organization. In an enterprise-wide digital document implementation, for example, a centralized department may create document images or character-coded text, while index data-entry is performed by the individual departments that originate or use the documents.

Depending on the application, key-entry of index data may be performed from source documents or from digital documents. The latter approach allows data-entry to be combined with inspection of digital images and verification of character-coded text. In either case, key-entry of index data is controlled by software. A data-entry workstation displays a formatted screen with field names and adjacent blank spaces. The data-entry operator fills in the blanks, using the tab key or another designated key to advance from field to field. As explained in Chapter 2, key-entry rates are affected by operator skill, data-entry procedures, source document characteristics, and other factors. Verification may be performed by double-keying or proofreading. As previously discussed, double-keying is more reliable but more time-consuming and costly. The two verification methods are not mutually exclusive, however. Double-keying can be limited to specific fields, such as key fields that require a high degree of accuracy for reliable retrieval performance, while proofreading is used for document summaries or other nonkey fields. Double-keying can also be used for index fields that contain numbers, personal names, or other information that is resistant to accurate proofreading.

Whether performed by double-keying or proofreading, **data verification** involves the detection and correction of incorrectly typed characters. **Data validation**, by contrast, checks the appropriateness of field values that are typed correctly. Data validation is performed by software during data-entry. Certain validation capabilities are widely supported by database management software used for document indexing as shown in Figure 3.1.

Barcoding

To minimize or eliminate key-entry requirements, some digital document implementations employ auto-indexing methods, by which index values are automatically

Data Validation
Routines

Figure 3.1

Data Validation Routines

Among commonly encountered examples, data validation routines can confirm

- that entries are made in mandatory fields;
- that entered field values are of a specified type such as alphabetic or numeric;
- that entered field values fall within a specified numeric or chronologic range;
- that entered field values are contained in a table of approved values.

- A simple data validation routine can confirm that a social security number or telephone number contains the correct number of digits.

- More complex routines can check internally stored data to confirm that field entries for city and ZIP Codes or for area code and state are compatible.

extracted from digital documents themselves. Barcode recognition, one of the oldest and simplest auto-indexing methods, is compatible with digital documents in image formats only. It provides an accurate, fast, and easily implemented alternative to key-entry for certain types of index information. In addition to digital imaging installations, barcoding has been successfully employed in various records management and document control applications, including computer-assisted microfilm retrieval, file circulation, and library circulation systems.

In barcode recognition, characters that comprise a specific field value are encoded by predetermined patterns of vertical lines that vary in width and spacing. Barcodes may be printed directly onto source documents or onto labels that are affixed to documents. In either case, the barcodes appear within electronic images when documents are scanned. Depending on application characteristics, documents may contain multiple barcodes, each representing a different field value.

The meanings of specific barcode patterns are defined by the symbology, or line patterns, employed in a particular system. Examples of barcode symbologies include Codabar, Code 39, Code 93, Code 128, Interleaved 2 of 5, and UPC/EAN. Some barcode symbologies are limited to numeric digits and selected nonalphabetic characters such as currency symbols and hyphens. Other symbologies can encode both alphabetic and numeric characters, but such usage is rarely encountered. In digital imaging implementations, barcodes typically represent numeric field values such as case numbers, order numbers, project numbers, batch numbers, or sequentially assigned document numbers. In some cases, a single barcode attached to a folder applies to all documents inside. Often, human-readable numbers are printed beneath the line patterns. Depending on symbology, a barcode may contain up to 30 characters. Higher capacity two-dimensional barcodes have been developed, but they are not used in digital imaging applications.

Although some document scanners can read barcodes, auto-indexing capabilities are usually implemented by software that locates and interprets barcodes within digitized images following scanning. The software runs on the scanning workstation's host computer. The interpreted information is transferred into designated fields within database records associated with particular document images. Although barcoding is a straightforward technology with proven performance characteristics, the accuracy of barcode recognition software is affected by a number of factors, including the locations and orientations of barcodes within digitized images, the clarity of a barcode's vertical line patterns, the contrast between lines and spaces, the characteristics of the paper stock on which the barcode is printed, the scanning resolution employed in a given application, and page skewing during scanning. The most flexible recognition software can locate barcodes anywhere within digitized images. The barcodes may be oriented horizontally or vertically. They can employ multiple symbologies printed in different sizes. Recognition software can also read barcodes that are moderately skewed.

Barcode technology is highly reliable, but its usefulness in digital imaging applications is often exaggerated. Barcodes principally encode numeric field values, which are a subset of most index data in document imaging applications. Names, subject terms, and other alphabetic values must be key-entered or captured by OCR technology.

Barcode recognition is best suited to documents with preprinted barcodes. Separate printing of barcodes on adhesive labels that must be affixed to documents can require more time and effort than key-entry of numeric field values. Further, barcode labels must be carefully positioned within pages to avoid obscuring information. Although large barcodes are easier to interpret when scanned at 200 dots per inch, they may not fit onto a given page. Densely printed barcodes must be scanned at 300 dots per inch for consistently accurate recognition.

Optical Character Recognition

Optical character recognition (OCR) is often cited as a fast, economical alternative to key-entry of index data in digital imaging implementations. As described in Chapter 2, OCR is a data-entry methodology that combines scanning with image analysis to recognize or read characters contained in source documents. It is more flexible than barcode recognition. In most OCR implementations, the recognizable repertoire includes letters of the alphabet, numeric digits, punctuation marks, and other symbols encountered in correspondence, reports, business forms, publications, and similar textual documents. The recognized characters are converted to machine-readable, character-coded form, just as if they had been typed.

Since its introduction in the 1960s, OCR has offered a fast, potentially cost-effective alternative to key-entry for certain computing applications, such as remittance processing and order fulfillment, where the layout and typographic characteristics of source documents are specially designed for machine recognition. OCR can be used to create character-coded text from images of source documents. As an auto-indexing methodology for digital images, OCR can recognize textual information within designated areas of source documents, convert the information to character-coded form, and transfer it into specified fields within index records, thereby eliminating the need to type those field values. This approach to auto-indexing is sometimes described as *zonal OCR* because recognition is limited to readily identifiable zones within source documents. It requires highly formatted source documents such as invoices, purchase orders, and insurance claim forms. Recognition is guided by a template that specifies the locations within source documents where the indicated field values appear.

OCR combines document digitization with image analysis. Because document scanning is an essential prelude to recognition, the terms *OCR* and *scanning* are often used interchangeably, but that usage is imprecise and misleading. Document scanning is merely one work step in an OCR implementation. Like the image compression and enhancement algorithms described in the preceding chapter, OCR is performed by programs that process digitized images generated by document scanners. OCR programs may reside in processing circuitry built into a scanner that performs both document digitization and character recognition. Such scanners are sometimes described as *OCR readers* to distinguish them from conventional document digitizers. During the 1980s, OCR readers were employed in various digital imaging installations, but their popularity has since waned. Although they support fast recognition processing for high-volume applications, OCR readers are expensive.

Taking a more flexible and economical approach to auto-indexing, most digital imaging configurations now incorporate OCR software that operates on the scanning workstation's host computer or, more appropriately, on another network computer that functions as an OCR server. Operating as a dedicated, special-purpose system component, the OCR server receives digitized images from scanning workstations and performs recognition processing without affecting other imaging operations. In the absence of a dedicated OCR server, recognition processing may be performed at night or during other off-peak hours to avoid degrading system performance.

Compared to key-entry of index values, OCR is faster and requires less labor. However, OCR affects only initial data-entry; error detection, via proofreading, is still required. Unrecognized or suspect characters and words are highlighted or otherwise marked for operator examination and correction. As a supplement to proofreading, data validation scripts can check for correct character content and length in specified field values.

Where appropriate OCR accuracy is unattainable, application planners can reduce key-entry costs by eliminating unnecessary index fields or by typing abbreviated field values for names or subjects that can later be expanded to full forms by software. In some applications, index data can be downloaded into an imaging system from external databases that reside on mainframes, midrange computers, or network servers. The resulting savings in data-entry labor typically offsets the cost of customized programming required to accomplish such transfers.

Even better, an existing database that resides on an external computer can sometimes serve as an index to digital images. Thus, a purchasing database can serve as an index to images of requisitions, purchase orders, correspondence, and other procurement-related documents. When records are retrieved from the purchase order database, the searcher is given the option of viewing images of related documents. Similarly, a library catalog can serve as an index to images of books, journal articles, reports, and other publications. When a bibliographic record for a given title is retrieved from the catalog, the searcher can request images of the documents themselves. Such situations are increasingly commonplace. Data-entry for document images is limited to a single field value that uniquely identifies individual documents, possibly supplemented by fields for the document type and date. The digital document imaging system must be networked to the computer on which the external database resides, and customized programming is required to link the imaging system's index database with the external database application, which is then described as *image-enabled*. Most imaging vendors can provide the integration services required to link the computer systems and databases. Such integration need not be limited to imaging implementations. It can also be applied to character-coded text, CAD files, or other digital documents.

Forms Processing Software

OCR programs can extract field values from designated areas within business forms. A related product group, termed *forms processing software*, combines OCR with bar-code recognition and mark sense (optical mark recognition) capabilities to simplify data-entry and reduce keystroking requirements. They are employed in digital imaging implementations that involve highly formatted source documents such as medical history forms, laboratory test sheets, bills of lading, customer surveys, warranty registration forms, credit applications, time sheets, tax returns, and applications for permits and licenses.

In most implementations, a forms processing program operates on a dedicated computer, called a *forms processing server*. The program receives digital images generated by a scanning workstation. In applications involving intermixed forms of different types, the incoming form images are automatically categorized for processing purposes, based on a previously established set of form descriptions or templates. Once a form image is properly categorized, appropriate recognition technologies are applied to the form's contents. Forms processing programs can read barcodes in various symbologies and assign their contents to specified fields within database records. They also provide omnifont character recognition capabilities comparable to those of the most highly functional OCR software. Going beyond OCR, however, some forms processing programs can read handprinted information, particularly uppercase alphabetic characters and numeric digits, provided they are clearly articulated and neatly positioned in boxes provided within the form for that purpose. Forms processing programs can also detect marks in checkboxes. Data validation rules can be defined for specific fields.

Chapter 4

Storage and Retrieval of Digital Documents

From a hardware perspective, a digital document implementation must include storage peripherals and recording media for digital images, character-coded text, CAD files, and other digital documents, as well as for the database records that index them. To be useful, digital documents must be quickly and reliably retrievable when needed. This chapter examines the characteristics and capabilities of storage and retrieval technologies and components incorporated into digital document configurations. It begins with a survey of storage requirements, formats, devices, and media for digital documents, including a detailed examination of factors that influence page storage requirements and the suitability of specific storage technologies, particularly hard drives and optical disks. Later sections discuss retrieval concepts and functionality, emphasizing database searching and document delivery characteristics that distinguish digital document implementations from other records management methodologies and technologies. The chapter closes with a survey of display and printing components for digital documents.

Calculating Storage Requirements

Determining storage requirements is an important part of the planning process for digital document implementations. Admittedly, storage requirements are less of a concern today than they were in the twentieth century, when storage devices were more costly and had less capacity. Nonetheless, a reasonable estimate of storage requirements is necessary to prepare hardware specifications for digital document repositories and to ensure that network servers are configured with sufficient capacity to accommodate existing document collections and future growth. Storage requirements for digital documents depend on several factors, including the number of pages to be stored, page characteristics, and the file format employed. The following sections present formulas for calculating storage requirements for digital documents in image and character-coded formats.

Image Storage Requirements

Although digital images offer a compact alternative to paper files, they can require large amounts of computer storage—far more, for example, than is required to store a given page as character-coded text. Storage requirements associated with specific documents depend on linear page dimensions and print densities, as well as the scanning resolution, scanning mode, and compression method employed in a particular imaging installation. Taking these variables into account, the formula provided in Figure 4.1 calculates the number of bytes required to store a single page.

The calculation $((H \times R) \times (W \times R) \times B)$ yields the uncompressed page storage requirement in bits. The value of B is determined by the scanning mode. As discussed in Chapter 2, binary-mode scanning of bitonal (black-and-white) pages is the most common scenario in digital imaging implementations. With binary-mode scanning, the value of B is 1. It has no effect on the calculation and can be omitted from the formula where bitonal documents are involved. More meaningful values for B are 8 for grayscale scanning of photographs and 24 for color-mode scanning.

The most common scanning resolutions for office records and engineering drawings are 200 dots per inch and 300 dots per inch, but lower or higher values are possible for R in the formula in Figure 4.1. Scanning resolution is usually, but not necessarily, identical for the horizontal (width) and vertical (height) dimensions of a page. Higher scanning resolutions increase the amount of information that must be stored per image. At 200 dots per horizontal and vertical inch, each square inch of a page contains 40,000 pixels; at 300 dots per horizontal and vertical inch, the number of pixels per square inch increases to 90,000. All other things being equal, the higher resolution image will require 2.25 times more storage space.

Storage requirements are similarly affected by page size. Larger documents require additional pixel coding and occupy more storage space at all scanning resolutions. All other things being equal, for example, a legal-size page will contain 27 percent more pixels than a letter-size page and will require 27 percent more storage space.

Storage Requirements Formula—Single Page—Digital Images

Figure 4.1

$$S = \frac{(H \times R) \times (W \times R) \times B}{8} \times \frac{1}{C}$$

Where:

S	=	the storage requirement per page in bytes
H	=	the page height in inches or millimeters
W	=	the page width in inches or millimeters
R	=	the scanning resolution in dots per inch or millimeter
B	=	the number of bits that encode each dot
C	=	an image compression factor

Approximate
Storage
Requirements in
Bytes for Pages
of Various Sizes
Scanned at 200
and 300 dpi.

Table 4.1

Page Size (in inches)	200 dpi Uncompressed	200 dpi Compressed*	300 dpi Uncompressed	300 dpi Compressed*
8.5 × 11	467,500	31,200	1,052,000	70,150
8.5 × 14	595,000	39,700	1,339,000	89,250
11 × 14	770,000	51,350	1,733,000	115,500
11 × 17	935,000	62,350	2,104,000	140,250
18 × 24	2,160,000	144,000	4,860,000	324,000
24 × 36	4,320,000	288,000	9,720,000	648,000
34 × 44	7,480,000	499,000	16,830,000	1,122,000

*Based on Group 4 algorithm

Applying the above formula to letter-size (8.5-by-11-inch) pages scanned in the binary mode at 200 dots per horizontal and vertical inch, the calculation $((11 \times 200) \times (8.5 \times 200) \times 1)$ yields an uncompressed storage requirement of 3.74 million bits per page. Division by 8 converts the uncompressed page storage requirement to bytes, the most common measure of computer media capacity. (A byte contains 8 bits.) In this example, the uncompressed page storage requirement is 467,500 bytes (467.5 kilobytes). When the same page is scanned in the binary mode at 300 dots per horizontal and vertical inch, the calculation $((11 \times 300) \times (8.5 \times 300) \times 1)$ yields an uncompressed storage requirement of 8.415 million bits or approximately 1.052 million bytes (1.052 megabytes) (see Table 4.1).

Storage requirements for images of engineering drawings and other large documents are significantly greater than for images of office records. For a D-size (24-by-36-inch) engineering drawing scanned in the binary mode at 300 dots per horizontal and vertical inch, the calculation $((24 \times 300) \times (36 \times 300) \times 1)$ yields an uncompressed storage requirement of 77.76 million bits or 9.72 megabytes. Color mode scanning of large documents can generate huge images. For a D-size color map scanned at 300 dots per inch, for example, the calculation $((24 \times 300) \times (36 \times 300) \times 24)$ yields an uncompressed storage requirement of approximately 1.9 billion bits or 238 megabytes.

The image sizes calculated in Table 4.1 must be multiplied by the reciprocal of a compression factor—that is, a fraction with an anticipated compression factor as the denominator and the value 1 as the numerator. The purpose of compression is to reduce the amount of storage space required for document images. Compression algorithms are applied before document images are recorded onto computer storage media. If electronic document images were not routinely compressed, they would overwhelm available storage capacity in high-volume applications. Compression also has a beneficial impact on retrieval and networking operations by increasing the effective transmission rate for electronic document images, thereby conserving network bandwidth.

In either case, the most widely encountered compression algorithms for bitonal images employ *run-length encoding methodologies,* so-called because they produce coded messages that indicate the number of successively encountered pixels of a given tonality within a digitized image. Many typewritten and printed pages contain relatively long, uninterrupted stretches of light or dark areas. Top and bottom page margins are an obvious example; if a letter-size page with a one-inch top margin is digitized in the binary mode at 200 dots per horizontal and vertical inch, the first 340,000 pixels will be white, and each will be encoded by a zero bit. Stored in uncompressed form, those 340,000 pixels would occupy 42,500 bytes.

Instead of generating a string of bits representing the tonal values of successively encountered pixels, run-length encoding records the line positions of alternating tonal values—indicating, in effect, how many pixels of a given tonality occur in sequence. Rather than storing 340,000 zero bits associated with a one-inch top page margin, the compression algorithm substitutes a much shorter code indicating that the digitized image begins with 340,000 white pixels in a row. The resulting reduction in storage requirements will vary with document characteristics. Pages with large amounts of contiguous light or dark space, such as typewritten documents with wide margins or other large blank areas, are well suited to run-length encoding and will yield high compression factors. On the other hand, densely printed documents with more frequent light-to-dark transitions offer much less compression potential. Business forms with vertical lines can prove particularly troublesome.

Widely cited compression factors are based on experience with correspondence, business forms, and other office documents, including certain test pages with characteristics particularly conducive to run-length encoding. As discussed in Chapter 2, they yield unrealistically high compression factors. When calculating storage requirements, more conservative estimates are advisable. For the widely used Group 4 algorithm, application planners should assume a compression factor of perhaps 12 to 15 for office records and 15 to 20 for engineering drawings. According to the compression formula cited previously, an uncompressed image requiring 467,500 bytes of storage will be compressed to as little as 31,200 bytes. To simplify calculations and allow for significant variations in printing density with a collection of office documents, some analysts assume that a compressed image of a letter-size page scanned at 200 dots per inch in the binary mode will require 50,000 bytes of storage. For densely printed business forms as well as books, journal articles, and other publications, compression factors of 5 to 8 are typical.

Storage Requirements for Character-Coded Text

The formula provided in Figure 4.2 computes the storage requirement for a single page stored in character-coded form.

Compared to electronic document images, storage requirements for character-coded pages are affected by fewer variables. The average number of characters per page depends on the typographic and page formatting characteristics of specific documents. Page size is also an important factor. When completely full, a double-spaced letter-size page will have 1,550 to 1,700 characters if printed in a monospaced typewriter font

Storage
Requirements
Formula—Single
Page—
Character-Coded
Form

Figure 4.2

$$S = C * I$$

Where:

S	=	the storage requirement in bytes;
C	=	the average number of characters per page; and
I	=	a factor that represents the amount of additional space required for full-text indexing.

such as Pica, Prestige Elite, or Courier. If a proportionally-spaced laser or inkjet printer font, such as Helvetica or Times Roman, is used, the same page will contain 2,300 to 2,500 characters. Single-spaced typewritten documents may have 3,100 to 5,000 characters per letter-size page, depending on the type font employed. A 6" by 9" book page contains 3,000 to 4,000 characters, depending on the type style and size. A 7" by 10" book page usually contains 4,000 to 5,000 characters. For all type fonts and page sizes, the character capacity per page is affected by margin widths. The character counts listed here must be reduced for pages that are partially full.

The index factor is only relevant for applications that employ full-text indexing of digital documents. If full-text indexing is not used, the value of the index factor is 1, which has no effect on the calculated storage requirement. Otherwise, the value of the index factor depends on the full-text indexing program utilized in a particular digital document implementation. As discussed in Chapter 3, full-text indexes contain words extracted from documents plus pointers to their text locations. Some software developers suggest a factor of 2 to 2.5 for index storage, plus an additional 0.5 for storage of working files and the full-text indexing itself plus associated working files. Some full-text indexing software employs data compression techniques to reduce the index storage factor to 1.5 to 1.8. In many situations, 2.3 is a reasonable value for the index factor in the Figure 4.2 equation.

Applied to single-spaced letter-size pages that are computer-printed in a proportionally-spaced font, the above formula yields a storage requirement of 4,600 to 6,250 bytes per page with full-text indexing. A collection of one million such pages, the contents of about 85 four-drawer filing cabinets, will require 4.6 billion bytes (4.6 gigabytes) to 6.25 billion bytes (6.25 gigabytes) of computer storage. Once considered formidable when computer storage was expensive, these estimates are almost negligible by modern standards. Storage requirements are greater but not out-of-bounds for digital document implementations that involve library materials. A small liberal arts college with a collection of 150,000 books averaging 300 pages each and 3,300 characters per 6" by 9" page will require about 150 gigabytes of computer storage without full-text indexing or 370 gigabytes with full-text indexing. For a large research library containing one million books with the same characteristics, the storage requirement is approximately one terabyte without full-text indexing or 2.5 terabytes with full-text indexing. Compared to electronic document images, character-coded text requires much less storage space for a given quantity of pages. As an example, the storage requirement for digitized images of 300 million book pages will exceed 15 terabytes.

Although it is not reflected in the above formula, some software products employ data compression to reduce storage requirements for character-coded documents as well as for indexes. The Lempel-Ziv-Welch (LZW) algorithm is the best-known and most widely used method for compression of character-coded text. It replaces character strings with shorter codes, thereby reducing storage requirements by a factor of 2 or more. The compression ratio attained in a given situation depends on the characteristics of the text being compressed. The LZW algorithm is most effective for repeating character strings, a characteristic of many textual documents. Unlike document images, which are routinely compressed to reduce storage requirements, compression of character-coded text has received little attention in recent years as the cost of computer storage has declined dramatically. It remains a useful option, however, for applications that involve very large quantities of digital documents. In addition to saving storage space, compression conserves bandwidth when large quantities of character-coded documents are transmitted over computer networks, but the documents must be decompressed for use at their reception point.

File Formats for Digital Documents

Depending on the software employed in a particular implementation, digital documents may be stored in a proprietary or nonproprietary file format. **Proprietary file formats**, sometimes termed *native formats*, are associated with specific application programs. They are developed by one vendor for its own software products. **Nonproprietary file formats**, by contrast, are supported by multiple vendors and software products. They may be based on published specifications prepared by cooperating software developers. Alternatively, a nonproprietary file format may be developed by one influential software company and subsequently adopted by others.

Proprietary and nonproprietary file formats are rarely exclusive options; many digital document implementations support multiple image and text formats. Further blurring the distinction between the two format categories, files stored in proprietary formats associated with very popular software products can often be imported (read) by competing or complementary products. Similarly, a given computer program may be able to export (write) files in the proprietary formats associated with other programs. Where the importing and exporting capabilities of a given computer program are inadequate, various companies offer translator programs or services that can convert files from one format to another.

The following sections describe common image and character-coded text formats for digital documents. This subject is important because file formats have a decisive impact on the future usability of digital documents. **Backward compatibility**—the ability of future software products to read information recorded in particular formats—is an obvious concern. Most software developers release new versions of, or replacements for, their products at regular intervals. These successor products may employ new or different file formats. The obvious concern is that digital documents stored in a particular file format may be rendered unreadable by product modifications and discontinuations.

Image File Formats

As previously described, document scanners generate two-dimensional digitized images composed of pixels that represent the tonal values of specific documents. The digitized images, variously described as *bit-mapped* or *raster images*, are recorded in computer files for storage and retrieval. Bit-mapped image files differ from *vector-based* or *object-oriented image files*, which define computer-processible images as points, lines, circles, or other geometric shapes. Vector-based image files are principally associated with CAD and computer-based drawing programs. Because they utilize different methods of representing images, bit-mapped and vector-based files are incompatible with one another. Subject to significant performance variations, conversion programs can generate bit-mapped images from vector-based files, and vice versa. Such image production is sometimes required in engineering-oriented document imaging installations.

The earliest document imaging programs, introduced in the 1980s, employed proprietary image file formats. Most newer products, by contrast, store images in the tag image file (TIF) format, also known as the *tagged image file format* and sometimes abbreviated as TIFF. The TIF format was developed jointly by Microsoft and Aldus Corporation, which was subsequently acquired by Adobe Systems Incorporated. Adobe Systems, which also owns the portable document format (PDF) discussed below, now publishes and maintains TIF specifications.

TIF is a flexible, multiplatform file format that is well suited to and widely supported by a variety of imaging applications, including OCR, desktop publishing, digitization of photographs for electronic manipulation, and PC-based facsimile transmission, as well as the digital imaging implementations discussed in this book. A TIF image file includes a header that describes the file's contents, size, and other characteristics. The TIF format is compatible with single- and multipage documents and with binary, grayscale, and color-scanning modes. TIF images can be stored in compressed or uncompressed form. The TIF format is compatible with the Group 3 and Group 4 compression algorithms discussed in Chapter 2. TIF images can be read by a variety of computer programs, including viewer software supplied with many personal computers and/or incorporated digital document software. Plug-ins for web browsers allow the TIF format to be used in Internet, intranet, and extranet implementations.

Since the late 1990s, the TIF format has become the de facto standard image file format for records management applications. Some state regulations require it for digital imaging systems implemented by government agencies subject to their jurisdiction. In theory, TIF files can be exchanged between otherwise incompatible document imaging products, thereby eliminating the need for customized image conversion services or rescanning of paper documents when existing systems are replaced or upgraded. In practice, however, compatibility problems are posed by permissible variations in TIF files and by different versions of the TIF specification that have developed over time. Further, some image viewer programs support a subset of the TIF specification. They may not be able to display all TIF files.

The JPEG file interchange format (JFIF) is the file format associated with JPEG compression algorithms, which were developed by the Joint Photographic Experts Group as discussed in Chapter 2. The JFIF file format and the JPEG compression method are often confused. Many vendors and publications incorrectly describe JPEG as a file format and omit any mention of JFIF. In some cases, the combined designation JPEG/JFIF is used. JPEG compression can be used with other file formats, such as TIF, but it is rarely done. Terminology aside, the JFIF format and the JPEG compression method are intended for photographs or other continuous tone images. They are supported by most digital cameras.

The graphics image file (GIF) format, also known as the graphical interchange file format, has become a widely utilized image format in Internet, intranet, and extranet implementations. Developed by CompuServe and supported by all web browsers, the GIF format is designed for rapid downloading and browsing of images. Its encoding method displays an approximation of images while complete information is downloaded from a web server. Designed to enhance the responsiveness of web pages, this progressive display approach generates low-resolution images that are gradually improved as more detailed information arrives.

The GIF format employs the Lempel-Ziv-Welch (LZW) algorithm for image compression. Until 2004, developers of GIF viewers had to license the LZW compression algorithm, which was patented by Unisys Corporation. To avoid this requirement and address other limitations of the GIF format, the World Wide Web Consortium (W3C) adopted the portable network graphics (PNG) format as a GIF replacement. Like GIF, PNG provides cross-platform compatibility, good image compression, and progressive display of images. The PNG format is freely usable without licensing arrangements. Unlike TIF, GIF and PNG are single-image formats. They do not support multiple images per file. This limitation is insignificant for most of the web pages where the GIF and PNG formats are used, but it can prove troublesome where digital images are produced by scanning multipage paper documents.

Other examples of file formats for bit-mapped images include BMP, the Windows Bitmap image format; PCX, which was developed by Z-Soft for its PC Paintbrush program; PCD, the Photo CD format developed by Eastman Kodak; PICT, the default image format for Macintosh graphics programs; RAS, a raster image format developed by Sun Microsystems; and Targa (TGA), which is supported by some computer painting programs. Principally associated with computer graphic applications, these file formats are support by some digital document software products.

File Formats for Character-Coded Text

Text files store information in a relatively unstructured manner. In many word processing applications, for example, a text file contains a single record—the computer-processible equivalent of a typewritten document that contains one or more pages. Alternatively, a text file may contain several or many documents created by word processing programs, electronic messaging software, or other systems; multiple electronic messages may be downloaded to a text file during an online session, for example. In such cases, individual records may be separated by page break commands or other delimiting characters. Their physical sequence within a text file may be based on their order of creation or logical interrelationships. Software typically imposes few significant restrictions on the length of text files. File sizes may be limited by available memory or other hardware characteristics, but such constraints are rarely meaningful.

Some text file formats are specific to the computer programs that create them. Word processing programs, for example, record documents in proprietary formats. Text files created by such programs combine textual characters with embedded characters that initiate page breaks, paragraph indentations, tabs, underlining, bold printing, italics, superscripts, subscripts, and other formatting features. Although the ASCII code is typically used for both text and control characters, the control characters associated with particular formatting operations are unique to specific programs. Consequently, a control character that initiates a page break or underlining with one word processing program may have a completely different meaning, or no meaning at all, with competing products. As a complicating factor, text file formats may differ among various versions of a given program. Successive releases of a word processing program may not be able to read and edit text files created by all previous versions. Incompatibility is likewise possible among versions of a given word processing program intended for different computer platforms.

Several software developers have introduced formats that promote compatibility among text files created by various competing or complementary products. They provide a canonical format in which text files can be saved and from which they can be translated. The most widely encountered example is Microsoft's rich text format (RTF). It records text and formatting instructions in a manner that compatible programs can correctly interpret—assuming, of course, that the target program possesses the requisite formatting capabilities. Designed to reproduce the content and appearance of files accurately during translation, the RTF format is supported by Microsoft programs and many competing and complementary products.

So-called *plain text files*, sometimes termed *ASCII text files*, represent the character content of word processing documents, electronic messages, or other computer-generated text, but they contain little additional information. Most word processing programs and many other software products support the plain text file format as an import or export option. It is typically available with carriage returns at the end of each paragraph or at the end of each line of text. In either case, most of the control characters that initiate formatting options are removed when files are saved in the plain text format. Paragraph indentations and tabs may be converted to spaces, but line centering, fonts, underlining, italics, and other potentially significant features are not preserved.

File Formats for Compound Documents

Text file formats are intended for alphanumeric information. Strictly defined, they cannot accommodate compound documents that combine text and graphics. Although newer word processing programs routinely support documents with embedded graphics generated by an internal drawing component or exported from other programs, the PDF is often a better choice for compound documents with complex formatting characteristics. Introduced by Adobe Systems in 1993, the PDF format is compatible with character-coded text and graphics, including digitized images, which can be combined within the same page. For character-coded information, PDF preserves fonts, styles, headers, margins, and other page formatting characteristics. PDF files are viewed with the Adobe Acrobat program, which is supplied with most new personal computers or can be downloaded from Internet sites without charge. The PDF format provides excellent functionality for document display, page navigation, printing, and security.

Although PDF was originally a proprietary format, it has been widely adopted and has become a de facto standard for digital documents. In January 2007, Adobe Systems, Inc., released the full 1.7 PDF specification to AIIM for publication as an ISO standard. Among its advantages, PDF is a cross-platform file format. Software for creating and reading PDF files is available for Windows, Macintosh, and Unix computers, and PDF documents can be reliably interchanged among those platforms. The PDF/Archival (PDF/A) format is a subset of PDF intended specifically for long-term preservation of digital documents. The applicable standard is ISO 19005-1, *Document Management—Electronic Document File Format for Long-Term Preservation—Part 1: Use of PDF 1.4 (PDF/A).*

So-called *markup formats* provide similar support for compound documents and are compatible with a variety of computer programs. They contain embedded instructions, called *markup codes* or *tags*, which describe various document components such as chapters, titles, headings, paragraphs, lists, and tables. Compatible computer programs interpret the markup instructions and display documents accordingly. Markup codes may be inserted manually or generated by special authoring tools. The syntax and semantics of specific markup codes are defined by sets of rules called *markup languages*. Some businesses, government agencies, and other organizations utilize markup languages and formats to facilitate the exchange of computer-processible documents.

The best-known markup languages are the *hypertext markup language (HTML)* and the *extensible markup language (XML)*. They are used for information on the World Wide Web, as well as on corporate and institutional intranets and extranets. HTML and XML codes are interpreted by web browsers that display the information as formatted text and graphics. Various software packages support the creation of web pages with specified content and embedded formatting codes. In addition, newer word processing programs can save digital documents in the HTML format. They automatically insert HTML codes that correspond to specific page, line, and character formats. In addition to text, many web pages incorporate photographs, illustrations, charts, or other graphics that are stored in one of the formats discussed next.

Markup languages promote the exchange of computer-processible documents by separating the content and appearance of information. Content is stored as plain text, while the embedded codes specify the appearance of pages. The encoded documents are not formatted; they contain formatting instructions that compatible software interprets. As a complication, however, different versions of a given markup language often incorporate special features and extensions that can pose compatibility problems. Some HTML extensions, for example, are incompatible with certain web browsers.

Storage Devices and Media

High-volume digital document implementations can require a large amount of computer storage; particularly where digital documents are stored in image formats:

- Assuming 50,000 bytes per letter-size page scanned in the binary mode at 200 dots per inch, a megabyte of computer storage will accommodate just 20 pages.

- Digitization of a four-drawer file cabinet containing about 12,000 pages will require 600 megabytes of computer storage, which is the approximate capacity of a CD.

- A million-page document collection, which is far from unusual in records management applications, will require 50 gigabytes plus additional storage for index data.

- Images of engineering drawings, maps, and other large-format documents are much larger than images produced from office records. A collection of 100,000 D-size drawings scanned at 200 dots per inch, for example, will require a terabyte of computer storage.

Character-coded documents are more compact than digital images, but large document repositories and their associated full-text indexes can occupy hundreds of gigabytes or even terabytes of storage.

Fortunately, developments in computer storage technology have kept pace with these demands. The following discussion surveys computer storage devices and media for digital documents. Index databases are typically stored on hard drives for rapid access. Like other types of computer-processable information, digital documents can be stored on any medium with sufficient capacity. For most records management applications, however, the only practical choices are hard drives or optical disks, in any of several formats described in this section. During the 1980s, several vendors introduced systems that employed magnetic tape for document storage. However, as briefly noted in Chapter 1, those products attracted few customers and have since been discontinued. Although magnetic tapes are available in multigigabyte formats appropriate to high-volume document repositories, their performance attributes are otherwise limited. They are principally used as backup media for digital document collections and index data.

Hard Drives

Hard drives are the principal storage devices in most computer configurations, and they are generally the preferred storage technology for digital documents. Hard drives' competitive position among computer storage devices is well established. Widely available and well understood, they provide the fastest, most convenient access to computer-processable information. This convenience is certainly a desirable attribute in digital document implementations, but widespread use of hard drives for document repositories is a relatively recent development.

In the early to mid-1980s, when digital imaging systems were initially commercialized, hard drives were expensive, and their capacities were too low for voluminous imaging applications. At that time, most midrange computer installations had a few hundred megabytes of hard disk storage, and multidrive gigabyte-level configurations were limited to the largest mainframe sites. Where present at all, hard drives for personal computers typically stored less than 20 megabytes—barely enough for the contents of a file drawer. In their initial product configurations, imaging vendors consequently reserved hard drives for index databases, which require relatively little space. Through the 1980s, document images were typically recorded onto optical disks, which were characteristically slower and less convenient than hard drives but offered higher capacity at lower cost.

Over the last decade, however, hard drive capacities have improved dramatically and their prices have plunged. Reasonably priced multigigabyte models have been commonplace since the mid-1990s, and hard drive capacities continue to double at short intervals. Hard drives for entry-level desktop computers can now store several hundred thousand digitized images, and network servers can accommodate multi-million-page document repositories. Multidrive RAID configurations combine high capacity with redundant recording and storage procedures for fault-tolerant operation and data protection. On a cost-per-megabyte basis for both equipment and media, hard drives compare very favorably with optical storage formats, and their performance advantages deliver added value. With hard drives, access times are measured in milliseconds; by contrast, access times for optical disk autochangers can exceed half a minute. When computer administrators are responsible for selecting or operating digital document systems, they often prefer hard drives for familiarity as well as for performance and cost.

Optical Disks

Optical storage technology uses lasers to record information by selectively altering the light reflectance characteristics of a platter-shaped storage medium. Within an optical disk drive, the recorded information is read by a laser and pickup mechanism that detects variations in reflected light, much as read/write heads sense variations in the alignment of metallic particles within magnetic disks and tapes. To prevent destruction of information, the playback laser operates at lower power or a different wavelength than the laser used for recording.

Digital imaging and optical disk technologies have been closely associated since the early 1980s. Given the then limited storage capacities of hard drives, the development of optical disks was a precondition for successful commercialization of digital imaging technology. The earliest digital imaging systems invariably incorporated optical storage components. During the same time period, optical disks were also used to store large collections of character-coded documents, particularly in library applications.

From their inception, optical disks have featured high *areal recording densities*; that is, individual bits are very closely spaced, allowing many bits to be recorded within a given area. The result is high media capacity; the earliest optical disks provided gigabyte-level storage at a time when most hard drives stored less than 100 megabytes. In recent years, hard drives have caught up, but optical disks still offer impressive storage capacities. They also provide the direct access capabilities associated with all platter-shaped media, but hard drives have faster access times for reading and writing information. Even where optical disks are used for document storage, hard drives are the principal storage devices for index data, which must be retrieved as quickly as possible and may be updated frequently.

At the time of this writing, the most widely encountered optical storage media were CDs and DVDs. Other types of optical disks have either been discontinued or remain in very limited use. Although all magnetic media support direct recording of computer-processable information, optical disks are available in read-only and recordable varieties. Read-only optical disks, as their name implies, have no recordable properties. They are limited to playback of prerecorded information generated by a mastering and replication process. Recordable optical disks, by contrast, permit direct recording of machine-readable information. In this respect, they resemble their magnetic counterparts.

Recordable optical disks may be write-once or rewritable media. Write-once optical disks are sometimes described as *WORM media*; the acronym variously stands for Write Once Read Many or Write Once Read Mostly. Such disks are not erasable. Once information is recorded in a given area of a write-once optical disk, that area cannot be reused. Rewritable optical disks, by contrast, are erasable and reusable. The contents of previously recorded media segments can be deleted or overwritten with new information.

Compact disc (CD) is the collective designation for a group of interrelated optical storage formats and products that are based on technology developed during the 1970s and 1980s by Sony and Philips. The most widely encountered type of CD is a rigid plastic platter that measures 4.75 inches (120 millimeters) in diameter. The various CD formats are distinguished by the type of information they contain. Compact disc-read only memory (CD-ROM), compact disc-recordable (CD-R), and compact disc-rewritable (CD-RW) are the compact disc formats for computer-processable information. As a read-only technology, CD-ROM is essentially a publishing and distribution medium for software, databases, or other computer-processable information. A 4.75-inch CD-ROM, the most common size, can store about 540 megabytes of computer-processable information. Some product specification sheets cite capacities up to 650 megabytes, which is unformatted capacity. A 3.5-inch (90-millimeter) CD-ROM, which can store about 190 megabytes, is rarely encountered in records management applications.

Compact disc-recordable (CD-R) and compact disc-rewritable (CD-RW) are recordable media. CD-R products are write-once optical disks. CD-RW media are erasable. Competitively priced and available from many suppliers, CD-R and CD-RW drives and media are widely encountered in personal computer installations where they may be used for data backup, data archiving, or other purposes. Their formatted storage capacities range from 540 megabytes to 660 megabytes, depending on the type of medium selected.

DVD—which originally stood for digital video disc and then digital versatile disc—is the replacement technology for compact discs, which they physically resemble. DVD specifications were developed in the mid-1990s by a group of cooperating companies. At the time of this writing, the technology was still evolving, and new formats and products with higher storage capacities than those cited here are expected. DVD media, which measure 4.75 inches in diameter, can store video, audio, or computer-processible information. Among the computer formats, DVD-ROM is the higher-capacity successor to CD-ROM. Intended for publication and distribution of large databases, clip art libraries, document collections, multimedia presentations, or other voluminous information, a single-sided DVD-ROM can store up to 4.7 gigabytes.

Among recordable DVD products, DVD-R and DVD+R are the counterparts of CD-R and CD-RW, which they will eventually supplant. As write-once media, they are not erasable. DVD-RW, DVD+RW, and DVD-Random Access Memory (DVD-RAM) are rewritable media. These DVD products are supported by different industry groups. Although some differences exist among them, their storage capacities are virtually identical: 4.7 gigabytes for single-sided media and 9.4 gigabytes for double-sided media. Most DVD drives can read and write media in multiple formats. DVD drives can also read and record CDs.

CDs and DVDs are removable media. Like magnetic tapes, they are stored offline when not in use and must be inserted into a compatible drive for reading and recording. *Autochanger units*, also known as *optical disk libraries* or *jukeboxes*, automate this process. By providing unattended access for reading and recording, autochangers give optical disks a distinctive position in the hierarchy of computer storage products. As nearline storage devices, optical disk autochangers fall between the high-performance online access provided by hard drives and the offline access offered by magnetic tape. Typical nearline access times range from 10 to 30 seconds. The actual time required to access a given optical disk is affected by several factors, including the disk's location within an autochanger. Smaller autochangers are faster than larger ones; their transport distances, an important determinant of access time, are characteristically short. To shorten the distance that media must travel, some autochangers are equipped with multiple optical disk drives, but the extra drives consume space that might otherwise be occupied by optical disks.

When selecting a storage technology for digital documents, records managers and vendors increasingly emphasize hard drives for availability, performance, and, in some cases, economy. Optical disks and hard drives are not mutually exclusive storage options, however. Often, the two technologies can be beneficially combined. In some digital imaging implementations, for example, hard drives provide a staging area for images that will eventually be recorded onto CDs or DVDs. Combining may be done to minimize inefficiencies associated with the slow recording speeds of some optical disk drives. Hard drives may likewise store digital documents for a relatively brief, predetermined period of intense retrieval activity. That approach is well suited to transaction processing applications where digital documents are referenced frequently for perhaps three to six months following an event such as the receipt of an order or submission of an insurance claim. In such cases, digital documents are stored on hard drives during the active reference period then archived onto optical disks.

Retrieval Functionality

In some implementations, as described in Chapter 3, digital documents are organized into folders by customer name, student name, patient name, project name, contract number, case number, or other readily identifiable parameters. At retrieval time, media directories are examined to locate appropriate folders, which are presumably arranged in a logical sequence, such as alphabetic or numeric order, and labeled to clearly indicate their contents. To locate a desired document, a searcher opens and browses through appropriate folders. In some applications, documents may be grouped in nested subfolders, which must likewise be opened and browsed.

These folder-based implementations replicate conventional filing methodologies. Apart from electronic delivery of documents, they offer few retrieval advantages over paper filing systems. Whether paper or digital documents are involved, browsing is tedious and time-consuming. As discussed in Chapter 1, faster retrieval when compared to paper filing systems is a strong motive for digital document implementations. In many installations, it is the principal motive and an anticipated source of enhanced productivity and improved operating efficiency. Such performance enhancements depend on indexing rather than filing methodologies. Assuming appropriate indexing as discussed in Chapter 3, software can quickly identify and retrieve digital documents. Digital document implementations permit complex retrieval operations that cannot be conveniently performed, and may not even be possible, with conventional paper filing methodologies. Once retrieved, digital documents can be routed to designated workstations or, if desired, imported into other information processing applications.

In digital document implementations, retrieval capabilities are embodied in database management programs, which also support the creation of index information about digital documents. Document retrieval operations begin with a search for database (index) records—and, by implication, digital documents—that satisfy specified parameters. The database records, which typically reside on a hard drive, contain pointers to digital documents stored on hard drives or on optical disks. The nature and complexity of database searches depend on the retrieval functionality supported by database management programs. The following discussion outlines commonly encountered retrieval requirements and capabilities.

Retrieval Concepts

Document retrieval operations are based on users' information requirements, which may vary in scope, specificity, complexity, and clarity of expression. In some cases, a retrieval operation involves specific documents that are known to contain required information. The documents may be identified by authors, recipients, dates, order numbers, customer names, or other straightforward parameters. With a little training, novice users can easily initiate and successfully execute such retrieval operations. More complex information requirements involve searches for documents pertaining to particular subjects, projects, events, transactions, or other matters, which may be described in vague terms or otherwise poorly articulated. Such ambiguous information requirements must be analyzed and clarified to develop an appropriate retrieval strategy. This process may require assistance from someone knowledgeable about information retrieval concepts and experienced with a particular implementation's indexing methodologies.

Ultimately, an information requirement must be expressed as a search specification to be executed by the database management software that indexes digital documents. Some software accepts **natural language queries** that consist of questions or instructions entered in a sentence format without regard to formal syntax. The software parses the query to identify search terms and determine the specific retrieval operations to be performed. More often, however, search specifications must be entered in a structured format. With field-based indexing, a typical search specification includes a field name, a field value, and a relational expression. Searchable fields, previously defined as key fields, are determined by the indexing plan developed for a particular collection of digital documents. Field values may be words, phrases, numbers, dates, or other index information to be matched. With some systems, they may be selected from a scrollable list of previously entered or permissible field values. Relational expressions, sometimes described as *relational operators*, specify the type of match desired. Relational expressions include:

- Equal to
- Not equal to
- Greater than
- Greater than or equal to
- Less than
- Less than or equal to

In an application involving technical reports, for example, a search statement of the form:

AUTHOR = SMITH

will initiate a search for index records that contain the character string "smith" in the author field. The equals sign, or an abbreviation such as EQ, is the most meaningful relational expression for index searches involving names, subjects, or other textual field values. It can also be applied to quantitative values, telephone numbers, social security numbers, and other numeric field entries. In most cases, the equals sign specifies an exact match of a designated field value, but it can be combined with other search capabilities to obtain different results. The "not equal to" operation is its opposite, but it is rarely used in document retrieval operations.

The other relational expressions may be represented by symbols, such as > or <, or by abbreviations such as GT for greater than or LT for less than. The relational expressions are obviously useful for numeric or date information, but they can be applied to textual field values as well. A textual field value that is greater than a specified character string, for example, follows it in alphabetic sequence. When combined with Boolean operators, relational expressions permit range searches that identify field values between an upper and lower numeric or alphabetic limit.

Depending on the retrieval software and user interface, a search specification—including a field name, field value, and relational expression—may be entered in a prescribed syntax at a command prompt or typed into a dialog box. Alternatively, retrieval software may display a search form with labeled fields accompanied by blank areas for entry of field values preceded by relational expressions. That approach is well suited to novice or occasional searchers, but both methods require some training for effective use. Both approaches are subject to considerable variation, and some systems combine them, supporting command-oriented retrieval operations for experienced searchers and form-based searches for novice users.

Boolean Operators

As an initial response to a search specification, most database management software displays a count of the number of index records and, by implication, the number of digital documents that satisfy the specification. Depending on this response, which is sometimes termed *hit prediction,* the searcher may reconsider the retrieval strategy and modify the search specification, broadening it if too few index records are identified or narrowing it if the number of retrieved index records is excessive. Most digital document implementations support the so-called Boolean operators for that purpose.

Named for a nineteenth-century mathematician and logician, the Boolean operators combine two or more search specifications in a single retrieval operation. Because their underlying principles are based on formal logical concepts and the algebra of sets, Boolean operations are sometimes described as *Boolean logic* or *Boolean algebra.* Although they have been criticized as difficult to understand, particularly for novice users, Boolean operators are essential for complex document retrieval requirements that transcend the capabilities of conventional paper filing methodologies.

The most common Boolean operators are AND, OR, and NOT. Of these, the AND operator—sometimes represented by the ampersand (&) or plus (+) sign—is the best known and most widely implemented. Virtually indispensable for effective retrieval operations in digital document implementations, it is supported by virtually all retrieval software, although it may be more or less convenient to use in a given implementation. In some implementations, the Boolean AND operator must be explicitly included in search specifications; in other cases, the AND operator is automatically applied to successively entered search specifications unless the retrieval program is instructed otherwise.

Variations aside, the Boolean AND operator limits the scope of a given retrieval operation by combining two or more search specifications, both of which must be satisfied. For retrieval of digital versions of technical reports in a research laboratory, for example, a search specification of the form:

AUTHOR = SMITH *AND* DATE > 1998

will limit retrieval to index records that contain the value "smith" in the author field and any value greater than "1998" in the date field. In effect, this search specification creates two sets of index records, one representing technical reports written by Smith, and the other representing technical reports written after 1998. In this context, the term *set* denotes a group of index records that contain a designated value in a specified field. The Boolean AND operator seeks the logical conjunction or intersection of two sets defined in a search specification; that is, it identifies index records that are members of both sets—in this case, technical reports written by Smith after 1998.

The Boolean OR operator, by contrast, broadens an index search by specifying two retrieval requirements, either of which must be satisfied. Thus, a statement of the form:

AUTHOR = SMITH *OR* AUTHOR = JONES

will retrieve index records that contain either or both of the two indicated values in the author field. The Boolean OR operator establishes a logical union of two sets; in this case, one set contains documents written by Smith, the other documents written by Jones. The Boolean OR merges the two sets to create a new set consisting of index records that are members of either set—that is, written by either Smith or Jones or both. Duplicate records are eliminated in the process. The Boolean OR operator is particularly useful for subject searches based on synonymous terms. (Some retrieval software automatically search for synonyms based on an online thesaurus or other term list.) Although it offers very convenient and highly desirable capabilities, the Boolean OR operator is not indispensable. The same results can be obtained, albeit in a more cumbersome way, by conducting separate retrieval operations based on two search specifications.

The Boolean NOT operator, which may be implicitly or explicitly combined with the AND operator, will narrow a database search by excluding records that contain specified values in designated fields. In the case of technical reports, a search specification of the form:

AUTHOR = SMITH *NOT* DATE < 1998

will limit retrieval to documents written by Smith in 1998 or later. The Boolean NOT operator seeks the logical negation or complement of two sets. It identifies index records that are members of a given set but that are not also members of another designated set. Other Boolean operators are more difficult to use effectively. Examples include the XOR (exclusive OR) operator, which identifies index records that satisfy either but not both of two search specifications; the NOR operator, which identifies index records that do not satisfy either of two search specifications; and NAND, which identifies index records that satisfy one or neither of two search specifications. They are seldom supported or needed in digital document implementations.

Depending on software capabilities, several Boolean operators may be combined in a given search specification, thereby permitting very complex retrieval operations involving multiple field matches. Parentheses can be used to control the sequence in which specific Boolean operations are performed, search specifications within parentheses being executed first. Thus, a search specification of the form:

(AUTHOR = JONES *OR* AUTHOR = SMITH) *AND* DATE > 1998

will retrieve documents written by either Jones or Smith after 1998. In the absence of parentheses, Boolean operations are performed in a default sequence defined by the retrieval program itself. Usually, NOT and AND operations are performed before OR operations. In such cases, the searcher's intent may be misinterpreted and inappropriate results obtained. Without parentheses, the above example would retrieve documents written by Smith after 1998 or all documents written by Jones regardless of date. Parentheses can be nested to several levels if necessary, but such complex search capabilities require training and practice for effective use.

Other Search Capabilities

Some digital document implementations support additional search capabilities to enhance retrieval flexibility. In addition to retrieving database records that match exact field values specified in search statements, some systems can identify field values that begin with, contain, or end with specified character strings. As a group, such capabilities broaden retrieval specifications.

Searches for field values that begin with a specified character string are particularly useful for retrieving subject terms, personal names, or corporate names with common roots, as well as singular and plural forms of field values. Thus, a search specification of the form:

SUBJECT = IMAG?

will identify index records that contain "IMAGE," IMAGES," or "IMAGING," among other words, in the subject field. Such retrieval operations are sometimes described as *right truncation* or *root word searches*. In some cases, right truncation must be explicitly stated, using a designated operator such as the question mark employed in the above example. In other cases, right truncation is the default search mode; field values that begin with a given character string are invariably retrieved unless an exact match is specified.

Retrieval operations based on left truncation of suffix searches—that is, searches for field values that end with a designated character string—are not as widely supported as those based on right truncation of field values, but they can prove useful in certain situations. In an application involving pharmaceutical research reports that are indexed with drug names, for example, a search specification of the form:

SUBJECT = ?MYCIN

will retrieve index records that contain certain antibiotic names (such as aureomycin, streptomycin, and teramycin) in the subject field. To obtain the same result without left truncation, the search specification would require individual antibiotic names linked by the OR operator.

Retrieval operations based on embedded character strings, sometimes described as *substring searches*, will match field values that contain a specified sequence of characters preceded or followed by other characters. Thus, a search specification of the form:

SUBJECT CONTAINS TAPE

will retrieve index records that contain "MAGNETIC TAPE," "MAGNETIC TAPES," "VIDEOTAPE," "VIDEOTAPES," "BACKUP TAPE," or "DIGITAL LINEAR TAPE," among other values, in the subject field. In some cases, substring searches can yield irrelevant or otherwise unintended results. The foregoing search statement, for example, would retrieve database records containing words such as "TAPER" or "TAPESTRY" in the subject field.

Wildcard characters broaden search specifications by using designated nonalphabetic symbols, such as asterisks or question marks, to denote positions within designated field values that can be matched by any characters. Thus, a search specification of the form:

SUBJECT = DIS*S

will retrieve index records with subject field values that begin with "DIS," followed by any character, and ending in "S." Possibilities include "DISKS" or "DISCS." Wildcard searches are particularly useful for field values with variant spellings. Depending on the system, wildcard symbols may match a single character in a designated position, multiple characters, or one or more characters from a specified list. With some systems, for example, a search statement of the form:

SUBJECT = DIS*CK*S

will match subject field values that begin with "DIS," followed by either a "C" or a "K," and ending in "S." Wildcard characters can be combined with term truncation or substring searches.

Some retrieval software supports *fuzzy search* capabilities, which will match field values that are similar to, but do not exactly satisfy, a given search specification. Fuzzy retrieval concepts recognize a continuum of possibilities when field values are matched against character strings. Distinctions between field values that match or do not match designated character strings are not delineated precisely. Partial matches are permitted. With some programs, the searcher can control the degree of fuzziness by entering a numeric value between two extremes to indicate the desired conformity of field values to search strings. The value 1, for example, may designate a very loose match, while the value 10 may specify an exact match. Like the wildcard symbols described above, fuzzy searches are particularly useful for subject terms with variant spellings—"color" and "colour," for example. They can also be used to retrieve misspelled field values or personal names of uncertain spelling. In digital imaging implementations that employ auto-indexing techniques based on optical character recognition, fuzzy searches can compensate for recognition errors. A related capability, *phonetic searching*, will match field values that sound like a specified search term and begin with the same character.

Specific search features aside, retrieved index records may be displayed as formatted screens with labeled fields or in tabular listings with labeled columns. Depending on software capabilities and the application planner's specifications, the displayed information may contain all or selected fields from within database records. If optical disks or other storage media must be manually mounted for retrieval, the displayed records will include disk numbers or other media identifiers. Retrieved index records can usually be sorted by an operator-designated field value in a specified sequence prior to display or printing. Some database management programs also provide report generation capabilities that can produce highly formatted output, although such capabilities are often more useful for general computing applications than for digital document implementations.

Depending on the type of computer monitor employed in a given installation, index records and their associated digital documents may be displayed simultaneously in adjacent or overlapping windows. Digital documents in image formats may be enlarged, reduced, rotated, or otherwise manipulated for display in a designated screen area. Some software provides annotation capabilities that let users type brief comments, instructions, corrections, or other notes to be appended to specific digital documents. A note indicator appears when its associated document is retrieved. Some software also permits voice annotation of digital documents.

Full-Text Searching

Where full-text indexing is employed, searches can be based on specific words contained in character-coded digital documents or document surrogates such as an abstract. Such full-text searches may employ relational expressions, Boolean operators, wildcard symbols, or other retrieval features described previously. Certain additional capabilities are unique to full-text searching. *Phrase searching*, a form of *proximity searching*, will retrieve documents that contain two adjacent words in a specified sequence—"magnetic tape," for example. With some software, proximity commands allow a searcher to specify the number of permissible intervening words between two search terms and/or the sequence in which the two terms appear. With some proximity commands, a searcher can specify that two terms appear in the same line, sentence, paragraph, or page within a digital document. This capability is sometimes described as *context searching*. With negative proximity commands, a searcher can specify that two terms be at least a specified number of words apart or that two terms not appear within the same line, sentence, or paragraph.

Some software products offer unusual full-text retrieval capabilities. Examples include index browsing to facilitate term selection, *case-sensitive searches*, automatic searches for synonymous or related terms based on an online thesaurus, conflation operators that automatically match different verb tenses or related forms of nouns, proximity searches for words that appear between two specified words, and *quorum searching* to locate documents that contain a specified number of listed terms such as any three search terms from a list of seven.

Software responds to full-text searches with a hit list of digital documents that satisfy specific retrieval parameters. Depending on the program, the hit list may be sorted chronologically, by specified fields, or by relevance, based on term weighting or statistical analysis of document content. Any listed document can be selected for a complete display with search terms highlighted. Alternatively, some programs will display short document segments that contain search terms surrounded by several lines of context. Documents may be displayed by launching their originating applications where present. Thus, a document created with Microsoft Word will be displayed in that application, assuming that it is installed on the retrieval workstation. Similarly, a PDF file will be displayed by launching Acrobat Reader. Where the originating application is not available, digital documents are displayed by viewing programs that accommodate computer files in a variety of text and image formats, including formats associated with unusual or discontinued applications as well as earlier versions of popular software.

Retrieval Workstations

Character-coded digital documents can be displayed on any computer workstation and printed by any printer. In digital imaging installations, by contrast, specially configured workstations support input and retrieval operations, including index data entry, image inspection, database searches, and document viewing. Such workstations are typically PC-based. Their input and output components include a computer monitor with a compatible controller, a keyboard, and a mouse or other pointing device. Input workstations may be configured with document scanners. Retrieval workstations may include printers for hardcopy output. Alternatively, networked printers may serve multiple retrieval workstations.

Whether they support input or retrieval operations, digital imaging workstations are categorized as *image-capable* or *nonimage-capable*, depending on their display capabilities. As the name suggests, an image-capable workstation can display computer-processible graphic images, including digitized document images. It can also display character-coded text or quantitative values contained in database records, word processing documents, spreadsheets, or other computer files. By contrast, nonimage-capable workstations can display only character-coded information. They lack graphic display capabilities. Examples of nonimage-capable workstations include the 3270-type terminals employed in some IBM mainframe computer installations and the VT series terminals employed in some Unix and OpenVMS computer installations.

Nonimage-capable workstations are less expensive than image-capable workstations, but they provide limited functionality for digital imaging implementations and are inappropriate for general-purpose computing applications that employ graphical user interfaces. In most work settings, nonimage-capable terminals have consequently been replaced by personal computers with image-capable components. In document input operations, nonimage-capable workstations can be used for entry or verification of index data, but they cannot display digitized images for inspection following scanning. As retrieval devices, nonimage-capable workstations can search index records to determine the existence of potentially relevant document images, but they cannot display the images themselves for operator viewing. Software permitting, however, document images can be routed to a designated printer for hard-copy output. Digital imaging implementations may include a combination of image-capable and nonimage-capable workstations. The latter may be marginally acceptable for users who principally interact with character-based applications but have occasional document retrieval requirements.

Image-Capable Displays

Graphic display devices incorporated into image-capable workstations are sometimes described as *bit-mapped monitors*. They store bit patterns for digitized document images in internal memory circuits and selectively illuminate or darken portions of the monitor's screen to match light and dark areas within the source documents from which the images were produced. The digitized images are, in effect, redrawn on, or mapped onto, the screen. Information areas within source documents appear as dark pixels or dots, while background areas are represented by light pixels.

Most of the bit-mapped monitors employed in image-capable workstations are CRT-based, although liquid crystal displays (LCDs)—once reserved for portable computing devices—are increasingly popular alternatives for desktop workstations. Monochrome monitors are suitable for applications involving textual documents or line art scanned in the binary mode. Featuring a white phosphor, they display document images in a positive-appearing format with dark information on a light background. Monochrome monitors were popular in imaging systems implemented through the mid-1990s. Although some monochrome models remain in use, color display capabilities are now the norm.

Conventional personal computer monitors are bit-mapped color devices. They can display digitized document images, but technical limitations, impede their functionality for some purposes. Certain bit-mapped monitors are designed specifically for digital imaging and other computer applications that require high-resolution graphic display capabilities. Once considered unusual devices, such high-resolution monitors are now widely available. Several companies manufacture high-resolution monitors and related components principally or exclusively. Others produce a broad line of computer monitors, including one or more high-resolution models suitable for digital imaging applications. Vendors of digital imaging systems purchase high-resolution monitors from one or more sources for integration into their systems. Consequently, competing digital imaging systems are rarely differentiated by distinctive display devices.

A high-resolution monitor requires a compatible high-resolution controller. A display controller, also known as a *display adapter* or a *graphics adapter*, contains processing components and memory to format, store, and display bit-mapped images at a particular resolution. Depending on product characteristics and application requirements, a given display controller may perform other image processing tasks, including decompression, reduction, enlargement, enhancement, and rotation. High-resolution display controllers are equipped with high-speed graphics processing chips. Sometimes described as *graphic accelerators*, these chips contain preprogrammed instructions for rapid execution of image generation and processing routines. A display controller must include sufficient memory to accommodate bit-mapped images. High-speed video random-access memory (VRAM) circuits are typically employed. Memory requirements vary with the type of images to be displayed and the desired resolution. As with newer bit-mapped video monitors, most display controllers increasingly provide grayscale and color capabilities. Such devices have greater memory capacities than their monochrome counterparts. To display an eight-bit grayscale image at 120 dots per inch, a controller requires approximately two megabytes of VRAM, as compared with approximately one-quarter megabyte of VRAM for a monochrome image. To display a 24-bit color image at the same resolution, a controller requires approximately six megabytes of VRAM.

Most manufacturers of high-resolution monitors offer one or more display controllers for use with their own products. Often, manufacturers market their high-resolution monitors with display controllers in bundled configurations, although a given controller may be purchased separately for use with compatible monitors of other manufacturers. Alternatively, display controllers may be purchased from companies that manufacture specialized image processing components. Such third-party display controllers are compatible with designated high-resolution monitors from various manufacturers. Although records managers and other information specialists should understand the purpose and desirable characteristics of high-resolution display controllers, the decision to employ a particular display controller in a given digital imaging implementation is usually made by a system developer or integrator. Vendors of digital imaging systems select specific monitor/controller combinations for use in their product lines. They acquire the desired components from their manufacturers and integrate them into systems marketed to prospective customers.

The design features, operating characteristics, and display capabilities of high-resolution monitors and display controllers have changed significantly since the early 1980s. Color display capabilities are routine. Flat, square picture tubes minimize distortions. Noninterlaced screens with high refresh rates eliminate flicker and facilitate prolonged viewing of electronic document images without eye fatigue. The Video Electronics Standards Association (VESA) specifies a minimum refresh rate of 70 Hertz. Newer bit-mapped video monitors satisfy that requirement at resolutions appropriate for the display of electronic document images. Some high-resolution monitors support refresh rates exceeding 80 Hertz. Newer high-resolution monitors also feature high-contrast screens with antiglare and antireflective treatments for improved viewing properties, as well as antistatic coatings to reduce dust accumulation. Energy-efficient monitors automatically invoke a standby mode following a predefined period of inactivity. Manufacturers of newer high-resolution video monitors likewise advertise compliance with requirements and recommendations for electromagnetic interference. Various after market products, such as antiglare and anti-emission filters that attach to a monitor's screen, are also available.

Most notably for digital imaging implementations, newer bit-mapped monitors differ from earlier models in screen size, screen orientation, and display resolution. Image-capable workstations have historically featured large screens that can display complete pages. The high-resolution monitors employed in the earliest digital imaging systems featured 15-inch (diagonally-measured) screens oriented in the vertical (portrait) mode. With approximate screen measurements of 8.5 inches wide by 11 inches high, such devices could display a letter-size page in its entirety. They were consequently described as *full-page* or *single-page monitors.* As their principal limitation, single-page monitors displayed data-entry forms or retrieval interaction in a separate window that overlapped and consequently obscured portions of the document image. Since the late 1980s, most vendors of digital imaging systems have emphasized high-resolution monitors with horizontally oriented (landscape mode) screens that measure 19 to 21 inches diagonally. These display devices are sometimes described as *dual-page monitors;* with screen areas that measure 11 to 12 inches wide by 14 to 15 inches high, they can display two letter-size page images side by side. In most applications, however, a dual-page monitor displays a single document image on one side of the screen; the other side displays one or more windows for data-entry, database searching, or other computer interaction.

Although screen sizes have increased since the early 1980s, display resolutions supported by the most widely installed high-resolution video monitors have declined. In technical specification sheets or other product literature, a monitor's display resolution may be measured in either of two ways: (1) as the number of pixels or dots along the display area's horizontal and vertical dimensions, or (2) as the number of displayable pixels or dots per inch. To operate at a given resolution, a monitor must be configured with a compatible display controller. Some bit-mapped video monitors support multiple resolutions and can operate with any of several controllers.

Although it denotes high-quality display capabilities, the adjective "high-resolution" is an imprecise descriptor. No standard definition distinguishes high-resolution monitors from lower-resolution devices. Indeed, users' resolution expectations and product capabilities have changed over time. Since the early 1990s, most vendors and users have considered 100 dots per inch to be the de facto dividing line between high-resolution and low-resolution video monitors. During the mid-1980s, however, records professionals assumed that the successful implementation of paperless document management systems required the highest quality display components. At that time, the 15-inch, portrait-mode monitors incorporated into image-capable worksta-tions displayed 2,200 dots vertically by 1,700 dots horizontally—the equivalent of 200 dots per inch, which was then, as now, the most common scanning resolution in digi-tal imaging implementations. Document images were consequently displayed at their full scanning resolutions. Industry analysts predicted that monitors with resolutions of 300 or even 400 dots per inch would soon become commonplace, thus permitting the very high-quality display of document images generated at those resolutions. Although such devices exist, they are seldom encountered in digital imaging configurations.

Since the early 1990s, vendors of digital imaging systems have favored bit-mapped monitors with resolutions ranging from 100 to 150 dots per inch. Among their significant advantages, such monitors and their display controllers are less expensive than devices that support higher resolutions. At the high end of current product offerings, several companies manufacture 19-to-21-inch landscape-mode monitors that can display 2,048 dots horizontally by 1,536 dots vertically, the equiv-alent of 150 dots per inch. Most digital imaging systems, however, use 19-to-21-inch, landscape-mode monitors that display approximately 1,600 dots horizontally by 1,200 dots vertically, the equivalent of 120 dots per inch. Such devices are widely available and competitively priced. Monitors that display 120 dots per inch cost about 30 percent less than monitors that display 150 dots per inch.

In most digital imaging implementations, source documents are scanned at 200 or 300 dots per inch. When the scanning resolution employed in a given application exceeds the resolution of display devices, document images must be adjusted or scaled to a lower resolution for display in a full-page format. Such scaling may be performed by a host computer when images are retrieved or by display controllers when images are transmitted to image-capable workstations. To eliminate process-ing delays associated with image scaling at retrieval time, some systems store images both at the full scanning resolution and in a scaled format. Thus, each image may be stored in a 300 dot-per-inch version for printing and in a 120- or 150-dot-per-inch version for full-page display. In such cases, scaling is performed following scanning but prior to image recording. As an alternative to scaling, document images may be displayed at full resolution, but a complete page cannot be displayed at one time.

Scaling of electronic document images invariably involves a degradation of image quality as pixels are omitted to accommodate lower-resolution display characteristics. Computer algorithms determine the pixels to be eliminated. To enhance the viewabili-ty of images at lower resolutions, some display controllers use scale-to-gray technology, which places gray dots around the edges of displayed characters to give the appearance of smoothness and enhance legibility. Scale-to-gray technology requires a grayscale or color monitor. Although grayscale models may offer better display characteristics for document imaging, color monitors are typically preferred for attractive display of win-dows, icons, toolbars, and other user interface components.

Prices have fallen for high-resolution bit-mapped video monitors of all types, steadily and significantly since the mid-1980s. The declining prices are attributable to several factors, including increased competition, lower costs for computer memories and other electronic components, and a broader market for high-resolution bit-mapped displays. In addition to digital imaging, image-capable bit-mapped monitors are employed in computer graphics, desktop publishing, multimedia, medical imaging, CAD, and other applications.

As an alternative or complement to high-resolution, image-capable worksta-tions, most digital imaging systems support the lower-resolution XGA and Super XGA displays that are commonly encountered in personal computer installations. As their principal attraction for digital imaging implementations, these monitors and their compatible controllers are much less expensive than higher-resolution display components. Vendors of entry-level digital imaging systems often promote the use of lower-resolution display components to reduce implementation costs and facilitate justification in low-volume applications. In large installations, lower-resolution monitors can provide access to electronic document images at individual desktops without hardware replacement.

Although lower-resolution bit-mapped monitors and controllers can be used in image-capable workstations, the results may prove unacceptable for some purposes. XGA screen resolution is 1,024 pixels (horizontal) by 768 pixels (vertical), while Super XGA monitors have a screen resolution of 1,280 pixels (horizontal) by 1,024 pixels (vertical). When displaying a complete letter-size page, the effective resolutions are 72 dots per inch for XGA monitors and 92 dots per inch for Super XGA monitors. Those resolutions provide marginal-to-acceptable character legibility when letter-size pages are displayed in their entirety, but they are too low for prolonged study of some docu-ment images. A resolution of 100 dots per inch is widely regarded as the dividing line between high-resolution and low-resolution displays, and 120 dots per inch is consid-ered the minimum acceptable display resolution for users with frequent image retrieval or prolonged image viewing requirements. For character legibility, XGA and Super XGA monitors must be able to display document images in a partial-page format. Cursor control keys or commands must be used to pan and scroll across each page.

Display limitations aside, the controllers employed with lower-resolution bit-mapped monitors do not support scaling, decompression, or other image processing capabilities required in digital imaging implementations. Typically, such functions must be performed by software installed on an image-capable workstation's host computer. The computer must be equipped with sufficient memory and hard disk capacity for that purpose.

Printers

Although digital document technologies are widely promoted as paperless alternatives to conventional filing methodologies, most records management applications will require paper copies of digital documents or index records for reference or other purposes. Sufficient printing equipment must consequently be available. Paper reference copies are especially important for lengthy documents that require careful study or where image retrieval workstations are configured with lower-resolution display components that are poorly suited to prolonged viewing of documents.

Character-coded documents can be printed by any device. Image printing, however, is more challenging. Image-capable printers must be equipped with a compatible controller, which may also function as a printer accelerator to increase output speed. Some controllers include decompression programs that reduce file sizes and conserve bandwidth in network printer installations. In the absence of such capability, images to be printed must be decompressed prior to network transmission. Based on instructions contained in the output stream, some controller cards can also rotate, scale, or otherwise manipulate images prior to printing.

Since the early 1980s, laser printing has been the technology of choice for hard-copy output in digital imaging implementations. Many newer models support black-and-white printing at resolutions exceeding 600 dots per inch. Scanning resolutions seldom exceed 300 dpi in records management applications, but printer software can simulate higher-resolution output through interpolation.

Image-capable laser printers are widely categorized by their operating speeds, which is usually measured in pages per minute. As might be expected, the least expensive digital imaging systems are configured with relatively slow printers. They usually produce four to six letter-size pages per minute and have a duty cycle comparable to a desktop copier; they can produce several thousand copies per month. Most models feature a single paper tray. Output is limited to letter-size copies. Faster, more expensive printers typically operate as shared peripherals in multi-workstation configurations. Medium-speed laser printers can produce 12 to 24 pages per minute. More ruggedly constructed than lower-speed models, their duty cycles range from 50,000 to 75,000 pages per month. To simplify operation, minimize interruptions in print jobs, and enhance throughput, some models are equipped with multiple, high-capacity paper trays. Some high-speed laser printers can produce 50 or more pages per minute. They are intended for high-volume centralized output in large-scale multiworkstation imaging installations. At all levels, output speed is affected by the amount of memory in the printer.

As an alternative to hard-copy output, digital documents can be printed directly onto microfilm using computer-output-microfilm (COM) technology. This type of COM recorder is shown in Figure 4.3. Character-coded documents can be printed by any COM recorder. Special graphic COM recorders can accept digitized document images in various formats, including TIF and PDF. Depending on the model, the resulting microimages may be recorded on 16mm microfilm, 35mm microfilm, microfiche, or aperture cards. As discussed in Chapter 5, some records managers and application planners want to rely on digital documents for active reference but prefer microforms to satisfy long-term retention requirements. In such situations, direct printing of digital documents by a COM recorder eliminates a separate operation to microfilm documents for retention.

COM Recorder—Prints Digital Images Directly onto Microfilm for Long-Term Retention

(Courtesy: Eastman Kodak)

Figure 4.3

Chapter 5

Implementation Issues

Although digital documents offer significant advantages for storage and retrieval of recorded information in a variety of applications, questions have been raised about the technology's records management implications and limitations. Digital document technologies are well developed, but successful implementations require careful planning. In particular, the selection of appropriate applications and qualified vendors is a critical consideration. Records managers and others responsible for the retention of information needed for legal reasons, business reference, or other purposes are understandably concerned about the continued usefulness of digital documents over time. The impact of product obsolescence and software modifications on the future usability of digital documents is an obvious concern. These issues, introduced briefly in Chapter 1, are examined in the following sections. This chapter also discusses the relationship between digital documents and other technologies, including workflow programming, COLD, and records management application (RMA) software.

Strategic Considerations

Digital document implementations are best suited to records that will be referenced frequently. Digital document technologies can identify and retrieve documents quickly for online display or printing. That advantage pertains to active records exclusively. For inactive records, which are seldom referenced, retrieval speed is inconsequential. Although conversion to digital images or character-coded text will reduce space requirements for inactive records when compared to retaining an equivalent quantity of paper documents, off-site storage or microfilming are usually more economical choices for that purpose. Generally, off-site storage is the least expensive option for inactive records that will be retained for less than 15 to 20 years. Microfilming should be considered for inactive records that must be kept for longer periods of time. Compared to retention long-term or permanent records in digital formats, microfilming avoids data migration requirements discussed later in this chapter.

Although ambitious enterprise-wide installations have been widely discussed, a conservative approach will increase the likelihood of a successful digital document implementation for most organizations. Because simultaneous implementation of multiple applications is complicated and risky, an organization should select one application for its initial digital document installation. The records management staff, computer personnel, and end-users can become familiar with the technology, evaluate the suitability of specific system components, determine training requirements, and develop procedures for subsequent well-selected applications to be phased in over time, once the initial application is fully operational.

Whenever possible, an organization should standardize on a single software platform for all its digital document applications. Although products of different vendors may utilize the same components and offer similar functionality, they differ in their input methods, indexing capabilities, retrieval procedures, and other characteristics. Organizations should avoid the implementation of incompatible systems in individual departments. Digital document technologies for different applications should not be procured separately. Instead, an organization should select one vendor as its sole provider of digital document capabilities and solutions. The vendor chosen for that purpose must offer a general-purpose product line that is readily scalable and suitable for a broad range of documents and applications. The vendor may provide an enterprise-wide system on which all digital document applications will be implemented. Alternatively, separate but compatible systems may be replicated in selected departments, operations, or locations within the organization.

Initial applications should involve a manageable number of documents with straightforward indexing, data-entry, and retrieval requirements. Word processing documents, e-mail messages, and other character-coded documents should be in commonly encountered file formats to facilitate full-text indexing as well as document viewing and printing. For imaging implementations, paper source documents should be in good condition and readily scannable. Large backfile conversions, which can prove complicated to manage and time-consuming to execute, should be avoided or at least postponed until digital document capabilities are fully implemented and operating reliably.

Self-contained records management applications that require little or no customized programming to interface with external software are easiest to implement. Applications that must be linked to other programs can require significant integration effort and should be deferred until the organization has acquired familiarity with digital document technology and specific software characteristics. In medium-size and large organizations, future implementations will likely require customized programming to link digital documents to third-party software or other programs that support specific business operations. Most digital document products include application programming interfaces or other software tools for this purpose. If software developers, systems integrators, or other contractors will perform this work, they must provide evidence of programming knowledge and experience appropriate to the organization's interface requirements.

Finally, effective records management programs are based on procedural rather than technological foundations. Digital document technology should not be implemented at the expense of other records management initiatives such as the preparation of retention schedules or the development of vital records protection programs. Technology is just one component of a systematic records management program. It should support rather than replace other customary responsibilities of records management.

Procurement Procedures

Software for digital document implementations is developed by dozens of companies, who may sell their products directly to customers or market them indirectly through value-added resellers, systems integrators, business partners, or other authorized representatives. Although competing products often incorporate identical hardware components and offer similar software functionality, vendor capabilities and prices for comparable system configurations can differ considerably. For most organizations, a competitive procurement based on a request for proposals (RFP) or other detailed statement of requirements will increase the likelihood of obtaining a qualified vendor and a favorable price. A model RFP for that purpose is presented in Appendix A. It specifies desirable characteristics and capabilities for hardware and software components to create, import, organize, store, retrieve, and otherwise manage digital documents in image and character-coded formats. It also includes procedural provisions, instructions to bidders, and other information applicable to digital document procurements.

Unlike an invitation to bid, which merely requests a price, an RFP describes a problem and solicits solutions from qualified suppliers. A well-prepared RFP will give vendors maximum flexibility in proposing digital document products and services to meet an organization's requirements while ruling out unacceptable hardware components and software capabilities. An RFP's specifications should be written in such a way that multiple vendors will be able to respond, which increases the likelihood that several acceptable proposals will be received.

RFPs for digital document implementations are typically detailed and lengthy. Time-consuming distribution of complete copies to dozens of vendors, some of whom may not choose to bid, is rarely advisable. Instead, a brief notice of the availability of an RFP can be mailed, e-mailed, or faxed to prospective bidders. Interested parties can then request copies of the full RFP, which can be transmitted to requesters as e-mail attachments, posted on a publicly accessible web site, or sent to requesters by mail service or overnight delivery. Some requests for the full RFP will be received shortly after its availability is announced. Others may come in over a week or two as the notice of availability is routed to appropriate parties within a vendor's organization or to authorized resellers and other representatives.

In addition to system specifications, an RFP for digital document products and services should provide detailed instructions for prospective bidders. Such instructions will increase the likelihood that proposals will be submitted in a format conducive to evaluation and comparison. In many cases, a proposed digital document implementation will replace a paper filing or micrographic system. Where appropriate, the RFP should invite prospective bidders to visit the customer's site to examine existing recordkeeping practices prior to submitting their proposals. A bidder's conference, which provides a public forum for questions about the RFP, is often advisable and may be required for procurements by government agencies. If a bidder's conference is not held, an organization must answer questions from individual bidders throughout the bid cycle.

Most vendors will require at least 45 days to prepare effective responses to a detailed RFP. A 30-day response interval will reduce the number of bidders, which is usually undesirable. Deadline dates for responses must allow ample time before and after holidays. If a bidder's conference will be held, it should be scheduled 30 to 35 days after the RFP is issued.

If a notice of availability of an RFP is sent to 50 prospective bidders, perhaps 15 to 20 will request a full copy, and 6 to 10 will actually submit proposals. Of these proposals, one or two will likely be incomplete, noncompliant, too expensive, or otherwise clearly unacceptable. From the remainder, an organization should create a short list of two or three finalists, who will be expected to make oral presentations of their proposals and to demonstrate their systems' capabilities. During the evaluation period, questions will presumably be raised and concerns resolved about specific proposals. Bidders' references will also be checked. Where procurement procedures permit, the finalists should be asked for their "best and final" offers at the conclusion of the evaluation process. Those prices may be lower than the initial bids. Depending on an organization's procurement procedures, 30 days or longer may be required to complete contract negotiations following selection of the successful bidder.

Legality

Concerns about the legal status of digital documents as substitutes for paper records or microfilm were introduced in Chapter 1. The principal issues involve the ability of digital documents to satisfy legally mandated recordkeeping requirements and the admissibility of digital documents as evidence in litigation, government investigations, administrative hearings, and other judicial and quasi-judicial proceedings. These issues are delineated and analyzed, in varying levels of detail, in numerous books, journal articles, and conference papers. The following discussion summarizes current thinking about the relationship of digital documents to legally mandated recordkeeping requirements. The acceptability of digital documents as evidence is considered in the next section.

Digital Documents and Recordkeeping Requirements

Legal statutes and government regulations specify that certain records must be kept for minimum periods of time. These legally mandated recordkeeping requirements apply to all private and public organizations that operate within a specific governmental jurisdiction. The ability to satisfy such requirements with digital documents is consequently subject to national and regional variations. In the United States, the relationship of digital documents to legally mandated recordkeeping requirements is based on the following principle: U.S. law permits the retention of documents in any form, provided that a particular form is not mandated or prohibited by legal statutes or government regulations. Although easily stated, this principle can be difficult to apply because the acceptability of digital documents is not always clearly delineated in recordkeeping laws and regulations. As a complicating factor, an organization's legal department, which often has approval authority over records retention practices, may interpret the mention of specific formats to mean nonacceptance of others for retention purposes.

Many recordkeeping laws and regulations predate widespread computerization of business operations. They are written in a manner that implies or is based on the assumption that the required information is contained in paper documents. As an example, the Uniform Preservation of Private Business Records Act, which was adopted by some states in the 1960s, equates the terms "business records" and "business papers." By contrast, newer recordkeeping laws and regulations, as well as recent revisions of older ones, approve digital documents for retention. The Uniform Electronic Transactions Act, which dates from 2000, is one example. It specifies that digital documents can satisfy legally mandated retention requirements, subject to reasonable conditions: The digital documents must be accessible for future reference when needed—a requirement that poses problems discussed later in this chapter—and the retention format must accurately reflect the information as it was originally generated, stored, sent, or received.

Recognizing the increasing prevalence and importance of digital documents, a growing number of government regulations address their acceptability as alternatives to paper or microfilm to satisfy specific recordkeeping requirements. Generally, these regulations stipulate that digital documents are acceptable, provided that they are readily available and indexed for convenient retrieval when needed; that appropriate retrieval equipment and software is available; and that paper copies can be produced in a reasonable amount of time on demand for audits or other purposes. Among the many examples that might be cited, 29 CFR 516.1 indicates that "automatic word or data processing memory" is acceptable for retention of records required by the Fair Labor Standards Act. Similarly, 21 CFR Part 11 permits the substitution of digital documents for certain paper records that the Food and Drug Administration requires pharmaceutical companies to create, maintain, or submit to the FDA under requirements of the Federal Food, Drug, and Cosmetic Act and the Public Health Service Act. Such substitution is limited, however, to documents identified in Public Docket No. 92S-0251 as accepted by the FDA in electronic form.

By disavowing any prescribed format for records retention, some regulations approve digital documents by implication. As cited in 29 CFR 1910.20, for example, the Occupational Safety and Health Act (OSHA) permits retention of employee exposure and medical records in any retrievable form, although it requires that chest X-rays be "preserved in their original state." In defining standards for retention of medical records, 42 CFR 482.24 specifies that hospitals participating in Medicare and Medicaid programs must keep accurate, complete, and accessible records for each patient. However, the regulation does not mandate a particular format for the records. It merely states that the hospital's recordkeeping system must ensure the authentication and security of all patient information. Other public health regulations include similar provisions without prescribing or limiting record formats. As an example, 42 CFR 485.60 requires that outpatient rehabilitation facilities keep accurate, complete patient records "in accordance with accepted professional standards and practices." It specifies the retention period for such records (five years after the patient is discharged) but not the retention format.

In some cases, regulations impose additional conditions on electronic recordkeeping, the most common being a requirement that digital documents not be alterable. The Securities and Exchange Commission (SEC), for example, accepts digital documents for records that must be retained by exchange members, brokers, and dealers pursuant to Rule 17a-4 of the Securities Exchange Act, but the digital documents must be stored on nonerasable media. According to 49 CFR 1220.3, the Surface Transportation Board of the Department of Transportation permits retention of documents by "any technology that is immune to alteration, modification, or erasure." Similarly, the Bureau of Export Administration of the Department of Commerce will accept "electronic digital storage" for reproduction of original paper records as specified in 15 CFR 762.5 provided that the information cannot be altered following its initial recording. This regulation applies to digital images rather than to character-coded digital documents. Although not explicitly mentioned, the latter may come within the scope of 15 CFR 762.4, which applies to original records rather than reproductions.

The foregoing examples apply to recordkeeping practices in the United States; however, the passage or revision of laws and government regulations to accept digital documents as alternatives to paper or microfilm is occurring internationally. As a widely cited example, the Model Law on Electronic Commerce, issued in 1996 by the United Nations Commission on International Trade Law (UNCITRAL), specifies that retention requirements for documents, records, or information can be satisfied by "data messages." According to the Canadian Personal Information Protection and Electronic Documents Act, which was passed in 2000, a government official, government body, or other responsible authority can issue regulations that accept digital documents to satisfy recordkeeping requirements associated with acts of Parliament. The Canadian Uniform Electronic Commerce Act accepts digital documents to satisfy retention requirements provided that they are maintained in a format that preserves the information "as originally made, sent, or received." The information must be in an accessible form and, where applicable, information must be retained about the origin, destination, date, and time the document was sent or received. Although a comprehensive survey is beyond the scope of this book, other countries have passed similar legislation. In Italy, for example, Presidential Decree No. 513, issued in 1997, provides legal recognition of digital documents and digital signatures. It expands upon Article 15 of Law No. 59, which addresses the simplification of public administration and permits the use of digital documents in government operations.

Digital Documents as Evidence

The purpose of evidence is to prove or clarify points at issue in court trials, administrative hearings, or other judicial or quasi-judicial proceedings. Documents are widely employed as evidence in such situations, often as a complement or supplement to testimony. Evidence, including documents, that a judge or jury can properly consider is termed *admissible.* Records managers, corporate and institutional attorneys, and other individuals responsible for planning and implementing recordkeeping systems that will effectively support legal actions are understandably concerned about the admissibility of digital documents, or printed copies made from them, as evidence. Compared to the previously discussed concerns about legally mandated recordkeeping requirements, admissibility issues typically affect a greater number of digital documents. Although retention periods specified in legal statutes and government regulations apply to a subset of an organization's digital documents, any record might prove useful as evidence.

The admissibility of digital documents is a facet of the broader issue of admissibility of electronic records, a subject examined in thousands of publications over the past three decades. Although commentators may differ on specific points, certain widely accepted principles apply to digital documents as a type of electronic record:

- To be admissible as evidence, digital documents, like their nondigital counterparts, must satisfy the two foundation requirements that apply to all evidence: (1) their contents must be relevant to the matter at issue, and (2) their authenticity must be firmly established—that is, a court must be convinced that the digital documents are what their proponents claim them to be. Relevance determinations are case-specific and typically outside the scope of records management responsibilities. The authentication of digital documents is a direct concern of records managers, who are responsible for the development and implementation of reliable recordkeeping systems.

- According to the Federal Rules of Evidence (FRE) and Uniform Rules of Evidence (URE), authentication requirements for digital documents or other records can be satisfied by describing the system or process that is used to produce a given record and by showing that the system or process produces an accurate result. Similar authentication provisions are contained in the Canadian Uniform Electronic Evidence Act and in the comparable laws of other countries.

- Digital documents are clearly admissible as evidence; it is confirmed by widely publicized lawsuits and government investigations where e-mail messages have been admitted into evidence, often to the detriment of the organizations that created and maintained them. Questions may arise, however, about the nature and extent of authentication required to establish the reliability of digital documents in specification situations. To demonstrate the accuracy and trustworthiness of digital documents, an organization may be expected to provide testimony and/or documentation pertaining to system administration, input procedures, equipment, software, security, and the competency of employees who create and retrieve the digital documents.

- Authentication issues are typically raised in the context of a hearsay objection. Hearsay is a statement made out of court that pertains to some matter that is raised in court. Because hearsay is not subject to cross-examination by the opposing party in a legal action, it is generally inadmissible under the rules of evidence that apply in federal and state courts. Because digital documents, like their nondigital counterparts, are usually created out of court, they are considered hearsay and will not be admitted into evidence unless they fall within one of the several exceptions to the rule against hearsay. Such exceptions exist for business and public records.

- In U.S. federal courts, the applicable provision is Rule 803(6) of the Federal Rules of Evidence, which is known as the *business records exception to the hearsay rule.* It is based on the premise that records created in the normal course of business activities possess a circumstantial probability of trustworthiness. Because organizations that create such records must rely on them, their accuracy is presumed. Rule 803(6) applies to business records, regardless of format. At the state level, identical provisions are included in the Uniform Rules of Evidence (URE), which have been adopted by approximately 60 percent of the states, and in various state codes. The Federal Rules of Evidence, Uniform Rules of Evidence, and some state-specific statutes include additional provisions that may be used to authenticate digital documents that cannot satisfy the requirements of Rule 803(6).

- These evidentiary rules interpret business records broadly. They apply to digital documents created and maintained by cultural institutions, charities, professional associations, and other nonprofit organizations. Although they also apply to digital documents created by government agencies, Rule 803 (8) of the Federal Rules of Evidence and Uniform Rules of Evidence provides an additional exception for public records, although the relationship between the two exceptions has not been fully explained. For records created by government agencies, the public records exception provides an additional method of overcoming hearsay objections.

- Evidentiary rules require that electronic records be made within a reasonable time after the transaction, business activity, or other event to which they pertain. Admissibility issues may involve paper printouts of word processing documents, PDF files, electronic messages, digital images, or other digital documents. As a potential complication, these printouts may be produced months or years after their digital source records were created. Courts and legal commentators have generally treated computer-generated printouts as electronic records, even though they are paper documents that contain human-readable information. Several authorities contend that the requirement for timely creation of electronic records applies primarily to the creation and recording of information rather than to the interval between input and printing. A long delay prior to creating computer printouts may increase the potential for tampering or errors, but such a delay alone should not impede admissibility of digital documents. In several cases, computer printouts have been judged admissible even though they were produced long after entry of the information they contain.

- Digital documents must be protected from physical damage or tampering that could impair their accuracy or raise questions about their trustworthiness. Concerns about the improper alteration of digital information have been widely publicized in discussions of computer crime. In nonelectronic record-keeping systems, such modifications are often difficult to make and easy to detect. By contrast, digital documents stored on rewritable magnetic or optical media may be changed, erased, or otherwise manipulated with little or no trace. Character-coded text and quantitative values can be easily overwritten with new information, while widely available software permits the undetected manipulation of digital document images and digital photographs. Where digital documents are stored by networked computers, such alterations may be performed by a remote perpetrator, thereby circumventing physical accessibility requirements associated with the alteration of paper records. Although these issues are significant, the possibility of tampering is not an invariable impediment to admissibility—computer records stored on rewritable media have been admitted into evidence for decades. For authentication purposes, an organization must demonstrate that, because of security provisions in place, tampering with digital documents, while possible, was extremely unlikely to have occurred. Specific protection measures, such as password and privilege controls, must be pervasively implemented, strictly enforced, and fully documented for all systems that create, store, and utilize digital documents. A list of authorized users and their access privileges, determined by need-to-know based on assigned duties, should be maintained and verified periodically. Software that manages digital documents should maintain a log of authorized and failed accesses to specific files.

- All aspects of system operation should be audited regularly for compliance with established procedures. Audit findings and the implementation of corrective actions should be fully documented.

The foregoing points apply to the admissibility of digital documents in federal and state courts. Some legal proceedings, however, are held before federal and state administrative agencies where court-oriented rules of evidence do not apply. Generalizing about the admissibility of digital documents in such situations is impossible. Federal administrative agencies are bound by the Administrative Procedures Act, which gives such agencies considerable discretion in determining the admissibility of records. Some federal administrative agencies have informal rules of evidence that must be evaluated on a case-by-case basis to determine their application to digital documents. At the state government level, the admissibility of evidence in administrative proceedings is typically governed by state administrative procedures acts and agency procedural rules. Significant variations in admissibility rules may be encountered from one state to another and, within a given state, from one agency to another.

Special Issues for Digital Images

The preceding discussion applies to digital documents of all types; however, several special issues relate to the legal status of digital images, which are considered copies of the documents from which they are made. In the United States, treatments of this subject have emphasized two uniform laws—the Uniform Photographic Copies of Business and Public Records as Evidence Act and the Uniform Rules of Evidence (and its counterpart, the Federal Rules of Evidence)—as the conceptual foundation for admissibility of digital document images in evidence:

- The Uniform Photographic Copies of Business and Public Records as Evidence Act, commonly known as the Uniform Photographic Copies Act and abbreviated as UPA, permits the substitution of photographic copies for original documents in judicial proceedings or for administrative purposes. The UPA applies to business records maintained by corporations, partnerships, sole proprietorships, nonprofit institutions, and other nongovernmental organizations. It also applies to copies of public records maintained by federal, state, and local government agencies. In every case, the copies must have been produced in the regular course of business, as part of an organization's established operating procedures. The UPA permits, but does not mandate, the destruction of original documents, allowing organizations to rely solely on copies. Destruction is prohibited, however, where preservation of the original documents is specifically required by law. Some states have added a clause to the UPA that prohibits destruction of original documents held in a custodial or fiduciary capacity; examples include case files, account files, and other records maintained for clients by law firms, public accountants, and other professional service firms. In such situations, the owner's permission is required for destruction of original documents following conversion to electronic images. Destruction of original documents must be performed in the regular course of business.

- Rule 1003 of the Uniform Rules of Evidence and Federal Rules of Evidence supports the admissibility of duplicate records in evidence as substitutes for original documents unless serious questions are raised about the authenticity of the original records or, in specific circumstances, it is judged unfair to admit a copy in lieu of an original. Unlike the UPA, Rule 1003 of the URE/FRE does not require that duplicate records be produced in the regular course of business. Rule 1003 neither authorizes nor prohibits the destruction of original records.

The Uniform Photographic Copies Act and Uniform Rules of Evidence apply only in those legal jurisdictions where they have been adopted. One or both of the laws have been adopted by 88 percent of the states. Their applicability to digital document images is based on interpretation rather than explicit provisions because both laws predate the commercial availability of digital document technologies discussed in this book. The Uniform Photographic Copies Act was written in 1949. The Uniform Rules of Evidence were written in 1953 and revised in 1974. (The Federal Rules of Evidence were passed by Congress in 1975.) The UPA applies to any copying process that "accurately reproduces or forms a durable medium for so reproducing" original documents. Rule 1001(4) of the URE/FRE defines a duplicate as "a counterpart produced by the same impression as the original, or from the same matrix, or by means of photography, including enlargements and miniatures, or by mechanical or electronic re-recording, or by chemical reproduction, or by other equivalent techniques which accurately reproduces the original." Digital document images satisfy the requirements of these broad definitions.

In developments likely to be repeated in other legal jurisdictions, several states have modified their existing laws concerning duplicate records to more specifically encompass digital images of documents. As examples:

- The definition of "copy" contained in section 8.01-391(F) of the Virginia Code Annotated has been changed to include "copies from optical disks" along with photographs, photostats, and microfilm. Although copies of digital images stored on magnetic media are not mentioned specifically, the definition does not exclude them; it broadly embraces "any other reproduction of an original from a process which forms a durable medium for its recording, storing, and reproducing."

- Section 109.120 of the Missouri Revised Statutes addresses reproduction of documents by "photographic, video, or electronic processes." The resulting copies must be "of durable material" and "accurately reproduce and perpetuate the original records in all details."

- Section 44.139(B) of the Louisiana Revised Statutes gives an "electronically digitized copy" equivalent evidentiary status with microfilm as a duplicate record. When properly authenticated, such copies are admissible in evidence in all courts and administrative proceedings in the jurisdictions governed by such law.

The UPA and Rule 1003 of URE/FRE can counteract objections to the admissibility of digital document images under the best evidence rule, which requires the introduction of an "original writing" into evidence unless its absence can be satisfactorily explained. Where paper documents are destroyed in the regular course of business following scanning and recording, digital images or printouts made from them may be admissible as trustworthy copies. Unless fraud is suspected, destruction of original records in conformity with an organization's established business practices is typically considered a satisfactory explanation for the substitution of a trustworthy copy in evidence. Even where the original paper documents remain available, the UPA and Rule 1003 support the admissibility of digital images in evidence as substitutes for originals in most cases. They place the burden of argument on the party seeking to exclude digital images rather than the party seeking to admit them.

Application of the best evidence rule to other types of digital documents poses conceptual problems. Although digital images are copies produced by scanning paper or microfilm records, many digital documents are not copies but "original writings;" obvious examples include word processing files, spreadsheet files, and electronic mail. The best evidence rule might be applied to paper printouts produced from such digital documents, but Rule 1001(3) of the Federal Rules of Evidence and Uniform Rules of Evidence treats computer printouts as original records, thereby precluding an objection to their admissibility under the best evidence rule.

Operational Retention Requirements

Although legal considerations are important, many records are retained because they may be needed to support future business operations. To satisfy such operational retention requirements, digital documents must be retrievable and usable throughout their retention periods. As discussed in Chapter 1, the continued retrievability of digital documents and their associated index records is affected by the stability of media on which such images and index records are recorded. Equally important is the continued availability of compatible hardware and software components for index searching, document display, document printing, and other retrieval operations. These complications are examined in the following sections.

Media Stability

As discussed previously, working copies of digital documents may be recorded onto hard drives or onto optical disks. Working copies of index data are usually recorded onto hard drives. For both documents and index data, backup copies suitable for offline storage may be produced on optical disks or on magnetic tapes.

Stability estimates, also termed *lifetime estimates* or *life spans*, define the time periods during which magnetic or optical media will support reliable retrieval of recorded information. With electronic storage media, reliability is determined by the preservation of signal strength and the absence of permanent read/write errors during recording and playback of information. Stability estimates are limited to storage copies; working copies of any medium can be damaged by use. Stability estimates are further limited to removable media such as optical disks and magnetic tapes. Although hard drives can provide rapid, convenient access to actively referenced documents and index records, they are, in effect, working media. Consequently, they cannot be considered stable. Incorporated into computer hardware, hard drives are replaced at relatively short intervals and, while in use, are subject to damage from various equipment malfunctions. For secure retention, digital documents and index data recorded onto hard drives must be copied onto removable media for offline storage. Such storage copies should be referenced as little as possible.

The stability of a given information storage medium depends on several factors, including the medium's chemical composition and the conditions under which it is stored and used. Optical disks and magnetic tapes are sometimes described as *archival media*, but they do not offer the permanence implied in that description. On the contrary, optical disks and magnetic tapes are vulnerable to significant time-dependent degradation that eventually will render them unsuitable for accurate retrieval of recorded information. Such changes may be induced by environmental effects or by defects associated with media manufacturing. Further, information recorded on optical disks and magnetic tapes can be damaged by improper media handling.

Environmental degradation of computer storage media is well documented in scientific publications. Magnetic tapes and recordable optical disks feature metallic layers that are susceptible to oxidation from exposure to air. Over time, oxidation promotes pinhole formation and other forms of corrosion that can significantly alter the signal-to-noise ratios, bit-error frequencies, and other recording and playback properties of magnetic and optical media. As a further complication, most optical recording materials are coated on plastic or glass substrates with rough spots, strains, or other defects that can promote localized corrosion. In addition, plastic substrates tend to absorb moisture. Although optical disk manufacturers may incorporate oxidation-resistant alloys and barrier coatings into their products, such measures only delay the onset of deteriorative processes. Over time, media degradation accompanied by the loss of recorded information is inevitable. Magnetic tape substrates, while more rugged than their optical disk counterparts, may stretch or shrink in response to environmental changes such as rapid fluctuations of temperature and humidity. The polyurethane binders that cause magnetic recording materials to adhere to tape substrates are easily damaged by inappropriate environmental conditions, particularly high humidity, which leads to particle shedding and information loss.

Generalizations about the stability of optical disks and magnetic tape are complicated by several factors. Available media employ a variety of technologies, each involving different recording materials, substrates, processes, and equipment. Write-once and rewritable optical disks, for example, may be composed of metal alloys, metal/polymer combinations, or dye-based materials coated on glass or plastic substrates. Information may be recorded by forming microscopic pits, bubbles, or bumps; by diffusion of dyes; by crystalline-to-amorphous transitions, or vice versa; or through a combination of heat and magnetism. In addition, specific implementations of a given recording technology vary from manufacturer to manufacturer. The various magnetic tape formats likewise employ different recording technologies and media.

Stability claims for optical disks are based on accelerated aging tests rather than operational experience. Accelerated aging calculations are discussed in ISO 18924, *Imaging Materials—Test Method for Arrhenius-type Predictions.* Because most optical disks have been in existence for less than two decades, direct observation of media in prolonged storage is impossible. Various publications estimate the life expectancy of CD-ROM media at about 25 years. Manufacturers provide a similar lifetime estimate for DVD-ROM media. Among other optical disks, CD-R is the most stable computer storage medium. Manufacturers claim lifetime estimates of 75 to 200 years for their CD-R media. DVD-R media manufacturers claim a comparable life span for their products, which, like CD-R, employ dye polymer recording materials. Stability estimates of 30 to 50 years are typical for rewritable CD-RW media. Some manufacturers of rewritable DVD products claim a lifetime estimate exceeding 100 years. Stability periods for other types of optical disks range from 10 to 40 years, with 30 years being a typical claim. Storage recommendations for optical disks are presented in ISO 18925, *Imaging Materials—Optical Disc Media—Storage Practices.*

Anecdotal evidence based on operational experience with magnetic tapes in prolonged use suggests the possibility of multidecade life spans. Audio and video tapes recorded more than a quarter century ago remain playable today. Computing facilities have likewise successfully retrieved data from magnetic tapes that have been in storage for several decades. Contradicting such claims, however, audible and visible distortions attest to the deterioration of some older audio and video tapes, while questions have been raised about the reliable retrieval of information from magnetic tapes maintained in large data archives. ISO 18923, *Imaging Materials—Polyester-base Magnetic Tape—Storage Practices* specifies extended-term storage conditions for the preservation of recorded information of permanent value, but it does not state or imply that magnetic tapes have permanent keeping properties. Published research and manufacturers' claims support lifetime estimates of 10 to 30 years, depending on format, for most magnetic tapes. Typically, newer formats, such as digital linear tape, have longer lifetime estimates than older formats such as nine-track reels.

Product Obsolescence

As computer storage media, optical disks and magnetic tapes are designed for use with specific hardware and software components that usually have shorter service lives than the media themselves. Although a given optical disk or magnetic tape may retain playback stability for multiple decades, no historical precedent exists for computer storage peripherals remaining in use for that length of time. Most optical disk drives and magnetic tape units are engineered for a maximum service life of ten years, and the frequency of repair and high maintenance costs associated with aging equipment will typically necessitate replacement before that time. The availability of new models with improved cost-performance characteristics, coupled with changing application requirements, also encourage replacement at relatively short intervals—within five years or less in many cases.

To maintain competitiveness, manufacturers of computer storage peripherals introduce new models at regular intervals. Based on continuing research and product development activities, such new models typically incorporate innovations, refinements, and improved capabilities. As a principal performance enhancement, successive generations of optical disk and magnetic tape devices have customarily supported higher-density recording formats than their predecessors. To preserve the utility of previously recorded media, new optical disk drives and magnetic tape units may offer backward compatibility for reading purposes; that is, they can retrieve information from media recorded by predecessor models in a given manufacturer's product line. Although such backward compatibility is customary, manufacturers give no guarantee that it will be continued in all future products. On the contrary, the history of computer storage peripherals suggests that, at best, backward compatibility provides a bridge between two or three generations of equipment. Eventually, support for older media and recording formats will be phased out.

As a further constraint, backward compatibility does nothing to address retrievability problems associated with discontinued computer products. Since the early 1980s, manufacturers of optical disk drives and magnetic tape units have discontinued certain models or product lines without providing replacements or migration paths, and some manufacturers have ceased operation entirely. As an example, none of the write-once optical disks manufactured before 1988 could be read by optical disk drives that were available for sale ten years later.

As an additional complication, digital documents and their associated index records are designed for retrieval or other processing by specific application software. Even more than hardware components, software may be updated or otherwise changed in a manner that can render previously recorded information unusable. The latest releases of a given vendor's application programs may not be able to read digital documents or index records produced by all earlier versions. Since the early 1990s, some software developers have migrated their product lines from mainframe and minicomputer platforms to client/server computing environments. This software redevelopment has posed compatibility problems for digital documents and index records created and maintained by earlier products.

Retention Alternatives

The limited stability of computer storage media and the complications posed by the hardware/software dependence of computer-processable information are widely acknowledged. Less agreement exists, however, about their significance for digital document implementations with multidecade retention requirements. The retrievability of digital documents and index data can be extended indefinitely by periodically converting them to new file formats or media, a process termed *data migration*.

Conversion of digital documents and index data to new file formats is intended to preserve the usability of recorded information when computer hardware and/or software components are upgraded or replaced. Copying digital documents and index data onto new storage media is intended to preserve the usability of recorded information where the stable life span of a given storage medium is shorter than the retention period for recorded information or where product modifications or discontinuations render a given storage medium unusable.* This form of data migration applies principally to inactive digital documents and index data that have been transferred from hard drives to removable media, such as magnetic tapes or optical disks, for offline storage. Digital documents and index data stored on hard drives will presumably be migrated to new equipment when servers or hard drives are replaced. Digital documents and index data stored on hard drives are presumably backed up on magnetic tapes, which will be replaced at frequent intervals with new backup copies.

Data migration will likely be required where one or more of the following conditions apply:

- The scheduled destruction date for digital documents or index data is greater than five years from the initial installation date or last major upgrade of the computer storage device or software that reads, processes, or maintains the documents. Thus, if digital documents or index must be read by an optical disk or magnetic tape drive that was installed in 2005, data migration will likely be required if the records will be retained until 2010 or later. Similarly, if digital documents or index data are organized, stored, retrieved, or otherwise managed by software that was upgraded in 2003, data migration will be required if the documents will be retained until 2008 or later.

- The total retention period for digital documents or index data is greater than ten years from the date that the records were created. Thus, digital document or index data created in 2006 will likely require data migration if they will be retained until 2016 or later.

---

* In most implementations, file format migration is more important than periodic recopying of digital documents onto new media. Where computer hardware is upgraded or replaced at relatively short intervals to take advantage of improved technology embodied in new products, the stability of particular storage media and the continued availability of compatible equipment and software have little significance for records retention practices. A computer system installed today is likely to be replaced or significantly upgraded within five or six years. Before media life spans have elapsed or specific hardware or software components are discontinued, digital documents and their associated index records will have been converted to media and formats required by the replacement system.

- The usability of digital documents or index data will be affected by replacement, upgrades, or other changes in computer hardware or software components before the specified retention periods for the records elapse.

These data migration guidelines apply only to digital documents designated as official copies to satisfy an organization's retention requirements. Data migration is not required for digital documents that are considered duplicate records.

Data migration requirements should be assessed during the planning phase for digital document implementations. At a minimum, the planning process should consider the following:

- Types of digital documents that require data migration,
- the organizational unit that will be responsible for performing the migration,
- the anticipated migration intervals,
- functional requirements for data migration tools to be developed or acquired,
- functional requirements for storage media to be used in the migration process, and
- procedures for testing and verifying that data migration was performed accurately and reliably without loss of information from digital documents.

Data migration plans should be reviewed periodically and revised, as necessary, based on experience or other considerations. At a minimum, data migration plans should be reevaluated whenever computer hardware and/or software components are upgraded or replaced or whenever recorded information is transferred to new storage media.

The use of data migration to satisfy retention requirements is based on the assumption that digital documents and their associated index information can be conveniently and reliably transferred from one medium or file format to another, that the cost of such transfer is not prohibitive, and that the required media and format migrations can be incorporated into an organization's work routines and prioritized at a sufficiently high level to ensure its completion at scheduled intervals. The time and effort to accomplish the periodic transfer of digital documents to new file formats or media should not be trivialized, however. In most digital document implementations, the migration effort will be pyramidal. As the number of digital documents increases, successive data migrations will involve greater volumes of information and will require more time to complete.

Dual-media implementations offer an alternative method of satisfying long records retention requirements. In the **dual-media approach**, a digital document implementation addresses an organization's active reference or workflow requirements while retention requirements are satisfied by paper or microfilm. Because paper and microfilm are stable media that contain human-readable information, the dual-media approach minimizes the impact of hardware/software dependence and prevents the irrevocable loss of information recorded in discontinued file formats or on obsolete computer media. The dual-media approach is best suited to imaging implementations. Following scanning, paper records can be transferred to off-site storage or microfilmed for retention. Depending on the application, the cost of off-site storage or microfilming may increase the implementation cost of an imaging system by a small percentage. The dual-media approach is problematic for word processing files, e-mail messages, and other documents that are born digital. These digital documents must be printed out or recorded onto COM for retention.

The choice between paper and microfilm as retention media will depend on a case-by-case analysis of application characteristics and requirements. Typically, off-site storage of paper documents following scanning will prove less expensive than microfilming for records with single-decade retention periods. Where documents are retained longer than 15 years, the accumulated cost of off-site storage will eventually exceed microfilming costs.

Where microfilm will be used for records retention, the required digital and microphotographic images can be produced in several ways:

- Documents can be scanned and microfilmed in separate operations. This approach involves some duplication of labor, but it may be the easiest to implement. Many corporations, government agencies, and other organizations currently operate micrographics production facilities. They can continue to utilize their existing equipment, trained personnel, and microfilming procedures. Depending on the type of camera utilized, roll microfilm, microfiche, or aperture cards may be produced.

- An integrated scanner/filmer can digitize documents and record them onto microfilm in a single pass. Compared to scanning and microfilming in separate operations, scanner/filmers can save labor and time, but they cost as much or more than separately purchased document scanners and microfilmers with comparable capabilities. Scanner/filmers are best suited to high-volume document conversion applications where their cost can be offset by labor savings.

- Documents can be microfilmed by rotary or planetary cameras. Using a microform scanner, the resulting microimages can be digitized for input to digital document implementation. As discussed in Chapter 2, microform scanners are available for roll microfilm, microfiche, and aperture cards. Such devices are capable of semi- or fully automated operation. As a potential inconvenience, however, conversion of microfilmed documents to electronic images must wait until the microforms are completely exposed, inspected, and processed.

- Using graphic COM technology, as discussed in Chapter 4, microforms can be produced from digital document images. This work can be done by an in-house COM recorder or by a service bureau.

Related Technologies

Records managers and information specialists are increasingly interested in the relationship between and integration of information technologies. By combining the strengths of two or more technologies, integration can facilitate the management of recorded information. They can also provide useful solutions to information problems that cannot be addressed by one technology alone. The following sections examine the relationship between digital documents and related technologies.

Records Management Application (RMA) Software

Broadly defined, a records management application (RMA) is a category of computer software that organizes, stores, retrieves, and otherwise manages records. Although this definition also characterizes document imaging and content management software, an RMA provides retention functionality that is absent from those products. As described below, an RMA can identify records that are eligible for destruction in conformity with an organization's retention schedules. Although RMA products can track the retention status of paper and photographic records stored in file rooms or off-site locations, they are more closely associated with digital documents and other types of electronic records. At the time of this writing, RMA products were offered by several dozen vendors. When they were first introduced in the 1990s, RMA programs were marketed as self-contained products that could import digital documents from a variety of applications. Such product configurations remain available; however, RMA software's retention capabilities are increasingly integrated into document imaging and content management products, either as a standard feature or, more commonly, as an optional module. In effect, RMA software operates as a back-end retention component for digital documents managed by those products. As its principal advantage, this approach combines document organization, storage, retrieval, and life-cycle management in a single software platform.

Baseline functionality and desirable characteristics of RMAs are delineated in DoD 5015.2-STD, *Design Criteria Standard for Electronic Records Management Software Applications*, issued by the U.S. Department of Defense in 1997 and subsequently revised in 2002 to include provisions for classified government records and other enhancements. Future revisions are anticipated. The Defense Information Systems Agency's Joint Interoperability Test Command tests RMA products to verify compliance with requirements specified in DoD 5015.2-STD. The National Archives and Records Administration (NARA) has endorsed DoD 5015.2-STD for use by U.S. government agencies when selecting RMA software to store electronic records as official copies and to facilitate the transfer of permanent electronic records to the National Archives. Other organizations, including corporations, not-for-profit institutions, and state and local government agencies, have also found DoD 5015.2-STD useful in establishing criteria for evaluation and selection of RMA products.

RMA software is compatible with many types of digital content, including database records, web pages, audio files, and video files. As it relates to the topic of this book—digital document management, RMA software creates an organized repository for digital documents, which may be transferred to the repository from office productivity software, e-mail systems, CAD programs, imaging software, workgroup collaboration software, or other originating applications. An RMA repository is organized into folders that correspond to categories in a user-defined file plan, which is based on the hierarchical folder / subfolder model previously described in Chapter 3. As an example, a file plan for contract records would provide a master folder for each contract with subfolders for proposals, signed contracts, amendments, invoices, payment authorizations, and other types of contract-related documents.

A carefully designed file plan for digital documents is a precondition for successful implementation of RMA software. File plan development is a significant effort that involves investigative, prototype, and test phases:

- In the *investigative phase*, the developer must identify record types to be stored in an RMA repository, as well as issues and concerns to be addressed by the file plan. For contract documents, for example, the investigative phase will require a detailed examination of records and filing methods for selected active and/or terminated contracts. The developer must also interview persons who are knowledgeable about contract documentation requirements and filing practices. Whenever possible, the developer will obtain and study file plans developed by government agencies and other organizations for comparable document collections.

- In the *prototype phase*, the developer will prepare a draft file plan, accompanied by instructions and appropriate supporting procedures. The draft file plan will specify how the document repository will be organized and indexed as well as retention periods keyed to file categories at the folder, subfolder, or document level. The draft plan should also include procedures that define responsibilities for transferring digital documents to the RMA repository and instructions for filing specific types of digital documents. The draft file plan will be circulated among knowledgeable persons for review and suggestions. One or more group meetings may be needed to clarify the reviewers' comments and criticisms, which will be incorporated into a revised draft to be recirculated for further review and comment. Several additional drafts may be required to produce an acceptable prototype file plan.

- In the *test phase*, the prototype file plan will be implemented using the selected RMA product and tested on several collections of digital documents. The developer will monitor this pilot implementation, discuss the prototype plan with users and other interested parties, and make further revisions to the file plan in order to ultimately produce an operational version, which will be reviewed periodically and modified as necessary to address changing requirements.

RMA repositories can import digital documents in a variety of file formats. Digital documents may be transferred into a repository in batches or they may be individually dragged and dropped into appropriate subfolders from their originating applications. The latter approach is suitable for small quantities of digital documents or where an entire folder from an originating application can be dragged and dropped into one of the repository's subfolders. Depending on the method employed, an RMA repository may contain the actual documents, or it may store links to word processing files, PDF files, e-mail messages, spreadsheets, or other documents that are located elsewhere—on a network file server, for example.

Regardless of format and storage location, digital documents transferred to an RMA repository are considered the official copies for reference and retention purposes. As determined by an application planner, authorized persons have read-only access to specific documents, but they cannot modify, replace, or delete them. Access privileges can be defined for individuals or groups at the folder, subfolder, or document level. Digital documents can be retrieved by browsing through subfolders, as is the case in paper filing installations. Alternatively, most RMA software allows folders, subfolders, and documents to be indexed by user-defined fields. As an example, master project folders may be labeled with project names and indexed by project number, the name of the sponsoring organization, and other parameters. Similarly, a subfolder label may identify the contents as "reports," with individual reports being indexed by the name of the author, the date, the type of report, or other descriptors. Some RMA programs also support full-text indexing of word processing files, e-mail messages, and other character-coded documents. RMA software also provides a conclusive method of identifying successive versions of reports, specifications, contracts, and other digital documents that are subject to revision.

Retrieved documents are displayed by launching their originating applications where available. Alternatively, most RMA software incorporates viewing modules that can display digital documents in a variety of file formats, including text, image, and CAD formats. Depending on RMA software capabilities and user privileges, retrieved documents may be printed, copied, annotated, attached to e-mail messages, or transferred to other applications. RMA software provides an audit trail for importing, retrieving, printing, exporting, copying, and other activity involving specific digital documents, including unsuccessful retrieval attempts as well as completed operations. The audit trail indicates the date the activity occurred, the type of activity, and the identity of the user who initiated the activity.

As noted previously, retention functionality is RMA software's distinctive characteristic. Authorized users can specify retention periods for digital documents in conformity with an organization's approved retention policies and schedules. Retention periods may be specified at the folder, subfolder, or individual document level. Retention periods may be based on elapsed time or events. In the former case, digital documents are eligible for destruction after a fixed period of time. In the latter case, digital documents are eligible for destruction after a designated event, such as termination of contract or completion of a project, plus a specified number of years. To address evidentiary requirements, RMA software allows authorized users to suspend destruction of or extend retention periods for specific digital documents or groups of documents that are relevant for litigation, government investigations, audits, or other purposes.

Destruction of records is not automatic: RMA programs generate lists of digital documents that are eligible for destruction on a specified date. The list is submitted to designated persons for approval before destruction is executed. RMA software provides safeguards against the unauthorized destruction of digital documents by issuing a warning to the user when such destruction is attempted. RMA programs can print lists, certificates of destruction, or other documentation for digital documents that were destroyed in conformity with an organization's retention policies and schedules.

Workflow Programming

As discussed in Chapter 1, workflow programming provides automatic control and coordinated management of the document or data flows associated with specific information processing transactions or tasks. Workflow programming concepts, technologies, and methodologies have been closely associated with digital documents since the early 1980s when workflow capabilities were incorporated into document imaging implementations. In a workflow implementation, document images, word processing files, e-mail messages, and other digital documents are routed under software control to workstations that require them for specific purposes. Workstation operators examine the routed documents to obtain information required to complete an assigned portion of a task.

Although workflow programming is widely promoted as a benefit of digital document technology, it is limited to a subset of digital document implementations. Workflow programming is best suited to highly-structured transaction-processing or production-oriented operations that are governed by clearly defined procedures for document preparation, review, and approval. Examples include claims processing, insurance policy underwriting, order fulfillment, payment processing, budget reviews, and loan approval. In such applications, documents are routed from one worker to another in a prescribed sequence in order to complete a specific transaction or other operation. Often, information obtained from the routed documents is key-entered into displayed work forms to create database records from which payment authorizations, purchase orders, reports, or other documents may subsequently be printed.

Some analysts and software developers distinguish between production-type workflow implementations, which involve well-defined tasks that are performed frequently and repeatedly, and ad hoc workflow implementations, which are developed for specific purposes of defined duration. The transaction-oriented business processes cited above are examples of production-type applications in which workflow automates well-established document routing procedures. Once implemented, production-type workflow applications may operate with little or no modification until their associated business processes are altered or discontinued. Ad hoc workflow applications may be designed to improve communication among members of a project team by expediting the movement of documents or other information. Examples include collaborative preparation of design specifications by architects or the writing of technical reports by pharmaceutical researchers.

Whether production-type or ad hoc, a workflow implementation must be preceded by a thorough analysis of the target application to identify the specific digital documents and work steps necessary to complete a transaction or other operation, as well as the sequence and time frames in which the work steps must be performed. Using a high-level scripting language, a programmer or other application designer must specify routing patterns for digital documents, work forms, and other information among participating workstations. The resulting workflow program is a set of rules that define the way in which information is to be routed, as well as the specific operations to be performed at each stage in the route. Depending on system capabilities and the application being automated, workflow routing rules may be based on document types, on the activities to be performed, on the field values contained in database records, or on external events such as elapsed time or the arrival of new documents.

As a simple example of a workflow implementation, invoice documents received by the accounts payable department of a project-oriented engineering firm might be processed by a workflow program in the following sequence:

- Incoming vendor invoices and supporting documents are scanned and indexed by purchase order number, customer invoice number, vendor name, date, and an identifying number for the project to which they pertain. The resulting document images and index records are stored on hard drives.

- A workflow program automatically routes document images to an accounts payable queue for the indicated project. A designated clerk retrieves images from the queue and checks each invoice for correctness and completeness. If additional information is required, an inquiry is prepared, printed, and sent to the vendor that submitted the invoice. Further processing of the invoice is temporarily suspended, pending receipt of the additional information.

- When an invoice is judged complete, the pertinent document images are routed to a designated project manager who confirms delivery of the invoiced goods or services and completes a displayed work form to approve payment. If the goods or services were not delivered as invoiced, an exception work form is prepared and routed, with the document images, to the accounts payable clerk who notifies the vendor or takes other appropriate action. Processing is suspended until the exceptional condition is resolved.

- When delivery of the invoiced items is confirmed, the document images are routed to a disbursements supervisor who authorizes check writing. Accounting records are updated to indicate that the invoice was paid.

As with the RMA capabilities described previously, workflow functionality is typically offered as an optional module with document imaging and content management products. Although not as difficult as conventional computer programming, the preparation of workflow scripts does require familiarity with variable types, conditional branching, and other programming concepts. Many workflow modules include programming aids that allow customers to develop their own workflow applications. Modeling and visualization tools, in particular, can minimize coding requirements. Specific tasks and decision points, represented by icons or other symbols, are interconnected to specify document routing patterns or other aspects of workflow implementations. Properly designed, workflow programs will check to determine that a given process has been completed before routing a digital document to the next workstation. They can perform simultaneous routing of documents for tasks that need not be performed in a prescribed sequence. Dates, times, and workstation identifiers are recorded for all document retrievals and workflow entries, thereby creating an audit trail. Workflow programs monitor the progress of transaction processing to detect and report delays. Documents routed to specific work queues can be prioritized for processing in a designated sequence. A dynamic routing feature allows a workstation to specify a successor where document flow is unpredictable or the normal flow must be suspended.

COLD / ERM

Computer-output laser disk (COLD) technology creates and manages a specific type of digital document: page-formatted, computer-generated reports. Rather than printing such reports, COLD software records them onto computer media for retrieval, retention, distribution, or other purposes. The COLD designation, which reflects the technology's origins in the 1980s, is outdated and confusing. Originally, COLD installations recorded computer-generated reports onto optical disks, hence the laser disk designation. Newer COLD implementations, however, utilize hard drives or any of several types of optical disks, including CDs and DVDs. In these situations, COLD technology is increasingly termed *enterprise reports management (ERM)* to more accurately represent its purpose.

Regardless of terminology and storage media, COLD / ERM offers an online alternative to paper printouts and COM. COLD / ERM software processes information generated by computer programs that operate in the batch mode. Such programs, some of which date from the 1960s or 1970s, are widely associated with so-called legacy systems that run on mainframes or minicomputers. COLD / ERM information is recorded in the character-coded form associated with data and text files. Unlike a conventional computer database, however, COLD / ERM information is formatted as report pages, much as it would be transmitted to a paper printer or COM recorder. When retrieved, the information is displayed in a printout-page format. Some COLD / ERM products can store images of business forms or organizational logos. Such images are superimposed on report data at the time specific pages are retrieved, in the manner of the form slides employed by COM recorders.

During the 1980s, COLD / ERM was marketed as its own technology. The earliest COLD / ERM products were self-contained software packages that provided online access to computer-generated reports produced by IBM mainframes and popular minicomputers. Although such products remain available, COLD / ERM technology is increasingly offered as an add-on component with document imaging and content management products. The combination of document imaging and COLD / ERM capabilities is widely considered complementary; customers seeking a completely computerized approach to storage and retrieval of documents are often interested in comparable methods of managing computer-generated reports.

Records managers and other information specialists have long recognized the storage and retrieval problems associated with computer-generated reports, which are among the most cumbersome business records. With large pages packaged in thick binders, computer-generated reports are characteristically difficult to handle. Many reports are printed in multiple copies at frequent intervals, daily or weekly in some cases. Computing departments must allocate resources to these print jobs and distribute the reports to user departments when completed. Among its advantages, COLD / ERM technology provides convenient online access to computer-generated reports and promotes information sharing in network installations. COLD / ERM technology provides compact storage of voluminous reports, an advantage that is also associated with COM-generated microfiche. COLD / ERM implementations eliminate the time and labor required for production of paper printouts or

COM-generated microforms and their distribution to user sites. Consumption of paper and other printing supplies will be minimized, while reduced workload will extend the service life of computer printers and lengthen replacement intervals.

The most flexible COLD / ERM software permits extensive page indexing and retrieval by designated fields. Users can also browse through report pages. Reference copies of specified pages can be printed on demand. As a potentially useful feature, report pages can be exported to other application programs as text files; for example, a table from a computer-generated report can be incorporated into a word processing document or transferred into a spreadsheet.

Chapter 6

Implementation Costs

Like other information management projects, digital document implementations involve a combination of start-up and ongoing costs. *Start-up costs,* also known as *upfront costs* or *initial capital investments,* are nonrecurring charges incurred at the inception of an imaging implementation. Examples include the purchase price of equipment and software, the cost of networking or other data communication components, charges for electrical improvements or other site modifications required to prepare work areas for the installation of computers and peripheral devices, and the cost to convert existing documents to digital form or to import digital documents from other systems. By definition, start-up costs precede any receipt of revenues or cost savings to be derived from an activity. They typically require a special appropriation.

All start-up costs must be clearly identified in proposals and budgets for digital document projects, because the required funds must be made available as soon as the project is authorized. A proposal to purchase equipment and software for $200,000, for example, will require that amount of funding at the inception of the project, regardless of anticipated future savings or other benefits to be derived from the digital document implementation. Although start-up costs must be available at a project's inception, they are usually paid in increments linked to specific project events such as the signing of a contract, delivery of equipment, installation and operation of specific software components, completion of customized programming, and final acceptance of a fully operational system. Start-up costs are usually fixed in amount for an implementation with specific characteristics. A notable exception is the cost to convert a backfile of paper documents to digital images or character-coded text in advance of system operation. Such backfile conversion charges will vary with the quantity of documents to be converted.

Ongoing costs are incurred on an annual or other periodic basis throughout the life of a digital document implementation. Ongoing costs may be fixed or variable amounts. Examples of fixed ongoing costs include equipment lease or rental charges, annual software license renewal fees, and annual maintenance contract charges for equipment and software components. Examples of variable ongoing costs include supply costs for removable storage media and labor costs for digitizing newly received documents and entering index information. Such variable costs depend on application characteristics, including the quantity of documents to be digitized and the amount of index data to be entered. Although start-up costs usually require special appropriations, the ongoing costs associated with a digital document implementation may be covered by an organization's existing operating budget or by anticipated revenues or savings to be generated by the implementation itself.

To facilitate system planning and budget preparation, this chapter presents a series of 12 worksheets that provide a step-by-step method of calculating start-up and ongoing costs for digital document implementations with specified characteristics. The worksheets, labeled A through L, cover specific start-up and ongoing cost components. The following sections present line-by-line explanations and instructions for worksheet entries. A cost calculation example based on the worksheets is presented in Appendix B.

Start-Up Costs

Worksheet A calculates start-up costs for computer hardware and software components employed in a digital document implementation. Digital document technology may be purchased as a preconfigured combination of computer hardware and software or, more commonly, as software for installation and operation on a customer-supplied computer configuration. In either case, the purchase prices of equipment and software are considered start-up costs. If the equipment or software are leased or rented, the lease or rental payments are treated as annual fixed costs. They are to be included in Worksheet B as described below. Worksheet A applies to hardware and software components that are purchased outright.

Line A1

The total purchase price for digital document technology, including all hardware and software components, is to be entered on line A1. This information is typically obtained from vendor proposals or bids. Government agencies and quasi-governmental organizations may qualify for purchase prices listed in prenegotiated contracts for specific products. The Federal Supply Schedules negotiated by the U.S. General Services Administration and comparable contracts negotiated by various state governments are examples. Amounts entered on Line A1 are limited to hardware and software components that are intended exclusively for the digital document implementation, as opposed to components that will be shared with other applications.

Line A2

Start-up costs other than those included in line A1 are to be entered in line A2. Such costs may include installation charges for computer hardware or software components; application analysis, database set-up, system initializations, or customized programming performed by software vendors, systems integrators, or other contractors; customer training; and other services related to system installation and implementation. Some vendors may embed these charges in the hardware or software prices entered on line A1. Others enumerate such implementation-related charges separately, in which case they are to be entered on line A2.

Line A3

Digital document implementations may require building modifications or other site preparation for equipment components included in line A1. Examples include:

- Construction or movement of interior walls to create or demarcate computer installation or personnel work areas;
- Electrical improvements to accommodate specific equipment components such as servers, document scanners, retrieval workstations, or printers;
- Installation or upgrading of air-conditioning and other environmental controls required for reliable operation of computer hardware; and
- Installation of wiring or networking facilities to interconnect system components.

These one-time site preparation charges are treated as start-up costs to be entered on line A3.

Line A4

A digital document implementation may share certain computer components with other information processing applications. This type of sharing is the case, for example, where digital document technology coexists with other applications on a mainframe, mid-range computer, or other server operated by a corporation, government agency, or other organization. In a network environment, a specific server may be dedicated to a digital document implementation, but desktop computers that retrieve digital documents may also be used for word processing, e-mail access, or other office applications. Similarly, networked printers accessed by a digital document implementation may serve multiple applications. Certain software components, such as database management programs, may likewise be shared with other applications. The purchase price of shared system components (including the cost of any site preparation or special services associated with implementation of the components) is to be entered on line A4.

Line A5

The cost of shared system components must be apportioned to a digital document implementation based on the estimated percentage of the shared components' resources utilized for digital documents. That percentage is to be entered as a decimal value on line A5. As an example, 75 percent of network printing resources may be used for a digital document implementation, while the remaining 25 percent will support other information processing applications. In that case, the value to be entered on line A5 is 0.75.

Allocation of shared resources may be determined by the amount of server or personal computer time spent on a digital document implementation as opposed to other computer applications, by the number of workstations associated with the digital document implementation, by the percentage of available storage resources consumed by digital documents and their associated database records, by the quantity of digital documents to be printed in relation to total printing activity, or by a combination of these and other factors.

Line A6

The decimal value on line A5 is multiplied by the amount on line A4 to obtain a dollar amount for shared components utilized by the digital document implementation. That amount is to be entered on line A6. This amount is to be charged to the digital document implementation. The remaining amount for each shared resource will presumably be incorporated into budgets for other activities the resources support.

Line A7

Line A7 calculates the total start-up cost for hardware and software in a digital document implementation. That amount is the sum of the purchase price of hardware and software components dedicated to the implementation (line A1), other system-related charges (line A2), site preparation costs (line A3), and the apportioned cost of shared system components (line A6).

Annual Fixed Costs

Worksheet B calculates annual (ongoing) fixed costs associated with a digital document system. Examples of such costs include periodic payments for leased or rented equipment, software license fees that are subject to annual renewal, and charges for equipment maintenance and software upgrades to take effect when the warranty period elapses.

Line B1

The annual total of lease or rental payments for computer hardware and software licenses to be used exclusively for a digital document implementation is to be entered on line B1. As with purchase prices, these amounts are typically obtained from vendor proposals, bids, or prenegotiated contracts. Leasing plans involve payments of a specified amount for an agreed-upon period, at the end of which time the leasing party assumes ownership of the leased items. Rental plans provide a method of acquiring equipment for which a customer has a short-term need rather than a continuing requirement; document scanners might be rented for a backfile conversion project of short duration, for example. Lease or rental charges for data communication facilities, networking software, and other data communication components employed in a digital document implementation should be included in line B1.

Line B2

Post-warranty repair and enhancement of specific system components are important annual fixed costs in digital document implementations. Annual charges for maintenance contracts for hardware, software, and data communication components used exclusively for a digital document implementation are to be entered on line B2. Maintenance contracts include equipment repair contracts and software upgrade agreements. Software license renewal fees, where priced separately from maintenance contracts, should be included in line B1.

Maintenance contract charges are treated as annual fixed operating costs for purchased, leased, or rented system components. To ensure proper maintenance of system components in which they retain a property interest, some vendors require the purchase of annual maintenance contracts for leased and rented equipment. In some cases, the cost of maintenance contracts is embedded in the lease or rental payments entered on line B1, making a separate entry on line B2 unnecessary. If maintenance contracts are not purchased, an amount equal to their annual cost should be budgeted for system repair on a per-incident basis. That amount is to be entered on line B2.

Line B3

The annual value of floor space occupied by a digital document implementation's hardware components and associated work areas is to be entered on line B3. For installations in leased or rented buildings, the total square footage occupied exclusively by digital document equipment is multiplied by the annual lease or rental cost per square foot. For owned buildings, the amortized value of the floor space, on a cost-per-square-foot basis, must be determined.

Line B4

Annual lease or rental charges for digital document hardware and software shared with other computing applications are to be entered on line B4. Lease or rental charges for shared networking and other data communication components should be included in that amount.

Line B5

The annual cost of maintenance contracts for post-warranty repair or enhancement of shared system components is to be entered on line B5. If maintenance contracts are not purchased, an amount equal to their annual cost should be budgeted for repairs or enhancements on a per-incident basis. That amount is to be entered on line B5.

Line B6

The annual value of floor space occupied by shared computer equipment, such as a mainframe, mid-range computer, or network server that supports a digital document implementation plus other information processing applications, is to be entered on line B6.

Line B7

Line B7 calculates the annual total of lease and rental charges, maintenance contract payments, and floor space costs for digital document components shared with other applications.

Line B8

For shared system components, the percentage of lease or rental payments, maintenance contract charges, and floor space costs attributable to the digital document implementation is to be entered as a decimal value on line B8.

Line B9

Based on the amounts entered in lines B7 and B8, line B9 calculates the apportioned dollar value of the shared system components utilized by the digital document implementation. This amount is to be charged to the digital document implementation. The remaining amount for each shared resource will presumably be incorporated into budgets for other activities the resources support.

Line B10

Line B10 totals the annual fixed costs associated with dedicated and shared system components in a digital document implementation.

Backfile Preparation and Disposition Costs

Many organizations want to convert existing collections of paper records, including microfilm images of documents, to digital images or character-coded text for inclusion in digital document implementations. As discussed in Chapter 2, such conversion may be accomplished by scanning, key-entry, or optical character recognition. *Existing document collections*, termed *backfiles*, often require substantial preparation prior to scanning or optical character recognition, which presumes scanning. Preparation requirements are typically less significant where key-entry methods will be used to convert the contents of existing documents to character-coded text, but such documents must still be removed from their storage locations, transported to key-entry workstations, and returned to storage, destroyed, or otherwise disposed of when backfile conversion is completed. Worksheet C calculates preparation and disposition costs for conversion of an existing document backfile to digital form.

Line C1

Backfile size can be measured in pages or documents, depending on the conversion method employed. Where documents will be scanned to convert them to digital images or, via OCR, to character-coded text, the number of pages in the organization's backfile is to be entered on line C1. Where key-entry will be used to convert documents to character-coded text, the number of documents in the organization's backfile is to be entered on line C1. If the number of pages is entered on line C1, that measure must be used for other calculations in Worksheet C. If the number of documents is entered on line C1, that measure must be used in the remainder of this worksheet.

Line C2

The estimated preparation rate in pages or documents per hour, depending on the measure selected for line C1, is to be entered on line C2. In digital imaging and OCR implementations, typical preparatory work steps include removing documents from file cabinets or other containers; removing staples, paper clips, or other fasteners; stacking documents for insertion into a scanner's automatic page feeder; keeping records of the documents removed for backfile conversion; and transporting documents to a scanning area. Some brittle or damaged pages may require photocopying, repair, or other special preparation prior to scanning. Preparation requirements are less extensive where key-entry is used to convert documents to character-coded text. In particular, removal of page fasteners, a time-consuming work step, is not usually necessary.

Line C3

Preparation time is calculated by dividing the preparation rate into the number of pages or documents in the organization's backfile. The result is to be entered on line C3.

Line C4

Additional time must be allocated for backfile disposition following conversion of documents to digital images or character-coded text. Examples of such disposition include destroying backfile documents, returning documents to their original locations, packing and inventorying documents for removal to off-site storage, or transporting documents to an in-house microfilming operation or a microfilm service bureau. In some situations, backfiles may be reassembled, with pages being restapled and reinserted into folders, following scanning or conversion to character-coded text. In any case, the disposition rate, in pages or documents per hour, is to be entered on line C4.

Line C5

Line C5 calculates the time required for document disposition by dividing the disposition rate into the number of pages or documents in the organization's backfile.

Line C6

Line C6 calculates the total number of hours required for backfile preparation and disposition.

Line C7

The hourly wage rate for employees performing backfile preparation and disposition is to be entered on line C7. If wage rates vary from worker to worker, an average rate should be entered. Throughout these calculations in all worksheets, hourly wages should include fringe benefits where applicable.

Line C8

Line C8 calculates the labor cost for backfile preparation and disposition based on productivity and wage information from the preceding lines.

Line C9

An organization's backfile may include books, reports, or other bound volumes. In imaging and OCR implementations, such documents may be unbound, temporarily or permanently, for scanning. The time required for such unbinding is to be included in the document preparation rate entered on line C3. Alternatively, bound documents may be photocopied for input into sheetfed scanners. For certain unbound documents, photocopying can facilitate scanning of fragile or damaged pages. For security reasons, documents may also be photocopied before sending them to a service bureau if backfile conversion is to be outsourced.

The percentage of backfile pages to be photocopied prior to scanning is to be entered as a decimal value on line C9. If 15 percent of pages will be photocopied, for example, the value to be entered on line C9 is 0.15. If all pages will be photocopied, the amount to be entered on line C9 is 1.00. If no pages will be photocopied, skip lines C9 through C11.

Line C10

The photocopying cost, in cents per page, is to be entered as a decimal value on line C11. Thus, a photocopy cost of 10 cents per pages is to be entered as 0.10. The cost should encompass purchase or rental charges for photocopying equipment, supply costs, and labor charges.

Line C11

Line C11 calculates photocopying costs for the number of pages specified on line C9.

Line C12

The cost of equipment, supplies, and related services for backfile preparation and disposition tasks is to be entered on line C12. Backfile preparation may require sorting tables, chairs, carts, packing containers, and such conventional office supplies as pens, tablets, and labels. Backfile disposition may require shredders, document destruction services, or transportation services if documents will be sent to off-site storage or a microfilm service bureau when backfile conversion is completed.

Line C13

Line C13 calculates the cost of labor, photocopying, equipment, and supplies to prepare an organization's backfile for conversion to digital documents.

Line C14

Throughout these worksheets, supervisory costs are estimated as a percentage of the cost of the activity to be supervised. The percentage of backfile preparation and disposition costs to be added for supervision of preparation activities is to be entered as a decimal value on line C14. If 25 percent of backfile preparation costs will be added for supervision, for example, the value to be entered on line C14 is 0.25.

Line C15

Line C15 calculates the supervisory cost for backfile preparation and disposition as a specified percentage of labor, photocopying, equipment, and supply costs, as previously calculated on line C13.

Line C16

Line C16 calculates the combined cost of backfile preparation, disposition, and supervision.

Line C17

To allow for unforeseen events, delays, or other problems that can increase backfile preparation and disposition costs, a contingency percentage can be entered as a decimal value on line C17. If the desired contingency is 5 percent, for example, the value to be entered on line C17 is 0.05. If no contingency amount is desired, skip lines C17 and C18.

Line C18

Line C18 calculates the contingency amount based on the percentage specified on line C17.

Line C19

Line C19 calculates the total cost of backfile preparation and disposition, including labor, photocopying, equipment, supplies, services, supervision, and the contingency amount.

In-House Backfile Conversion

Conversion of an organization's backfile to digital images or character-coded text can be performed in-house or by a service bureau. A given digital document implementation may employ a combination of both methods for backfile conversion. Worksheet D calculates the cost of in-house backfile conversion. Service bureau costs are calculated in Worksheet E.

Line D1

The number of backfile pages to be converted to digital images by in-house scanning is to be entered on line D1. The entered value must include pages that will be scanned for storage and indexing as images as well as pages that will subsequently be converted to character-coded text via OCR. As previously explained, document scanning is a precondition for OCR. If in-house scanning will not be used for backfile conversion, go to line D15.

Line D2

The desired elapsed time, in working days rather than calendar days, to perform the backfile conversion by in-house scanning is to be entered on line D2.

Line D3

Line D3 calculates the number of pages that must be converted per day in order to complete in-house scanning in the desired time.

Line D4

The average number of pages that can be scanned per hour—the scanning throughput rate—is to be entered on line D4. In addition to actual scanning time, the scanning throughput rate includes the time required for positioning and removal of pages, inspection of digital images following scanning, recording of images on magnetic or optical media, and any required rescanning. As discussed in Chapter 2, many of these tasks are time-consuming; image inspection, for example, can require 10 seconds or longer per page. A document scanner may operate at a rated speed of three seconds per page or 1,200 pages per hour. When all scanning-related tasks are considered, however, the total scanning time may be 20 to 30 seconds per page, which equates to a scanning throughput rate of 120 to 180 pages per hour.

Line D5

The number of daily operating hours per scanning workstation is to be entered on line D5. A scanning workstation used for two 8-hour shifts, for example, will have a maximum of 16 operating hours per day. In actual practice, however, some time must be allocated for preventative maintenance or repair of equipment. Thus, a two-shift operation will provide less than the maximum number of operating hours—perhaps 15 to 15.5 hours per day on average.

Line D6

Line D6 calculates the number of pages that can be scanned per workstation per day.

Line D7

Line D7 calculates the number of scanning workstations required to complete the backfile conversion in the desired time. If the calculation yields a decimal value, the result is to be rounded up to the next integer (nondecimal) value. For example, if the calculated result is 2.25, the amount to be entered on line D7 is 3.

Line D8

Some scanning workstations may have been included in the purchased, leased, or rented digital document configurations previously entered on lines A1, A4, B1, and B4. The number of those workstations, if any, is to be entered on line D8.

Line D9

Line D9 deducts those workstations from the number required for backfile conversion. The result is the number of additional scanning workstations that must be purchased, leased, or rented specifically for backfile conversion. If the result is zero or a negative value, skip lines D10 and D11.

Line D10

The cost per scanning workstation, including equipment and software, is to be entered on line D10.

Line D11

Line D11 calculates the equipment and software cost for the number of scanning workstations specified on line D9.

Line D12

Line D12 calculates the number of hours of labor required for the in-house scanning workload specified on line D1 at the scanning rate specified on line D4.

Line D13

The hourly wage rate for scanning workstation operators is to be entered on line D13. If wage rates vary from worker to worker, an average rate should be entered. As previously noted, hourly wage rates should include fringe benefits where applicable.

Line D14

Line D14 calculates the labor cost for backfile conversion by in-house scanning.

Line D15

The number of pages to be converted in-house to character-coded text via OCR is to be entered on line D15. Because document scanning is a precondition for OCR, the entry on line D15 cannot exceed the value previously entered on line D1 unless backfile scanning is performed by a service bureau as provided in Worksheet E. If no pages will be converted via OCR, skip lines D15 through D29.

Line D16

Backfile conversion will require the purchase of OCR software, which recognizes text contained in digitized images as explained in Chapter 2. The assumption is that OCR software will operate on a network server, which may be the same server utilized for other digital document operations or a device purchased specifically for OCR. The combined cost of OCR software and the server on which it will operate is to be entered on line D16, omitting the cost of OCR hardware and software components, if any, that are included in the purchased, leased, or rented digital document configurations previously entered on lines A1, A4, B1, and B4.

Line D17

The desired elapsed time, in working days rather than calendar days, to perform the backfile conversion by OCR is to be entered on line D17.

Line D18

Line D18 calculates the number of pages that must be converted to character-coded text via OCR per day in order to complete the backfile conversion in the desired amount of time.

Line D19

The average number of pages that can be converted to character-coded text via OCR per hour, including verification of recognized text and error correction, is to be entered on line D19.

Line D20

The assumption is that personal computer workstations will be used for verification of recognized text and error correction. The number of daily operating hours per OCR workstation is to be entered on line D19.

Line D21

Line D21 calculates the number of pages that can be verified and corrected per OCR workstation per day.

Line D22

Line D22 calculates the number of OCR workstations required to complete the backfile conversion in the desired time. If the calculation yields a decimal value, the result is to be rounded up to the next integer (nondecimal) value. For example, if the calculated result is 2.25, the amount to be entered on line D22 is 3.

Line D23

Some personal computers suitable for use as OCR workstations may have been included in the purchased, leased, or rented digital document configurations previously entered on lines A1, A4, B1, and B4. The number of those workstations, if any, is to be entered on line D23.

Line D24

Line D24 deducts those OCR workstations from the number required for verification and correction of character-coded text. The result is the number of additional OCR workstations that must be purchased, leased, or rented specifically for backfile conversion. If the result is zero or a negative value, skip lines D25 and D26.

Line D25

The cost per OCR workstation, including equipment and software, is to be entered on line D25.

Line D26

Line D26 calculates the equipment and software cost for the number of OCR workstations specified on line D24.

Line D27

Line D27 calculates the number of hours of labor required for in-house backfile conversion via OCR for the number of pages specified on line D15 at the processing rate specified on line D19.

Line D28

The hourly wage rate, including applicable fringe benefits, for OCR workstation operators is to be entered on line D28. If wage rates vary from worker to worker, an average rate should be entered.

Line D29

Line D29 calculates the labor cost for in-house backfile conversion via OCR.

Line D30

The number of backfile pages to be converted to character-coded text by in-house key-entry is to be entered on line D30. If no pages will be converted via in-house key-entry, skip lines D31 through D45.

Line D31

The average number of characters per page is to be entered on line D31. As previously defined, characters include the letters of the alphabet, numeric digits, punctuation marks, and other textual symbols plus such invisible characters as blank spaces, tabs, and carriage returns.

Line D32

Line D32 calculates the total number of characters to be converted to character-coded text by in-house key-entry.

Line D33

The key-entry rate in characters per hour is to be entered on line D33. As discussed in Chapter 2, key-entry rates range broadly from 6,000 to 15,000 characters per hour, depending on operator skill, the characteristics of source documents, and other factors. Key-entry rates of 10,000 to 11,000 characters per hour sustained throughout the workday are attainable by full-time experienced data-entry operators.

Line D34

Line D34 calculates the actual key-entry rate in characters per hour including the time required for data verification and error correction. If verification by double-keying will be used, the amount on line D33 is to be divided by 2.25. By this calculation, an initial key-entry rate of 10,000 characters per hour yields an actual key-entry rate of 4,445 characters per hour when double-keying and error correction are included. Put another way, a backfile conversion involving 1,000 hours of initial key-entry will require a total of 2,250 hours when double-keying and error correction are included. If sight verification (proofreading) will be used, the amount on line D33 is to be divided by 1.6. Thus, an initial key-entry rate of 10,000 characters per hour will be reduced to 6,250 characters per hour when proofreading and error correction are included.

Line D35

Line D35 calculates the total number of hours required for backfile conversion by in-house key-entry, including verification and error correction.

Line D36

The hourly wage rate, including fringe benefits, for key-entry personnel is to be entered on line D36. If wage rates vary from worker to worker, an average rate should be entered.

Line D37

Line D37 calculates the labor cost for backfile conversion by in-house key-entry.

Line D38

The assumption is that personal computer workstations will be used for initial key-entry, verification, and error correction. The number of daily operating hours per workstation is to be entered on line D38.

Line D39

Line D39 calculates the number of characters that can be key-entered, verified, and corrected per key-entry workstation per day.

Line D40

Line D40 calculates the number of working days required to complete the work at the rate calculated on line D39.

Line D41

The desired elapsed time, in working days rather than calendar days, to perform the backfile conversion by in-house key-entry is to be entered on line D41.

Line D42

Line D42 calculates the number of key-entry workstations required to complete the backfile conversion in the desired time. If the calculation yields a decimal value, the result is to be rounded up to the next integer (nondecimal) value. For example, if the calculated result is 0.8, the amount to be entered on line D21 is 1.

Line D43

Some personal computers suitable for use as key-entry workstations may have been included in the purchased, leased, or rented digital document configurations previously entered on lines A1, A4, B1, and B4. The number of those workstations, if any, is to be entered on line D43.

Line D44

Line D44 deducts those workstations from the number required for key-entry, verification, and correction of character-coded text. The result is the number of additional key-entry workstations that must be purchased, leased, or rented specifically for backfile conversion. If the result is zero or a negative value, skip lines D45 and D46.

Line D45

The cost per key-entry workstation, including equipment and software, is to be entered on line D45.

Line D46

Line D46 calculates the equipment and software cost for the number of key-entry workstations specified on line D44.

Line D47

Line D47 calculates the total cost—including labor, equipment, and software—for in-house backfile conversion via scanning, OCR, and key-entry.

Line D48

As previously explained, supervisory costs are estimated as a percentage of the cost of the activity to be supervised. The percentage to be added for supervision of in-house backfile conversion by scanning, OCR, and key-entry is to be entered as a decimal value on line D48. If 25 percent of backfile preparation costs will be added for supervision, for example, the value to be entered on line D48 is 0.25.

Line D49

Line D49 calculates the supervisory cost for in-house backfile conversion as a specified percentage of the labor, equipment, and software costs previously calculated on line D47.

Line D50

Line D50 calculates the combined cost of labor, equipment, software, and supervision for in-house backfile conversion.

Line D51

To allow for unforeseen events, delays, or other problems that can increase backfile conversion costs, a contingency percentage can be entered as a decimal value on line D51. If the desired contingency is five percent, for example, the value to be entered on line D50 is 0.05. If no contingency amount is desired, skip lines D51 and D52.

Line D52

Line D52 calculates the contingency amount based on the percentage specified on line D51.

Line D53

Line D53 calculates the total cost of in-house backfile conversion, including labor, equipment, software, supervision, and the contingency amount.

Backfile Conversion by a Service Bureau

Backfile conversion projects are well-suited to outsourcing. Many service bureaus offer document scanning, key-entry, and OCR services for conversion of paper or microfilm records to digital images or character-coded text. Worksheet E calculates the cost of backfile conversion by a service bureau. If a service bureau will employ combinations of scanning, key-entry, and OCR to produce both digital images and character-coded text, Worksheet E should be separately completed for each conversion method.

Although it was developed to estimate backfile conversion costs, Worksheet E can also be used if scanning, OCR processing, and/or key-entry operations will be outsourced to a service bureau on an ongoing basis.

Line E1

The total number of pages to be converted by a service bureau is to be entered on line E1.

Line E2

Total service bureau's charges for backfile conversion are to be entered on line E2. This information will typically be obtained from a proposal, bid response, or other firm price quotation provided by a service bureau. The amount entered on line E2 must encompass all service bureau charges, including scanning, key-entry, data verification, error correction, document preparation, shipping charges, and media costs.

Line E3

Packing and shipping costs for sending documents to the service bureau are to be entered on line E3. Such costs include, but are not necessarily limited to, in-house labor, containers, postage or freight charges, and insurance.

Line E4

Although service bureau rates include the cost of data verification and error correction, work performed by a service bureau must be inspected by the customer for correctness and completeness. Defective work will presumably be returned to the service bureau for correction. In some implementations, inspection will be limited to a sample of the service bureau's work. The percentage of the service bureau's work to be inspected is to be entered as a decimal value on line E4. If one-half of the service bureau's work will be inspected, for example, the value to be entered on line E4 is 0.50. If all pages will be inspected, the value to be entered is 1.00.

Line E5

Line E5 calculates the number of pages to be inspected based on information previously entered on line E1.

Line E6

The average inspection rate, in pages per hour, is to be entered on line E6.

Line E7

Line E7 calculates the number of hours required for inspection based on the workload specified on line E5.

Line E8

The hourly wage rate for employees performing inspections is to be entered on line E8. If wage rates vary from worker to worker, an average rate should be entered.

Line E9

Line E9 calculates the labor cost for inspection of the service bureau's work.

Line E10

The assumption is that personal computers will be used as inspection workstations. Lines E10 through E13 calculate the number of workstations required for page inspection. The desired time, in days, to complete the inspection is to be entered on line E10.

Line E11

Line E11 calculates the number of hours of inspection that must be performed each day in order to complete the work in the desired time.

Line E12

The number of daily operating hours per inspection workstation is to be entered on line E16. An inspection workstation used for two 8-hour shifts, for example, will have 16 operating hours per day.

Line E13

Line E13 calculates the number of pages that can be inspected per workstation per day.

Line E14

Line E14 calculates the number of workstations required to complete inspection of the service bureau's work in the desired time. If the calculation yields a decimal value, it should be rounded up to the next integer.

Line E15

Some workstations suitable for inspection may have been included in the purchased, leased, or rented computer configurations previously entered on lines A1, A4, B1, and B4. One or more scanning, OCR, and key-entry workstations previously entered on lines D9, D24, and D43 may also be suitable for inspection. The number of these workstations, if any, is to be entered on line E15.

Line E16

Line E16 deducts those workstations from the number required for inspection. The result is the number of workstations that must be purchased specifically for inspection of digital documents produced by a service bureau. If the result is zero or a negative value, skip lines E17 and E18.

Line E17

The cost per inspection workstation, including equipment and software, is to be entered on line E17.

Line E18

Line E18 calculates the cost for the number of workstations specified in line E16.

Line E19

Line E19 calculates the combined cost of service bureau charges, packing and shipping, in-house inspection labor, and inspection workstations for backfile conversion by a service bureau.

Line E20

The percentage of backfile conversion costs to be added for supervision of work related to conversion by a service bureau is to be entered as a decimal value on line E20. If 15 percent of backfile conversion costs will be added for supervision, for example, the value to be entered on line E20 is 0.15.

Line E21

Line E21 calculates the supervisory cost for backfile conversion by a service bureau as a specified percentage of service bureau charges, in-house inspection labor, inspection workstations, and packing and shipping costs, as previously calculated on line E19.

Line E22

Line E22 calculates the cost of backfile conversion by a service bureau, including supervision.

Line E23

To allow for unforeseen events, delays, or other problems that can increase backfile conversion costs, a contingency percentage is to be entered as a decimal value on line E23. If the desired contingency is five percent, for example, the value to be entered on line E23 is 0.05.

Line E24

Line E24 calculates the contingency amount based on the percentage specified on line E23.

Line E25

Line E25 calculates the total cost of backfile conversion by a service bureau, including service bureau charges, packing and shipping costs, in-house inspection labor, inspection workstations, supervision, and contingency.

Backfile Indexing Costs

Worksheet F calculates the cost of indexing and index data-entry in backfile conversions where digital documents will be indexed by manual selection of index values associated with specific index categories. In such applications, a computer database serves as an index to digital documents.* As explained in Chapter 3, the index database contains one record for each document, which may be stored as an image or as character-coded text. Each database record is composed of fields that correspond to predetermined index categories.

For the calculations in Worksheet F, indexing denotes the analytical tasks that culminate in the selection of field values for specific digital documents. Data-entry denotes the conversion of index values to computer-processable form—done via key-entry.

Worksheet F calculates costs for in-house indexing and index data-entry in backfile conversion. If indexing and index data-entry will be performed by a service bureau or other contractor, those costs were presumably included in line E2 of Worksheet E. Although service bureaus are well equipped to convert backfiles to digital images or character-coded text, they may lack the requisite knowledge to index the resulting digital documents. Consequently, document indexing and index data-entry may be performed in-house for digital documents created by a service bureau.

Worksheeet F does not apply to full-text indexing of character-coded documents. As previously discussed, full-text indexing software extracts index terms from word processing files, e-mail messages, and other character-coded documents—automatically. The software does not require manual selection or key-entry of index terms.

Line F1

Although scanning, OCR, and key-entry are performed at the page level, indexing is done at the document level. The number of documents in an organization's backfile is to be entered on line F1. A document may contain one or more pages. The assumption is that multipage documents will be indexed as a unit. Except where a backfile consists entirely of single-page documents, the value entered on line F1 will be a fraction of the page amounts previously entered on lines D1, D15, D30, and E1.

Line F2

An organization's backfile may include some documents that will be linked to previously created database records, as well as others that require indexing. The percentage of a given backfile for which indexing is required is to be entered as a decimal value on line F2. If the entire backfile will be indexed, the value to be entered on line

---

*   As discussed in Chapter 3, some digital document implementations employ structured file plans that allow documents to be dragged and dropped or otherwise relegated to specific folders in a predefined taxonomy. In such implementations, selection of an appropriate folder is equivalent to selecting an index category for a given document. In many cases, file plans are supplemented by field-based indexing. In addition to selecting the folder in which a given document will be stored, an indexer must select index values associated with specific fields.

F2 is 1.00. If document indexing is not required—as would be the case where an existing database will serve as an index to digital images or where documents were previously indexed—skip lines F2 through F7.

Line F3

Line F3 calculates the number of backfile documents for which indexing is required.

Line F4

The average indexing rate, in documents per hour, is to be entered on line F4. Indexing involves the selection of values for specific fields within database records. Indexing difficulty and time will depend on the content, purpose, comprehensibility, and other characteristics of documents being indexed as well as the knowledge and experience of the person doing the indexing.

Line F5

Line F5 calculates the total indexing time, in hours, for the document backfile based on the indexing workload specified in line F3 and the indexing rate specified in line F4.

Line F6

The hourly wage rate, including fringe benefits, for indexing personnel is to be entered on line F6. If wage rates vary from worker to worker, an average rate should be entered.

Line F7

Line F7 calculates the labor cost for the specified indexing workload at the wage rate entered on line F6.

Line F8

The remainder of Worksheet F calculates costs for in-house key-entry of database records (index data) associated with digital documents. The average number of characters per database record is to be entered on line F8. That amount is the total of the average number of characters for each field within database records. Some key-entry of index values is required in every backfile conversion. Even where digital documents will be linked to previously created database records, a unique linking field value—such as an account number, purchase order number, or invoice number—must be entered for each document.

Line F9

Line F9 calculates the data-entry workload, in keystrokes, for the number of documents specified on line F1.

Line F10

The expected key-entry rate, in characters (keystrokes) per hour, is to be entered on line F10. As previously discussed, key-entry rates range broadly from 6,000 to 15,000 characters per hour. Rates of 10,000 to 11,000 characters per hour are attainable by full-time, experienced data-entry personnel.

Line F11

Line F11 calculates the time required, in hours, for initial key-entry of database records based on the volume of work specified on line F9 and the typing rate specified on line F10.

Line F12

Line F12 calculates the total number of hours required for key-entry of database records, including data verification and error correction. If data verification by double-keying will be used, the amount on line F11 is to be multiplied by 2.25. Thus, a backfile conversion involving 500 hours of initial key-entry will require a total of 1,125 hours for initial key-entry, verification by double-keying, and error correction. If sight verification (proofreading) will be used, the amount on line F11 is to be multiplied by 1.6. A backfile conversion involving 500 hours of initial key-entry will require 800 hours for initial key-entry, sight verification, and error correction.

Line F13

The hourly wage rate for data-entry personnel is to be entered on line F13. If wage rates vary from worker to worker, an average rate should be entered.

Line F14

Line F14 calculates the labor cost for key-entry of index data associated with backfile conversion of digital documents.

Line F15

Lines F15 through F18 determine the number of workstations required for the data-entry workload specified on line F12. The number of daily operating hours per data-entry workstation is to be entered on line F15. A workstation that is used for two 8-hour shifts, for example, will have 16 operating hours per day.

Line F16

Line F16 calculates the data-entry time in days for the workload specified on line F12.

Line F17

The desired elapsed time, in days, to complete the backfile conversion is to be entered on line F17.

Line F18

Line F18 calculates the number of workstations required to complete data-entry in the desired time. If the calculation yields a decimal value, the result is to be rounded up to the next integer value. For example, if the calculation yields 2.1, the amount to be entered on line F18 is 3.

Line F19

Some data-entry workstations may have been included in the purchased, leased, or rented computer configurations previously entered on lines A1, A4, B1, and B4. One or more workstations, previously entered on lines D9, D24, D43, or E16, may likewise be available for data-entry. The total number of those workstations, if any, is to be entered on line F19.

Line F20

Line F20 deducts those data-entry workstations from the number required for backfile conversion. The result is the number of additional data-entry workstations that must be purchased, leased, or rented specifically for backfile conversion. If the result is zero or a negative value, skip lines F21 and F22.

Line F21

The cost per data-entry workstation, including equipment and software, is to be entered on line F21.

Line F22

Line F22 calculates the cost for the number of data-entry workstations specified on line F20.

Line F23

Line F23 calculates the combined cost of labor and workstations for document indexing and in-house key-entry, verification, and correction of database records associated with backfile conversion.

Line F24

The percentage of backfile conversion costs to be added for supervision of document indexing and data-entry is to be entered as a decimal value on line F24. If 10 percent of document indexing and data-entry costs will be added for supervision, for example, the value to be entered on line F24 is 0.1.

Line F25

Line F25 calculates the supervisory cost for document indexing and data-entry as a specified percentage of labor and workstation costs, as previously calculated on line F23.

Line F26

Line F26 calculates the cost of backfile indexing and data-entry, including supervision.

Line F27

To allow for unforeseen events, delays, or other problems that can increase document indexing and data-entry costs, a contingency percentage is to be entered as a decimal value on line F27. If the desired contingency is five percent, for example, the value to be entered on line F27 is 0.05.

Line F28

Line F28 calculates the contingency amount based on the percentage specified on line F27.

Line F29

Line F29 calculates the total cost of backfile indexing and data-entry, including labor, data-entry workstations, supervision, and contingency.

Backfile Storage Costs

Worksheet G calculates storage requirements and costs for digital documents and index records associated with backfile conversion.

Line G1

The number of backfile pages to be converted to digital images is to be entered on line G1 by adding lines D1 and E1. The value on line E1 indicates the number of backfile pages to be converted by a service bureau. That value may include both digital images and character-coded text, in which case the entry on line G1 must be limited to digital images. If no backfile pages will be converted to digital images, skip lines G2 and G3.

Line G2

The number of digital images per megabyte of storage is to be entered on line G2. As previously discussed, image storage requirements vary with document characteristics, scanning resolution, and compression methodologies. Assuming that a single-spaced, typewritten, letter-size page scanned at 200 dots per inch with Group 4 compression requires 50,000 megabytes of storage, a megabyte will contain 20 such pages. With larger documents and/or those scanned at higher resolutions, fewer pages will be stored in each megabyte.

Line G3

Line G3 calculates the backfile storage requirement, in megabytes, for digital images.

Line G4

The number of backfile pages to be converted to character-coded text via OCR or key-entry is to be entered on line G1 by adding line D15, D30, and the number of pages from line E1 that are to be converted to character-coded text as opposed to digital images. If the value on line G4 is zero, skip lines G5 and G6.

Line G5

The number of pages of character-coded text per megabyte of storage is to be entered on line G5. As with digital images, storage requirements will vary with page characteristics. As previously explained, each character will require a byte of storage. Assuming that a single-spaced, typewritten, letter-size page contains approximately 3,800 to 4,000 characters, a megabyte can store 250 to 260 such pages. The number of pages per megabyte will increase if the pages are double-spaced and/or less than completely filled.

Line G6

Line G6 calculates the backfile storage requirement, in megabytes, for character-coded text.

Line G7

The amount of index data associated with backfile documents was previously calculated on line F9. Line G7 calculates the storage requirement, in megabytes, for database records that index backfile documents.

Line G8

The percentage of character-coded backfile documents for which full-text indexing will be used is to be entered as a decimal value on line G8. If full-text indexing will be used for all character-coded backfile documents, the value to be entered on line G8 is 1.00. If full-text indexing will not be used, skip lines G9 through G10.

Line G9

Line G9 calculates the amount of character-coded data, in megabytes, to which full-text indexing will be applied.

Line G10

Line G10 calculates the storage requirement, in megabytes, for full-text indexing of character-coded backfile documents. Full-text indexes and their associated overhead are estimated to occupy 1.3 times as much storage as the documents being indexed.

Line G11

Line G11 calculates the storage requirement for backfile documents and their associated index data, including full-text indexing where applicable.

Line G12

The assumption is that hard drives will store backfile documents and their associated index data. Some unused hard drives may have been included in the purchased, leased, or rented computer configurations previously entered on lines A1, A4, B1, and B4. The amount, in megabytes, of such unused capacity is to be entered on line G12.

Line G13

Line G13 deducts the unused capacity from the amount required for backfile storage. The result is the amount of computer storage, in megabytes, that must be purchased specifically for backfile documents and index data. If the result on line G13 is zero or a negative number, skip lines G14 and G15.

Line G14

The cost per megabyte for hard drive storage of backfile documents and index data is to be entered on line G14.

Line G15

Line G15 calculates the additional cost of hard drives for backfile documents and their associated index data.

Line G16

One or more backup copies of backfile documents and index data will be stored offline. Magnetic tapes are the widely used media for that purpose. Alternatively, optical disks may be used as backup copies. The cost per megabyte for media to be used for backup copies of backfile documents and index data is to be entered on line G16.

Line G17

Line G17 calculates the cost of backup media for the quantity of information specified on line G11.

Line G18

The number of sets of backup copies to be produced is to be entered on line G18.

Line G19

Line G19 calculates media costs for the specified number of backup copies.

Line G20

Line G20 calculates total online storage and backup media costs for backfile documents and their associated index data.

Ongoing Document Conversion Costs

Worksheet H calculates ongoing costs associated with the conversion of newly acquired paper documents to digital images or character-coded text. These costs will be incurred on a recurring basis in successive years following the initial digital document implementation. (Backfile conversion, as previously discussed, is treated as a nonrecurring, start-up cost). Annual costs are associated with specific document conversion tasks such as document preparation and disposition, photocopying, document scanning, OCR, and key-entry of document content.

Line H1

The number of documents or pages to be converted to digital images or character-coded text per year is to be entered on line H1.

Line H2

The estimated preparation rate in documents or pages per hour is to be entered on line H2. As previously discussed, typical preparatory work steps in imaging and OCR applications include removing documents from file cabinets or other containers; removing staples, paper clips, or other fasteners; stacking documents for insertion into a scanner's automatic page feeder; and transporting documents to a scanning area. Preparation requirements are less extensive where key-entry is used to convert documents to character-coded text. In particular, removal of page fasteners, a time-consuming work step, is not usually necessary. Some brittle or damaged pages may require photocopying, repair, or other special preparation prior to scanning. Photocopying costs, where applicable, are calculated later in this worksheet.

Line H3

Line H3 calculates the annual preparation time, in hours, for the workload specified on line H1.

Line H4

The estimated disposition rate, in documents or pages per hour, is to be entered on line H4. Examples of disposition tasks include destruction of documents following scanning or key-entry, return of documents to their original locations, packing and inventorying of documents for removal to off-site storage, or transporting of documents to an in-house microfilming operation or microfilm service bureau. In some situations, documents may be reassembled, with pages being restapled and reinserted into folders, following scanning or conversion to character-coded text.

Line H5

Line H5 calculates the annual disposition time, in hours, for the workload specified on line H1.

Line H6

Line H6 calculates the total annual time, in hours, for document preparation and disposition.

Line H7

The hourly wage rate for employees performing document preparation and disposition is to be entered on line H7. If wage rates vary from worker to worker, an average rate should be entered. The hourly rate wage should include fringe benefits where applicable.

Line H8

Line H8 calculates the annual labor cost for document preparation and disposition based on productivity and wage information from the preceding lines.

Line H9

The percentage of pages from the annual workload that must be photocopied prior to conversion to digital form is to be entered as a decimal value on line H10. Bound documents may be photocopied for input to sheetfed scanners, for example. For certain unbound documents, photocopying can facilitate scanning of fragile or damaged pages. For security reasons, documents may be photocopied before sending them to a service bureau if scanning, OCR, or key-entry will be outsourced. If all documents will be photocopied, the value to be entered on line H9 is 1.00. If no documents will be photocopied, skip lines H9 through H13.

Line H10

Line H10 calculates the total number of pages to be photocopied annually prior to scanning.

Line H11

The photocopying cost, in cents per page, is to be entered as a decimal value on line H11. The cost should encompass purchase or rental charges for photocopying equipment, supply costs, and labor charges, including fringe benefits where applicable.

Line H12

Line H12 calculates photocopying costs for the number of pages specified on line H10.

Line H13

Document scanning may be performed in-house, by a service bureau, or by a combination of both methods. The number of annual pages to be scanned in-house is to be entered on line H13. The entered value must include pages that will be scanned for storage and indexing as images as well as pages that will subsequently be converted to character-coded text via OCR. If in-house scanning is the only method used to create digital documents, the value to be entered on line H13 will equal the value previously entered on line H1. If in-house scanning will not be used, skip lines H13 through H17.

Line H14

The average number of pages that can be scanned per hour is to be entered on line H14. In addition to actual scanning time, the scanning rate must include the time required for positioning and removal of pages, inspection of digital images following scanning, recording of images on computer media, and any required rescanning. These time-consuming supporting tasks will degrade throughput. Although a given document scanner may operate at 3 seconds per page or 1,200 pages per hour, the total scanning time may be 20 to 30 seconds per page when all scanning-related tasks are considered. Image inspection alone, for example, may require 10 seconds or longer per page.

Line H15

Line H15 calculates the number of hours of labor required annually for in-house document scanning.

Line H16

The hourly wage rate, including fringe benefits, for scanning workstation operators is to be entered on line H16. If wage rates vary from worker to worker, an average rate should be entered.

Line H17

Line H17 calculates the annual labor cost for document conversion by in-house scanning.

Line H18

The number of pages to be converted in-house to character-coded text annually via OCR is to be entered on line H18. Because document scanning is a precondition for OCR, the entry on line H18 cannot exceed the value previously entered on line H13. If no pages will be converted via OCR, skip lines H18 through H22.

Line H19

The average number of pages that can be converted to character-coded text via OCR per hour, including verification of recognized text and error correction, is to be entered on line H19.

Line H20

Line H20 calculates the number of hours of labor required for in-house document conversion via OCR for the number of pages specified on line H18 at the processing rate specified on line H19.

Line H21

The hourly wage rate, including fringe benefits, for OCR workstation operators is to be entered on line H21. If wage rates vary from worker to worker, an average rate should be entered.

Line H22

Line H22 calculates the labor cost for in-house document conversion via OCR.

Line H23

The number of pages to be converted to character-coded text by in-house key-entry is to be entered on line H23. If no pages will be converted via in-house key-entry, skip lines H23 through H30.

Line H24

The average number of characters per page is to be entered on line H24. As previously defined, characters include the letters of the alphabet, numeric digits, punctuation marks, and other textual symbols plus such invisible characters as blank spaces, tabs, and carriage returns.

Line H25

Line H25 calculates the total number of characters to be converted to character-coded text by in-house key-entry.

Line H26

The key-entry rate in characters per hour is to be entered on line H26. As previously explained, key-entry rates range broadly from 6,000 to 15,000 characters per hour, depending on operator skill, the characteristics of source documents, and other factors. Key-entry rates of 10,000 to 11,000 characters per hour sustained throughout the workday are attainable by full-time experienced data-entry operators.

Line H27

Line H27 calculates the actual key-entry rate in characters per hour including the time required for data verification and error correction. If verification by double-keying will be used, the amount on line H26 is to be divided by 2.25. By this calculation, an initial key-entry rate of 10,000 characters per hour yields an actual key-entry rate of 4,445 characters per hour when double-keying and error correction are included. Put another way, a backfile conversion involving 1,000 hours of initial key-entry will require a total of 2,250 hours for initial key-entry, proofreading, and error correction. If sight verification (proofreading) will be used, the amount on line H26 is to be divided by 1.6. Thus, an initial key-entry rate of 10,000 characters per hour will be reduced to 6,250 characters per hour when proofreading and error correction are included.

Line H28

Line H28 calculates the total number of hours required for document conversion by in-house key-entry, including verification and error correction.

Line H29

The hourly wage rate, including fringe benefits, for key-entry personnel is to be entered on line H29. If wage rates vary from worker to worker, an average rate should be entered.

Line H30

Line H30 calculates the labor cost for backfile conversion by in-house key-entry.

Line H31

Line H31 calculates the number of annual pages to be converted by a service bureau. If a service bureau will not be used, skip lines H31 through H39.

Line H32

The service bureau's charges for document scanning are to be entered on line H32. This information will typically be obtained from a proposal, bid response, or other firm price quotation provided by a service bureau. The amount entered on line H32 must include all service bureau charges, including scanning, key-entry, data verification, error correction, document preparation, shipping charges, and media costs.

Line H33

Packing and shipping costs for transporting documents to the service bureau are to be entered on line H33. Such costs include, but are not necessarily limited to, in-house labor, containers, postage or freight charges, and insurance.

Line H34

Work performed by a service bureau must be inspected for correctness and completeness. Defective work will presumably be returned to the service bureau for correction. In some implementations, inspection will be limited to a sample of the service bureau's work. The percentage of the service bureau's work to be inspected is to be entered as a decimal value on line H34. If one-half of the service bureau's work will be inspected, for example, the value to be entered on line H34 is 0.50. If all pages will be inspected, the value to be entered is 1.00.

Line H35

Line H35 calculates the number of pages to be inspected, based on the specified percentage of work performed by a service bureau.

Line H36

The average inspection rate, in pages per hour, is to be entered on line H36.

Line H37

Line H37 calculates the required inspection time, in hours, for the number of pages specified on line H35.

Line H38

The hourly wage rate, including fringe benefits, for employees performing inspection is to be entered on line H38. If wage rates vary from worker to worker, an average rate should be entered.

Line H39

Line H39 calculates the annual labor cost for in-house inspection of the service bureau's work.

Line H40

Line H40 calculates the combined annual cost of document preparation and disposition; photocopying; and labor for in-house document conversion by scanning, OCR, and key-entry; and labor to inspect service bureau work.

Line H41

The percentage of annual costs to be added for supervision of document preparation, disposition, photocopying, conversion, and inspection is to be entered as a decimal value on line H41. If 25 percent of annual document preparation, disposition, and scanning costs will be added for supervision, for example, the value to be entered on line H41 is 0.25.

Line H42

Line H42 calculates the annual supervisory cost for document preparation, disposition, photocopying, conversion, and inspection.

Line H43

Line H43 calculates the annual cost of labor and supervision plus service bureau charges for document conversion.

Line H44

To allow for unforeseen events, delays, or other problems that can increase document conversion costs, a contingency percentage is to be entered as a decimal value on line H44. If the desired contingency is five percent, for example, the value to be entered on line H44 is 0.05.

Line H45

Line H45 calculates the contingency amount based on the percentage specified on line H44.

Line H46

Line H37 calculates the total annual cost of document conversion, including labor, supervision, service bureau charges, and the contingency amount.

Annual Indexing Costs

Worksheet I calculates the annual cost of document indexing and entry of index records. This worksheet does not apply to full-text indexing, which automatically extracts index terms from character-coded documents.

Line I1

Indexing is done at the document level rather than the page level. The number of digital documents to be indexed annually is to be entered on line I1. A document may consist of one or more pages. The assumption is that multipage documents will be treated as a unit for purposes of indexing and index data-entry. If document indexing is not required—as would be the case where an existing database will serve as an index to digital images or where documents have already been indexed—skip lines I2 through I5.

Line I2

Indexing denotes the analytical tasks that culminate in the selection of field values for specific documents. Indexing difficulty and time will depend on the characteristics of documents being indexed. The average indexing rate, in documents per hour, is to be entered on line I2.

Line I3

Line I3 calculates the number of hours required to index the quantity of documents specified on line I1.

Line I4

The hourly wage rate for indexing personnel is to be entered on line I4. If wage rates vary from worker to worker, an average rate should be entered.

Line I5

Line I5 calculates the annual labor cost for the specified quantity of document indexing at the indicated wage rate.

Line I6

The remainder of Worksheet I calculates annual costs for key-entry of database records (index information) associated with digital documents. The number of documents for which index data-entry is required is to be entered on line I6. If index data is not required—as would be the case, for example, if full-text indexing is used exclusively—skip lines I7 through I13.

Line I7

The average number of characters per database record is to be entered on line I7. That amount is the total of the average number of characters for each field within the database records. Where digital documents will be linked to previously created database records, key-entry requirements will typically be limited to a unique linking field value such as an account number, an invoice number, or a purchase order number.

Line I8

Line I8 calculates the annual data-entry workload for the number of documents specified on line I6.

Line I9

The expected key-entry rate, in characters (keystrokes) per hour, is to be entered on line I9. As discussed in Chapter 3, key-entry rates range broadly from 6,000 to 15,000 characters per hour. Rates of 10,000 to 11,000 characters per hour are typical for full-time, experienced data-entry personnel.

Line I10

Line I10 calculates the time required, in hours, for initial key-entry of database records for the annual volume of work specified on line I8 and the typing rate specified on line I9.

Line I11

Line I11 calculates the total number of hours required for entry of database records, including data verification and error correction. If data verification by double-keying will be used, the amount on line I10 is to be multiplied by 2.25. If sight verification (proofreading) will be used, the amount on line I10 is to be multiplied by 1.6.

Line I12

The hourly wage rate, including fringe benefits, for data-entry personnel is to be entered on line I12. If wage rates vary from worker to worker, an average rate should be entered.

Line I13

Line I13 calculates the annual labor cost for entry of database records associated with newly received documents.

Line I14

Line I14 calculates the combined annual labor cost for document indexing and entry of database records associated with newly received documents.

Line I15

The percentage of annual costs to be added for supervision of document indexing and data-entry activities is to be entered as a decimal value on line I15. If 25 percent of annual document indexing and data-entry costs will be added for supervision, for example, the value to be entered on line I15 is 0.25.

Line I16

Line I16 calculates the annual supervisory cost for document indexing and data-entry.

Line I17

Line I17 calculates the annual cost of document indexing and data-entry, including supervision.

Line I18

To allow for unforeseen events, delays, or other problems that can increase document indexing and data-entry costs, a contingency percentage is to be entered as a decimal value on line I18. If the desired contingency is five percent, for example, the value to be entered on line I18 is 0.05.

Line I19

Line I19 calculates the contingency amount based on the percentage specified on line I18.

Line I20

Line I20 calculates the total annual cost of indexing and data-entry for newly acquired documents, including labor, supervision, and the contingency amount.

Additional Equipment Costs

Worksheet J calculates the cost of additional scanning, inspection, and data-entry equipment required for annual document input activities.

Line J1

Lines J1 through J7 determine the number of additional workstations required for in-house scanning of newly acquired documents on an ongoing basis. The number of hours of labor required annually for in-house scanning of documents, including inspection, is to be entered on line J1 as previously calculated on line H15. If in-house scanning will not be used, skip lines J1 through J10.

Line J2

The number of daily operating hours per scanning workstation is to be entered on line J2. A scanning workstation used for two 8-hour shifts, for example, will have 16 operating hours per day. However, some time must be allocated for preventative maintenance or repair of equipment. Thus, a two-shift operation will provide less than the maximum number of operating hours—perhaps 15 to 15.5 hours per day on average.

Line J3

The number of days of scanner operation per year is to be entered on line J3. Depending on holidays observed and weekend work schedules, most organizations have 240 to 250 working days per year.

Line J4

Line J4 calculates the maximum number of annual operating hours per scanning workstation.

Line J5

Line J5 calculates the number of workstations required to accommodate the scanning workload specified on line J1. If the calculation yields a decimal value, it should be rounded up to the next integer. Thus, if the calculation yields 1.2, the value to be entered on line J5 is 2.

Line J6

Some scanning workstations may have been included in the purchased, leased, or rented digital document configurations previously entered on lines A1, A4, B1, B4, and D9. The number of unused scanning workstations, if any, is to be entered on line J6. In this context, a workstation is "unused" if it is not being used for tasks discussed in other worksheets. Such workstations are presumably available for scanning operations.

Line J7

Line J7 deducts those workstations from the number required to scan the number of pages specified on line J1. The result is the number of additional scanning workstations that must be purchased. If the amount on line J7 is zero or a negative value, skip lines J8 and J9.

Line J8

The cost per scanning workstation, including equipment and software, is to be entered on line J8.

Line J9

Line J9 calculates the total cost for the number of additional scanning workstations specified on line J7.

Line J10

The number of hours required annually for in-house conversion of documents to character-coded text via OCR is to be entered on line J10 as previously calculated on line H25. Because document scanning is a precondition for OCR, the entry on line J10 cannot exceed the value previously entered on line J1 unless a service bureau will be used for scanning. If no pages will be converted in-house via OCR, skip lines J11 through J18.

Line J11

The number of daily operating hours per OCR workstation is to be entered on line J11. An OCR workstation used for two 8-hour shifts, for example, will have 16 operating hours per day. However, some time must be allocated for preventative maintenance or repair of equipment. Thus, a two-shift operation will provide less than the maximum number of operating hours—perhaps 15 to 15.5 hours per day on average.

Line J12

The number of days of OCR operation per year is to be entered on line J12. Depending on holidays observed and weekend work schedules, most organizations have 240 to 250 working days per year.

Line J13

Line J13 calculates the maximum number of annual operating hours per OCR workstation.

Line J14

Line J14 calculates the number of OCR workstations required to accommodate the workload specified on line J10. If the calculation yields a decimal value, it should be rounded up to the next integer. Thus, if the calculation yields 1.2, the value to be entered on line J14 is 2.

Line J15

Some OCR workstations may have been included in the purchased, leased, or rented digital document configurations previously entered on lines A1, A4, B1, B4, and D24. In addition, scanning workstations entered on lines J7 may be used as OCR workstations when not being used for scanning. The number of unused OCR workstations, if any, is to be entered on line J6. As previously explained, a workstation is "unused" if it is not being used for tasks discussed in other worksheets. Such workstations are presumably available for OCR operations.

Line J16

Line J16 deducts those workstations from the number specified on line J14. The result is the number of additional OCR workstations that must be purchased to accommodate the annual workload. If the amount on line J16 is zero or a negative value, skip lines J17 and J18.

Line J17

The cost per OCR workstation, including equipment and software, is to be entered on line J17.

Line J18

Line J18 calculates the total cost for the number of additional OCR workstations specified on line J16.

Line J19

The number of hours required annually for conversion of documents to character-coded text by in-house key-entry, including verification and error correction, is to be entered on line J19 as previously calculated on line H28. If no pages will be converted via in-house key-entry, skip lines J20 through J29.

Line J20

The number of daily operating hours per key-entry workstation is to be entered on line J20. A key-entry workstation used for two 8-hour shifts, for example, will have 16 operating hours per day. Because some time must be allocated for preventative maintenance or repair of equipment, a two-shift operation will provide less than the maximum number of operating hours—perhaps 15 to 15.5 hours per day on average.

Line J21

The number of days of operation per year for key-entry workstations is to be entered on line J21. Depending on holidays observed and weekend work schedules, most organizations have 240 to 250 working days per year.

Line J22

Line J22 calculates the maximum number of annual operating hours per key-entry workstation.

Line J23

Line J23 calculates the number of key-entry workstations required to accommodate the workload specified on line J19. If the calculation yields a decimal value, it should be rounded up to the next integer. Thus, if the calculation yields 1.2, the value to be entered on line J23 is 2.

Line J24

Some key-entry workstations may have been included in the purchased, leased, or rented digital document configurations previously entered on lines A1, A4, B1, B4, and D43. The number of unused key-entry workstations, if any, is to be entered on line J24. In addition, scanning and OCR workstations entered on lines J7 and J16 may be used for key-entry of character-coded text when not being used for their intended purposes. As previously explained, a workstation is "unused" if it is not being used for tasks discussed in other worksheets. Such workstations are presumably available for key-entry operations.

Line J25

Line J25 deducts those workstations from the number specified on line J23. The result is the number of additional OCR workstations that must be purchased to accommodate the annual workload. If the amount on line J25 is zero or a negative value, skip lines J26 and J27.

Line J26

The cost per key-entry workstation, including equipment and software, is to be entered on line J26.

Line J27

Line J27 calculates the total cost for the number of additional key-entry workstations specified on line J25.

Line J28

The number of hours required annually for entry of index data associated with digital documents in image or text formats, including verification and error correction, is to be entered on line J28 as previously calculated on line I11. If index data-entry is not required (as would be the case if full-text indexing of character-coded documents is used exclusively), skip lines J29 through J36.

Line J29

The number of daily operating hours per data-entry workstation is to be entered on line J29. A data-entry workstation used for two 8-hour shifts, for example, will have 16 operating hours per day. Because some time must be allocated for preventative maintenance or repair of equipment, a two-shift operation will provide less than the maximum number of operating hours—perhaps 15 to 15.5 hours per day on average.

Line J30

The number of days of operation per year for data-entry workstations is to be entered on line J30. Depending on holidays observed and weekend work schedules, most organizations have 240 to 250 working days per year.

Line J31

Line J31 calculates the maximum number of annual operating hours per data-entry workstation.

Line J32

Line J32 calculates the number of data-entry workstations required to accommodate the workload specified on line J28. If the calculation yields a decimal value, it should be rounded up to the next integer. Thus, if the calculation yields 1.2, the value to be entered on line J28 is 2.

Line J33

Some data-entry workstations may have been included in the purchased, leased, or rented digital document configurations previously entered on lines A1, A4, B1, B4, D43, E16, and F20. In addition, scanning, OCR, and key-entry workstations entered on lines J7, J16, and J25 may be used for key-entry of character-coded text when not being used for their intended purposes. The number of unused workstations, if any, is to be entered on line J33. As previously explained, a workstation is "unused" if it is not being used for tasks discussed in these worksheets. Such workstations are presumably available for data-entry operations.

Line J34

Line J34 deducts unused workstations from the number specified on line J32. The result is the number of additional workstations that must be purchased to accommodate the annual data-entry workload. If the amount on line J34 is zero or a negative value, skip lines J35 and J36.

Line J35

The cost per data-entry workstation, including equipment and software, is to be entered on line J35.

Line J36

Line J36 calculates the total cost for the number of additional data-entry workstations specified on line J34.

Line J37

Line J37 calculates the combined cost of additional workstations to accommodate the annual workload of document scanning, conversion of documents to character-coded text, and index data-entry.

Annual Storage Costs

Worksheet K calculates the cost of computer storage to accommodate successive annual accumulations of digital images, character-coded documents, and database records.

Line K1

The number of digital images to be added to the digital document implementation per year is to be entered on line K1, as transcribed from line H13. If no digital images will be added, skip lines K2 and K3.

Line K2

The number of digital images per megabyte of storage is to be entered on line K2. Image storage requirements vary with document characteristics, scanning resolution, and compression methodologies. Assuming that a single-spaced, typewritten letter-size page scanned at 200 dots per inch with Group 4 compression requires 50,000 megabytes of storage, a megabyte will contain 20 such pages. With larger documents and/or those scanned at higher resolutions, fewer pages will be contained in each megabyte.

Line K3

Line K3 calculates the storage requirement, in megabytes, for each year's accumulation of digital images.

Line K4

The number of pages of character-coded text to be added to the digital document implementation per year is to be entered on line K4. That number is the total of values previously entered on lines H18 and H23 plus any documents created in digital form by word processing or other software. If no character-coded documents will be added, skip lines K5 and K6.

Line K5

The number of pages of character-coded text per megabyte of storage is to be entered on line K5. As with digital images, storage requirements will vary with page characteristics. Assuming that a single-spaced, typewritten, letter-size page contains approximately 3,800 to 4,000 characters, a megabyte can store 250 to 260 such pages. The number of pages per megabyte will increase if the pages are double-spaced and/or less than completely filled.

Line K6

Line K6 calculates the storage requirement, in megabytes, for each year's accumulation of character-coded documents.

Line K7

The number of digital documents that will require indexing each year is to be entered on Line K7. In this context, indexing refers to the creation of structured database records with values for specific index categories entered into predetermined fields. Typically, all imaged documents will be indexed in this manner. In addition, some character-coded documents may require field-based indexing, even if full-text indexing is used. As explained elsewhere in this book, field-based indexing is performed at the document level. Multipage documents will be indexed as a unit. Unless single-page documents are involved, the amount entered on line K7 will be lower than the amounts on lines K1 and K4. If no digital documents will require indexing, skip lines K8 and K9.

Line K8

The average number of characters per index record is to be entered on line K8. That amount is the total of the average number of characters for each field within index records.

Line K9

Line K9 calculates the amount of field-based index data to be added per year.

Line K10

The percentage of character-coded pages for which full-text indexing will be used is to be entered as a decimal value on line K10. If full-text indexing will be applied to all character-coded pages, the entry on line K10 should be 1.00. If full-text indexing will not be used, enter zero on line K10 and skip lines K11 and K12.

Line K11

Line K11 calculates the amount of character-coded text to which full-text indexing will be applied.

Line K12

Line K12 calculates the amount of full-text index data to be added per year. The assumption is that full-text indexes and their associated overhead will require 1.3 as much storage as the digital documents being indexed.

Line K13

Line K13 calculates the amount of field-based and full-text index data to be added per year.

Line K14

Line K14 calculates the storage requirement, in megabytes, for each year's accumulation of index data.

Line K15

Line K15 calculates the storage requirement, in megabytes, for each year's accumulation of digital documents and index data.

Line K16

Some unused storage capacity may have been included in the purchased, leased, or rented computer configurations previously entered in lines A1, A4, B1, B4, and G13. The amount, in megabytes, of such unused capacity is to be entered on line K16.

Line K17

Line K17 deducts the unused capacity from the amount of storage required annually. The result is the amount of additional storage that must be purchased to accommodate annual accumulations of digital documents and index data. If the amount on line K5 is zero or a negative value, skip lines K18 and K19.

Line K18

The cost per megabyte for online storage is to be entered on line K18.

Line K19

Line K19 calculates the cost of online storage to accommodate each year's accumulation of digital documents and index data.

Line K20

One or more backup copies of digital documents and index data will be stored offline. Magnetic tapes or optical disks are suitable media for that purpose. The cost per megabyte for backup media is to be entered on line K20.

Line K21

Line K21 calculates the cost to produce one set of backup media for each year's accumulation of digital documents and index data.

Line K22

The number of sets of backup copies to be produced is to be entered on line K22.

Line K23

Line K23 calculates storage media costs for the indicated number of backup copies.

Line K24

Line K24 calculates annual costs for online storage and backup media to accommodate each year's accumulation of digital documents and index data.

Annualized Cost Summary

Pulling together the foregoing calculations, Worksheet L summarizes the cost of a digital document implementation on an annualized basis. Such annualized presentations can be useful for cost justification and analytical comparisons of records management methodologies.

Line L1

The start-up cost for purchased hardware and software for the digital document implementation is to be entered on line L1, as transcribed from line A7.

Line L2

The cost of computer storage for backfile conversion is to be entered on line L2, as previously calculated on line G20.

Line L3

The cost of additional scanning, image inspection, and data-entry equipment is to be entered on line L3, as transcribed from line J37.

Line L4

Line L4 calculates the total of these amounts.

Line L5

The useful life, in years, of the digital document implementation's hardware, software, and storage components is to be entered on line L5. The useful life is the period of time during which the implementation's components will remain in service without significant upgrading or replacement. A reasonable estimate for the useful life of digital document hardware, software, and storage components is three to five years. Beyond that time, computer systems are likely to be replaced in order to take advantage of technological innovations, to address changing application requirements, to improve reliability, to acquire new product capabilities, or for other reasons.

Line L6

Line L6 calculates the annualized cost of the purchased hardware, software, and storage components in a digital document implementation.

Line L7

Line L7 calculates the total cost of backfile conversion, including document preparation costs, in-house scanning costs, service bureau costs, and document indexing and data-entry costs.

Line L8

The useful life of the converted backfile is to be entered on line L8. The useful life of digital documents and index data will typically prove longer than the service lives of computer hardware, software, and storage components. If necessary, digital documents can be converted to new formats for input into a replacement system. Index data, being character-coded, is highly portable. The useful life of digital documents and their associated index data is typically determined by application-dependent retention requirements rather than technical factors. In most if not all cases, the useful life of digital documents is identical to their retention periods.

Line L9

Line L9 calculates the annualized cost of backfile conversion for a digital document implementation.

Line L10

Annual fixed costs for a digital document implementation are to be entered on line L10, as transcribed from line B10.

Line L11

Annual costs for document conversion are to be entered on line L11, as previously calculated on line H46.

Line L12

Annual costs for document indexing and entry of index data are to be entered on line L12, as transcribed from line I19.

Line L13

The annual cost of additional online storage and backup media is to be entered on line L13, as transcribed from line K24.

Line L14

Line L14 calculates the combined cost of computer hardware and software that is not covered by maintenance costs included on line B5.

Line L15

Line L15 estimates the annual maintenance cost for those system components at the rate of 18 percent of the purchase price (1.5 percent of the purchase price per month). Annual maintenance costs may be higher, up to 23 percent of the purchase price, for some hardware and software products. In that case, the decimal value used to calculate maintenance costs must be adjusted accordingly.

Line L16

Line L16 calculates the annualized cost—including amortized start-up costs and annual fixed and variable costs—for a digital document implementation with specified characteristics.

Cost Justification

Broadly defined, **cost justification** is an analytical procedure that evaluates the costs associated with a particular methodology or technology to determine whether such costs are defensible in terms of the benefits to be derived from them. In some cases, digital document implementations are justified at a broadly conceptual level as one component in an enterprise-wide business process improvement or productivity enhancement project. In many records management applications, however, digital document systems are proposed for a specific document storage and retrieval operation that currently relies on paper filing methodologies or microfilm technology. In such situations, digital document systems are implemented to achieve one or more information management objectives that presumably yield benefits to the implementing organization.

Examples of objectives and their associated benefits include, but are not necessarily limited to, the following:

- Faster access to documents reduces the number of employees required to perform a given number of retrieval operations. An organization can also accommodate increased retrieval workloads without corresponding increases in personnel.
- Improved workflow reduces the time and labor required to complete a given number of transactions or allows transactions to be completed more quickly, thereby improving customer service and/or cash flow.
- Compact storage of documents reduces office space requirements and minimizes purchases of new filing equipment and supplies.
- Online access to documents makes information available to users quickly and conveniently. It also minimizes photocopying and faxing requirements for document distribution.
- Through computer-based indexing, digital document systems can retrieve documents that cannot be effectively retrieved by other means. Consequently, more information is available to support business operations.
- Simplified file maintenance reduces administrative support requirements, eliminates misfiles, and promotes file completeness by eliminating the out-of-file condition.
- Digital document implementations can protect documents, such as engineering drawings, that are subject to damage from repeated handling.

In digital document implementations, as in computer implementations generally, the most readily quantifiable benefits lead to cost reductions (or cost avoidance in the case of costs not yet incurred). Alternatively, digital document implementations may yield quantifiable revenue increases through productivity improvement or the development of new products or services. Greater availability of information is often cited as a benefit of digital document systems, but its value is difficult to quantify. Presumably, greater availability of information enhances employee productivity, permits faster completion of specific tasks, reduces errors in decision-making, or has other measurable effects. Taking a reductionist view, greater availability of information is not a distinct benefit but a means of reducing costs or increasing revenues. To be justified, digital document technology implementation must ultimately have an impact on an organization's bottom line.

To illustrate these points, Appendix C analyzes cost justification parameters for a hypothetical but realistic digital document implementation involving technical reports and related research documents maintained by the library services department of a pharmaceutical company. The justification is based on costs calculated in Appendix B using the worksheets presented in this chapter. Appendix C confirms that digital document technologies have the potential to reduce costs when compared to a paper-based filing system for documents that are consulted frequently.

Model Request for Proposals for a System to Manage Digital Documents

Introduction

- This request for proposals (RFP) solicits proposals from qualified vendors to provide, install, and support a document management system and certain related products and services for use by XYZ Company, hereafter referred to as "the Company."
- The following definitions are used in this RFP.
  - A document consists of one or more pages.
  - A page is defined as one information-bearing surface of a sheet of paper. A sheet of paper that contains information on both sides counts as two pages.
  - The terms "page" and "image" are synonymous.
  - The terms "proposer," "vendor," and "bidder" are synonymous.
- This RFP specifies the required characteristics of a document management system to be implemented initially in a records management application involving technical reports and related research documents maintained by the Company's library services department. In the future, the Company intends to expand its use of document management technology to other business applications. Specific future applications and the timetable for system expansion have not been determined.
  - The expansion may involve the addition of one or more applications to the document management system purchased for the technical reports application. Alternatively, the Company may purchase additional, fully compatible document management systems for future applications at the Company's headquarters or at other locations, including Company facilities outside the

United States. Any proposed document management system must be available, from an authorized dealer or other qualified vendor, in those locations. Reliable local service and customer support for all system components must likewise be available in all U.S. and international locations where the Company does business. In their proposals, bidders must affirm that this service and customer support is available. A list of the Company's locations is appended to this RFP.

- The Company wants to avoid the implementation of different, potentially incompatible document management systems in its future applications. It consequently seeks a document management vendor with products and capabilities that transcend the initial application described in this RFP. The Company is seeking a document management vendor that can satisfy a broad range of application requirements in various business operations with fully compatible document management components.

- The Company's future document management applications may require hardware components (such as higher-capacity storage devices or faster document scanners) or software functionality (such as workflow programming or web content management) that are different from those included in the initial system configuration.

- Proposers must indicate whether, and to what extent, their products and capabilities will be compatible with the future implementation of additional document management applications. The Company understands that any future implementation of additional document management applications may require the addition of hardware and software components beyond those purchased through this RFP.

- This RFP contains information and instructions that will enable qualified document management system developers, resellers, systems integrators, and other vendors to prepare and submit proposals and supporting materials.

  - The RFP specifies characteristics and requirements for the system to be procured by the Company.

  - The RFP also specifies terms and conditions the successful bidder will be expected to accept.

  - Site visits to the Company's headquarters location will be arranged for interested bidders on request. A site visit will provide an opportunity for direct observation of the planned document management application and of the physical facilities in which the document management system will be installed and operated.

- If this RFP is amended, the Company will notify each proposer in writing.

- A nonmandatory bidder's conference will be held at the Company's headquarters on [insert date, time, and meeting location].

  - Proposers are strongly urged to attend the bidder's conference.

- Proposers are asked to provide advance notification of their intention to attend the bidder's conference. Call [insert name, telephone number, e-mail address, and fax number for contact person].

- Attendance will be limited to three representatives per proposer.

- The bidder's conference will provide a public forum for questions about system specifications or other matters contained in this RFP.

- Answers and interpretations presented at the bidder's conference will be considered authoritative.

- Written questions submitted prior to the bidder's conference will be answered first. To ensure consideration, written questions must be received by the Company at least three (3) days prior to the bidder's conference.

- Oral questions will be answered as time permits.

Preparation of Proposals

- Proposals submitted in response to this RFP must be received by the Company by [insert date and time].

  - Proposals may be submitted by e-mail, by physical delivery, or combinations thereof. For example, a vendor may submit cost information by e-mail and send detailed product specifications, Company information, or other supporting materials by regular mail. In that case, the cost information must arrive by the deadline date and time stated above. The supporting material must arrive within three (3) working days of the deadline date.

  - E-mail submissions are preferred. They should be sent to [insert name and e-mail address]. Proposals should be sent as attachments in the Word document format, RTF, or PDF.

  - For submissions by mail or package delivery services (such as Fedex or UPS), the address is [insert address], Attn: [insert name].

    - Proposals submitted by fax will not be accepted.

    - Proposals will not be opened until the deadline date and time specified above. Bidders may withdraw, modify, or submit alternate proposals prior to that date and time.

    - To prevent accidental opening of proposals prior to the deadline date and time, submissions should be clearly labeled as responses to this RFP.

- All responses to this RFP are prepared and submitted at the proposer's expense. The Company will not pay any costs incurred by proposers in connection with site visits, typing of proposals, photocopying, oral presentations, or any other activities associated with the preparation, submission, or evaluation of proposals solicited by this RFP.

- To be considered responsive, a vendor must submit a complete proposal that satisfies all requirements and addresses all system components specified in this RFP. Proposals to supply partial systems—selected hardware or software components, for example—are not acceptable.

- A vendor may submit more than one proposal, but each submission must satisfy the mandatory requirements of this RFP.

  - Alternate proposals may be used to present different system configurations, alternate hardware components, or system enhancements not presented in a vendor's initial proposal.

  - All alternative proposals must be separately packaged and clearly identified.

- The Company will base its evaluation entirely on information presented in each vendor's written proposal, and in any additional written or oral presentations which may be requested from a given proposer.

  - When preparing proposals, vendors should assume that the Company has no previous knowledge of their products or capabilities.

  - Proposers' descriptions of products and services must be clearly written and presented in sufficient detail to permit effective evaluation by the Company.

  - Emphasis should be placed on a clear, complete presentation of factual information.

- Proposals must be divided into technical, management, and cost sections. Each section must be clearly labeled. The report must include a table of contents that indicates the page locations for specific topics in each section.

  - The technical section must include complete descriptions of all hardware, software, and services to be provided by the proposer.

    o The technical section must provide clear, unequivocal confirmation of the proposer's compliance with particular specifications presented in this RFP.

    o Where this RFP specifies that a document management system must have a particular characteristic or capability, the proposer must state explicitly that the system has that characteristic or capability.

    o Vague expressions, such as "standard procedures will be employed" or "industry standards will be followed," are not acceptable.

    o The proposer must indicate the specific brands and models of all hardware components, such as document scanners or computer storage devices, to be provided in response to this RFP.

    o The proposer must indicate the names and versions of operating systems, programming languages, database management systems, software development tools, or other software components on which its document indexing and retrieval capabilities are based.

  - The management section must present information about the proposer and its approach to system implementation and project management.

- The proposer must provide clear evidence that it has experience and resources appropriate to the application described in this RFP and to the company's future document management requirements.
- The proposer must provide a brief company history, including information about its involvement with records management technologies in general and document management in particular.
- The proposer must describe the organization and staffing of its corporate headquarters, divisions, and operating units.
- The proposer must provide an audited financial statement for the latest complete fiscal year.
- The proposer must provide references for three (3) document management installations that are similar in scope and components to the system proposed for the Company.
    - The references must be for systems installed within the last three years. Installations within 120 miles of our headquarters location are preferred.
    - Each reference must include the name and address of the organization in which the document management system is installed, a brief description of the system, and the name and telephone number of a contact person at the installed site.
    - The list must also indicate the dates that the systems were sold and the current status (to be installed, implementation in progress, operational, etc.) of each installation.
    - If the proposer operates as an authorized agent, distributor, or value-added reseller for a document management system developer, the references can include installations undertaken by the document management system developer.
    - The Company reserves the right to request or contact additional or different reference installations.
    - The proposer must provide a project management plan with details of project design and system implementation.
    - The proposer must list and describe the specific tasks and milestones associated with delivery, installation, implementation, training, testing, and acceptance of products and services to be provided under this RFP. The proposer must provide a master schedule for completion of all system implementation tasks and milestones.
    - The proposer must indicate key personnel—by name, title, and qualifications—who will be responsible for specific tasks defined in its proposal. If key personnel cannot be identified by name for this project, the proposer must provide the name, title, and qualifications for current employees who are assigned to comparable projects. Qualifications of the named employees must be typical of personnel to be assigned to this project.

- The proposer must identify all subcontractors who will work on this project and their specific responsibilities.
- The management section of a vendor's proposal may include a list of exceptions to this RFP.
  - A proposer may present concerns that it believes will adversely impact system implementation or operation. Evaluation of a vendor's proposal will not be negatively influenced by presentation of such concerns.
  - Any requests to delete or change specific system requirements presented in this RFP must be fully explained in the management section.
- The cost section must clearly and completely enumerate costs and pricing options associated with products and services to be provided by the proposer.
  - Cost information must appear in the cost section only. Putting all cost information into this section will allow the Company to evaluate the technical and management aspects of a vendor's proposal on their own merits, without reference to costs.
  - Prices for specific hardware components, software components, system maintenance, customer training, and related services must be individually enumerated and clearly identified.
  - The proposer must be willing to honor all quoted prices for a period of 90 days from the deadline date for submission of proposals.
  - The proposer must supply a copy of a sample purchase contract. The sample is requested for reference purposes only. The Company will utilize its own contracting procedures.
  - The proposer must supply a copy of warranty provisions for all system components. The copies must clearly indicate the length of the warranty period. For purposes of this RFP, a warranty period is the amount of time during which system components will be repaired or replaced without charge to the customer.
  - The proposer must supply a copy of a sample annual maintenance contract for all hardware components. For purposes of this RFP, a maintenance contract is a repair, replacement, or preventative maintenance arrangement that takes effect after the warranty period has elapsed. The maintenance contract must indicate the specific hardware components and circumstances to be covered by repair, replacement, or preventative maintenance.
  - The proposer must supply a copy of a sample annual maintenance contract for all software components. The maintenance contract must indicate the specific software components and circumstances to be covered by repair or replacement. The software maintenance contract must include provisions for repair of defects in and enhancements to document management software supplied under this RFP.

- The proposer must indicate single-year prices for all maintenance contracts. The proposer must also provide firm prices for hardware and software maintenance contracts in the second and third year of system operation. The Company may elect to purchase multiyear maintenance agreements for some or all document management components as part of the initial system procurement.

- All sections of a vendor's proposal should be prepared and submitted in a straightforward, economical manner.

  - The Company does not impose a limit on the length of proposals; however, brevity is encouraged. Informative content and clarity of presentation are more important than quantity of pages.

  - Expensive binding, elaborate artwork, or other embellishments that improve a proposal's appearance without affecting its content are discouraged.

  - The first page of each proposal must be clearly labeled with the proposer's name, the name of a contact person within the proposer's organization, and the proposer's mailing address, telephone number, fax number, and e-mail address.

  - The proposal must include a table of contents that indicates the proposal's organization and identifies the page locations of major sections.

  - Proposers' responses must be prepared specifically for this RFP and address the points raised herein. Prewritten product descriptions and promotional materials, presented without reference to this RFP, are not acceptable. Technical specification sheets, product brochures, and similar printed materials, where provided, should be included in an appendix. Such materials should be included only to the extent that they directly pertain to information presented in the vendor's proposal.

- All proposals submitted in response to this RFP become the property of XYZ Company.

  - Proposals will not be returned.

  - Proprietary or confidential information should be clearly identified in each proposal. The Company will make all reasonable efforts to maintain such sections in confidence and will release them only to persons involved in the evaluation effort.

Proposal Evaluation

- All proposals will be initially evaluated for completeness and compliance with technical specifications, management capabilities, and other requirements presented in this RFP.

  - Minor problems of completeness or compliance will be called to the attention of proposers for discussion and correction.

- Substantial deviations from specifications or other requirements of this RFP will result in disqualification of the proposal.

- Proposers' references may be contacted during the initial evaluation of proposals or at a later stage in the evaluation process. The Company reserves the right to contact references without advance notice to the proposer.

- Cost information in all proposals will be evaluated for completeness and arithmetic accuracy. Minor problems of completeness or inaccuracy will be called to the proposer's attention for discussion and correction.

- Lowest cost will not be the sole consideration when selecting the successful bidder. Detailed evaluation of proposals will involve a determination of the most favorable combination of technical, management, and cost elements for those proposals in conformity with this RFP.

- Selected proposers will be required to provide an oral presentation of their proposals.

- Selected proposers will be required to provide a functional demonstration of hardware and software capabilities outlined in this RFP.
  - The demonstration must be conducted with the specific products included in the vendor's proposal.
  - The demonstration will involve document scanning, index data-entry, image recording, image display, image printing, and other capabilities as specified in this RFP.
  - The demonstration will involve documents to be supplied by the Company.

- The successful proposer must be prepared to complete the contract award within 30 days of selection as the best proposal.

- The successful vendor's proposal will be incorporated into the contract. Any false or misleading statements found in the proposal will be grounds for disqualification.

- The Company will contract only with the submitter of the best proposal, to be known as the prime contractor.
  - The prime contractor is solely responsible for contractual performance, including delivery, installation, implementation, maintenance, and other activities relating to hardware, software, or services specified in the proposal.
  - In the case of joint ventures between two or more vendors, one vendor must be designated the prime contractor for contractual purposes. That vendor must be clearly identified in the proposal.
  - For subcontracting arrangements, the prime contractor assumes full responsibility for all system components and services supplied by subcontractors. All subcontractors must be identified in proposals.

- The successful proposer must begin delivery of system components as soon as possible, but in no case later than 30 days after the contract is signed.

- The document management system must be fully installed and operational for those activities specified in this RFP as the proposer's responsibility within 90 days after the contract is signed.

- Unsuccessful proposers will be notified in writing following the completion of the contract award.

Description of Initial Application

- The document management application that is the subject of this RFP involves technical reports and related research documents maintained by the Company's library services department. Documents to be included in the proposed document management implementation are currently maintained in paper files grouped by their originating departments and arranged alphabetically by the name of the principal author. Copies of title pages for each report are filed separately by subject.

- The principal purpose of the Company's initial document management implementation is to improve retrieval of research documents needed by scientists, managers, or other authorized persons. In particular, the library services department wants to reduce the amount of time required to locate reports needed for a given purpose. At present, this type of search requires browsing through paper files.

- The Company intends to scan a backfile of 10,000 technical reports totaling 300,000 pages. In the future, the library services department will receive technical reports in digital formats from their originating departments.

- All document preparation, document scanning, image inspection, and data-entry will be performed by the library services department using Company-paid personnel. The labor cost of those operations is not part of this RFP. The Company may contract with an imaging service bureau to perform backfile conversion. In that case, the Company may issue a separate RFP for the required services.

- The library services department is developing an indexing plan and procedures for digital documents. Index fields may include, but will not necessarily be limited to, the following:
  - Document Date
  - Originating department
  - Author(s)
  - Subject (s)
  - Report Number

- The proposed document management system will be accessible to authorized persons at the Company's headquarters location through an existing local area network. It will also be accessible through wide area network linkages to authorized persons in other Company locations. Selected users may have desktop retrieval stations equipped with high-resolution monitors. Other authorized employees will use previously installed personal computers to access document images. Those personal computers are equipped with SVGA monitors.

- Note that the foregoing description applies to the Company's initial document management application only. As previously noted, the Company anticipates the future implementation of additional document management applications that may involve larger document collections or documents with different characteristics.

General Requirements

- Document management software must be complete, pretested, fully operational, and commercially available in a general-release version for at least 60 days prior to its acquisition by the Company. Experimental, developmental, and near-release products are unacceptable. This requirement applies to all software components, including products developed by a given vendor's business partners or other external parties.
  - Any document management software or related product proposed for use by the Company must be the latest available version of that product.
  - A single vendor must support all software components, including those developed by business partners and other external parties.
- Document management software must be fully compatible with the Company's computing and networking infrastructure. The software must operate on servers and clients with which the Company is familiar and is currently using. Document management software for other computing environments is unacceptable.
- Procurement of document management technology covered by this specification will be limited to software and related services such as product installation, training, and technical support. The Company will provide all computer hardware and networking components to be used in the document management implementation. Vendors must specify required and preferred hardware characteristics, such as the processor speed and amount of random-access memory for servers and clients, to run any proposed document management software.
- The Company's initial document management application will require software licenses for 50 concurrent users.
  - User licenses must allow authorized persons to add documents to and retrieve documents from designated repositories.
  - In addition, the Company may require one or more licenses for scanning paper documents if it elects to implement that capability as a document management component. Alternatively, the Company may elect to acquire separate scanning components, in which case the resulting images will be imported into the document management system.
  - Document management software's imaging components must be compatible with popular document scanners, including duplex models that can scan double-sided pages in a single pass.

- The vendor must indicate unit costs and incremental discounts for additional user licenses. The vendor must indicate whether an unlimited-use site license is available as a more economical alternative to individual user licenses.

- The proposed document management software must be easily learned and convenient to use by nontechnical personnel. Knowledge of programming concepts or other information systems expertise, apart from broad familiarity with computer operations in an office context, must not be required.

- Future applications may require the integration of document management capabilities with external databases, portals, or other content, including information maintained by custom-developed programs as well as prewritten software acquired by the Company from commercial developers.

  - Document management software must provide appropriate application programming interfaces or other tools to support such integration.

  - The vendor must describe those tools in sufficient detail to enable the Company to evaluate their ease of use and suitability for its purposes.

  - Written documentation must be provided for all software to be included in the system.

    o User documentation must be provided for all application software.

    o Developmental documentation, in the form of working papers and source code, must be provided for any customized programming paid for by the Company.

Document Organization / Indexing Requirements

- Document management software must permit the creation and maintenance of document repositories for purposes and applications to be determined by the Company. Each repository will be an organized, searchable collection of documents.

- Repositories must be compatible with Company-defined file plans that consist of hierarchically structured folders and subfolders nested to multiple levels.

- Document management software must provide a convenient method for implementing file plans by setting up and labeling folders and subfolders. Where the Company has defined a uniform taxonomy for folders or subfolders, a convenient method of importing that taxonomy into a given application without the necessity of manually recreating it for each application must be included.

- Document management software must support modification of file plans by authorized persons.

- Document management software must support metadata (index data) consisting of Company-defined fields at the folder, subfolder, and document levels. Document management software must support the modification of metadata, including the addition or deletion of fields, by authorized persons.

- Metadata characteristics—including file names, field names, field lengths, data types, and key fields—must be definable by the Company, thereby allowing the Company to create, implement, and operate additional document management applications without vendor assistance.

- Document management software must support full-text indexing of all or selected documents within a repository. The software must incorporate a suitable full-text indexing component for that purpose.

Input Requirements

- Repositories created by document management software must accommodate digital documents of all types including, but not necessarily limited to, the following:
  - Word processing documents
  - Spreadsheet files
  - PowerPoint presentations
  - PDF files
  - TIF images with or without compression
  - JPEG images
  - CAD files

- Document management software must provide convenient methods for importing digital content into designated repositories. Import alternatives must include, but need not be limited to, the following:
  - Batching import of digital content from designated directories or subdirectories on network servers.
  - Dragging and dropping individual documents or groups of documents into specific folders or subfolders within a designated repository.
  - Saving documents into a specific repository, folder, or subfolder from within word processing programs, e-mail systems, or other software to be specified by the Company.

- Document management software must provide a convenient method of capturing metadata related to specific folders, subfolders, and documents.
  - Whenever possible, metadata, such as the date a folder or document was created, should be derived automatically.
  - Other information can be key-entered into a formatted screen at the time a folder, subfolder, or document enters the repository. For that purpose, document management software must provide customizable formatted screens with labeled fields.
  - Document management software must support default values for designated metadata.

- Document management software must support automatically incrementing numeric values for designated metadata.

- Document management software must support the carry-over of specified metadata values from the previous data-entry screen.

- Document management software must provide a method of identifying different versions of documents.

Retrieval Requirements

- Authorized persons must be able to quickly identify and locate documents needed for a given purpose. Document management software must support the retrieval of documents from a given repository in the following ways:

  - By browsing through folders and subfolders. To support such browsing, document management software must display the file plan for a given repository. The displayed file plan must clearly represent the hierarchy of folders and subfolders for a given application.

  - By searching metadata associated with folders, subfolders, or documents.

  - By words or phrases contained in documents (where full-text indexing is utilized).

- At a minimum, metadata searches must support the following retrieval functionality:

  - Exact match of a specified field value.

  - Relational expressions "greater than" and "less than" in search statements.

  - The Boolean AND, OR, and NOT operators in search statements.

- Where full-text indexing is used, searchers must be able to locate documents that contain a specified word or phrase.

- All retrieval methods must be easily learned and used.

- For metadata and full-text searches, the initial response to a retrieval operation must indicate the number of documents that satisfy the search statement.

- Whenever possible, retrieved documents must be displayed in their native applications, which are to be launched automatically when a document is retrieved.

- Where a native application or a compatible equivalent is not available, document management software must provide a multiformat viewer for display of documents. The viewer must accurately represent the original appearance of documents.

- Document management software must provide a convenient method of printing documents without the necessity of viewing them.

- Authorized persons may append comments, instructions or other free-form annotations to folders, subfolders, or documents. Document management software must support this capability. The annotations must be displayable and printable when their associated folders, subfolders, or documents are opened.

- Document management software must support a web browser interface for all retrieval operations.

System Administration / Security

- Document management software must provide a convenient method of specifying access privileges with a minimum of repetitive effort.
- The Company must be able to designate "super users" who will have full access privileges at the repository, folder, subfolder, and document levels.
- The Company must be able to redefine access privileges at the repository, folder, subfolder, or document level.
- In general, a Company employee who is authorized to access a given folder will have access to all documents in that folder as well as in any embedded subfolders, but there may be cases in which certain subfolders or documents must be excluded. Document management software must provide a mechanism for limiting access to specific subfolders or documents without imposing corresponding limitations on other documents or folders.
- Search results must be limited to those documents the searcher is authorized to see. Searchers must not be able to determine the existence of unauthorized documents.
- Document management software must provide a reliable mechanism for authenticating users and verifying their access privileges.
- Document management software must maintain an audit log of document retrieval activity, including failed attempts as well as completed operations. The audit log must identify the date, the user, and the type of activity (view, add, move, delete, etc.).

Proposed System Requirements: Training

- The proposer must provide appropriate customer training for all aspects of system operation and use.
- Proposals must present a training plan and schedule with costs specifically enumerated for each training component.
- The proposer must provide descriptions of specific training sessions to be provided. The descriptions must indicate the purpose of each training session, the specific topics to be covered, the duration of the session (in hours or days), and the location where the session will be taught.
- The Company prefers on-site training involving the system components that it will actually utilize.
- The Company prefers live classroom training with instructors as opposed to audio-visual or computer-aided instruction.

- The proposer must indicate the specific instructional methods to be employed in each training session.

- The proposer must indicate the type of training materials to be utilized in each session.

- The proposer must indicate the number and type of Company employees who are to attend each training session.

- Training costs must be separately enumerated in the cost section of the vendor's proposal.

Proposed System Requirements: Maintenance

- The proposer must specify the warranty period and provisions for all proposed system components, including hardware, software, and communication components.

- Differences between manufacturers' warranties and proposers' warranties must be clearly stated.

- The proposer must specify post-warranty maintenance provisions, terms, and costs for all proposed system components, including hardware, software, and communication components.

- For hardware components the proposer must specify provisions, terms, and conditions for preventive maintenance and equipment repair.

- The proposer must specify the source of hardware maintenance service and the location of its service facilities. The proposer must identify any third-party maintenance organizations to be employed.

- The proposer must specify the hours that hardware maintenance service is available.

- The proposer must specify the response time for hardware maintenance service from the time the request for such service is received.

- For software, the proposer must specify provisions, terms, and conditions for repair or replacement of defective software.

- For software, the proposer must specify provisions, terms, and conditions for technical support in response to customer questions.

- For software, the proposer must specify provisions, terms, and conditions for new releases and other software upgrades.

- The proposed document management software will be implemented in applications critical to the Company's mission and daily operations. Prolonged downtime is consequently intolerable. For software malfunctions that result in system failure, the proposer must be able to restore system operability within 24 hours from the time the problem is reported. The proposer must state the cost and explain the method for satisfying this requirement. The proposer should also state the cost difference, if any, for longer repair intervals.

Worksheet-Based Cost-Calculation Example

Worksheet A

Start-Up Costs—Computer Hardware and Software

A1.	Purchase price of hardware and software components to be used exclusively for digital document implementation.	$250,000
A2.	System-related charges not included in line A1.	$30,000
A3.	Cost of site preparation for installation of system components included in line A1.	$5,000
A4.	Purchase price of hardware and software components shared with other computer applications.	$3,000
A5.	Percentage of amount on line A4 attributable to digital document application.	0.40
A6.	Amount on line A4 multiplied by decimal value on line A5.	$1,200
A7.	Total of amounts on lines A1, A2, A3, and A6—the total start-up cost for purchased hardware and software.	$289,200

Worksheet B

Annual Fixed Costs

B1.	Annual lease or rental payments for computer hardware and software used exclusively for digital document implementation.	$0
B2.	Annual cost of maintenance contracts for computer hardware and software used exclusively for digital document implementation.	$45,000
B3.	Annual value of floor space occupied by computer hardware used exclusively for digital document implementation.	$3,000
B4.	Annual lease or rental payments for computer hardware and software shared with other applications.	$0
B5.	Annual cost of maintenance contracts for computer hardware and software shared with other applications.	$540
B6.	Annual value of floor space occupied by computer hardware shared with other applications.	$0
B7.	Total of amounts on lines B4, B5, and B6.	$540
B8.	Percentage of amount on line B7 attributable to digital document implementation.	0.40
B9.	Amount on line B7 times decimal value on line B8.	$216
B10.	Total of amounts on lines B1, B2, B3, and B9—the annual fixed cost for a digital document implementation.	$48,216

Worksheet C

Start-Up Costs—Document Preparation for Backfile Conversion

C1.	Number of pages or documents to be converted to digital form.	300,000
C2.	Preparation rate, in pages or documents per hour.	1,000
C3.	Amount on line C1 divided by amount on line C2.	300
C4.	Disposition rate following conversion in pages or documents per hour.	2,000
C5.	Amount on line C1 divided by amount on line C4.	150
C6.	Total of amounts on lines C3 and C5—the number of hours required for backfile preparation and disposition.	450
C7.	Hourly wage rate for employees performing backfile preparation and disposition.	$16

C8.	Amount on line C6 times amount on line C7.	$7,200
C9.	Number of backfile pages to be photocopied for scanning or other conversion; if no pages will be photocopied, enter zero and go to line C12.	225,000
C10.	Photocopying cost, in cents, per page.	$0.08
C11.	Amount on line C9 times decimal value on line C10.	$18,000
C12.	Cost of equipment, supplies, and related services for backfile preparation.	$200
C13.	Total of amounts on lines C8, C11, and C12.	$25,400
C14.	Percentage of backfile preparation costs to be added for supervision.	0.10
C15.	Amount on line C13 times decimal value on line C14.	$2,540
C16.	Total of amounts on line C13 and line C15.	$27,940
C17.	Contingency percentage entered as decimal value.	0.05
C18.	Amount on line C16 times decimal value on line C17.	$1,397
C19.	Total of amounts on line C16 and line C18—the total cost of backfile preparation and disposition.	$29,337

Worksheet D

Start-Up Costs—In-House Backfile Conversion

D1.	Number of backfile pages to be converted to digital images by in-house scanning; if in-house scanning will not be used, enter zero and go to line D15.	75,000
D2.	Desired time, in working days, to perform backfile conversion by in-house scanning.	60
D3.	Amount on line D1 divided by amount on line D2—the number of pages to be converted per day.	1,250
D4.	Average number of pages scanned per workstation per hour, including make-ready time, image inspection, and image recording.	120
D5.	Number of scanning hours per workstation per day.	8
D6.	Amount on line D4 times amount on line D5.	960
D7.	Amount on line D3 divided by amount on line D6; if decimal value, round up to next integer.	2
D8.	Number of scanning workstations included in lines A1, A4, B1, and B4.	2

D9.	Amount on line D7 minus amount on line D8; if zero or negative value, go to line D12.	0
D10.	Cost per scanning workstation, including hardware and software.	
D11.	Amount on line D9 times amount on line D10.	
D12.	Amount on line D1 divided by amount on line D4.	625
D13.	Hourly wage rate for scanning workstation operators.	$17
D14.	Amount on line D12 times amount on line D13.	$10,625
D15.	Number of backfile pages to be converted in-house to character-coded text via OCR; if OCR will not be used, enter zero and go to line D30.	5,000
D16.	Cost of OCR software and server excluding OCR components included in lines A1, A4, B1, and B4.	$3,000
D17.	Desired time, in working days, to perform backfile conversion by OCR.	60
D18.	Amount on line D15 divided by amount on line D17—the number of pages to be converted per day.	83
D19.	Number of pages converted to character-coded text per hour, including verification and error correction.	12
D20.	Number of operating hours per OCR workstation per day.	8
D21.	Amount on line D19 times amount on line D20.	96
D22.	Amount on line D18 divided by amount on line D21; if decimal value, round up to next integer.	1
D23.	Number of OCR workstations included in lines A1, A4, B1, and B4.	4
D24.	Amount on line D22 minus amount on line D23; if zero or negative value, go to line D27.	-3
D25.	Cost per OCR workstation, including hardware and software.	
D26.	Amount on line D24 times amount on line D25.	
D27.	Amount on line D15 divided by amount on line D19.	417
D28.	Hourly wage rate for OCR workstation operators.	$17
D29.	Amount on line D27 times amount on line D28.	$7,083
D30.	Number of backfile pages to be converted to character-coded text via in-house key-entry; if in-house key-entry will not be be used, enter zero and go to line D46.	500

D31.	Average number of characters per page.	2,400
D32.	Amount on line D30 times amount on line D31.	1,200,000
D33.	Key-entry rate in characters per hour.	8,000
D34.	Amount on line D33 divided by 2.25 if double-keying will be used or by 1.6 if proofreading will be used—the number of characters that can be key-entered per hour including verification and error correction.	5,000
D35.	Divide amount on line D32 by amount on line D34.	240
D36.	Hourly wage rate for key-entry operators.	$17
D37.	Amount on line D35 times amount on line D36.	$4,080
D38.	Number of operating hours per key-entry workstation per day.	8
D39.	Amount on line D38 times by amount on line D34.	40,000
D40.	Amount on line D32 divided by amount on line D39.	30
D41.	Desired time, in working days, to perform backfile conversion by in-house key-entry.	60
D42.	Amount on line D40 divided by amount on line D41; if decimal value, round up to next integer.	1
D43.	Number of unused key-entry workstations included in lines A1, A4, B1, and B4.	3
D44.	Amount on line D42 minus amount on line D43; if zero or negative value, go to line D47.	-2
D45.	Cost per key-entry workstation, including hardware and software.	
D46.	Amount on line D44 times amount on line D45.	
D47.	Total of amounts on lines D11, D14, D26, D29, D37, and D46.	$21,788
D48.	Percentage of in-house backfile conversion costs to be added for supervision.	0.20
D49.	Amount on line D47 times decimal value on line D48.	$4,358
D50.	Total of amounts on line D47 and line D49.	$26,146
D51.	Contingency percentage entered as decimal value.	0.05
D52.	Amount on line D50 times decimal value on line D51.	$1,307
D53.	Total of amounts on line D50 and line D52—the total cost of backfile conversion by in-house scanning, OCR, and key-entry.	$27,453

Worksheet E

Start-Up Costs—Backfile Conversion by Service Bureau

E1.	Number of pages to be converted by a service bureau.	225,000
E2.	Service bureau charges.	$18,000
E3.	Packing and shipping costs for sending documents to service bureau.	$1,500
E4.	Percentage of service bureau work to be inspected on receipt entered as decimal value; if 100 percent, enter 1.00.	0.20
E5.	Amount on line E1 times decimal value on line E4.	45,000
E6.	Inspection rate, in pages per hour.	180
E7.	Amount on line E5 divided by amount on line E6.	250
E8.	Hourly wage rate for employees performing inspection.	$15
E9.	Amount on line E8 times amount on line E9.	$3,750
E10.	Desired time, in working days, to complete inspection of service bureau's work.	40
E11.	Amount on line E5 divided by amount on line E10—the number of pages to be inspected per day.	1,125
E12.	Number of operating hours per inspection workstation per day.	8
E13.	Amount on line E6 times amount on line E12.	1,440
E14.	Amount on line E11 divided by amount on line E13; if decimal value, round up to next integer.	1
E15.	Number of inspection workstations included in lines A1, A4, B1, B4, D9, D24, and D43.	2
E16.	Amount on line E14 minus amount on line E15; if zero or negative number, go to line E19.	-1
E17.	Cost per inspection workstation, including hardware and software.	
E18.	Amount on line E16 times amount on line E17.	
E19.	Total of amounts on lines E2, E3, E9, and E18.	$23,250
E20.	Percentage of conversion costs to be added for supervision.	0.20
E21.	Amount on line E19 times decimal value on line E20.	$4,650
E22.	Total of amounts on line E19 and line E21.	$27,900

E23.	Contingency percentage entered as decimal value.	0.05
E24.	Amount on line E22 times decimal value on line E23.	$1,395
E25.	Total of amounts on line E22 and line E24—the total cost of backfile conversion by a service bureau.	$29,295

Worksheet F

Start-Up Costs—Document Indexing and Data-Entry for Backfile Conversion

F1.	Number of backfile documents.	10,000
F2.	Percentage of backfile for which indexing is required; if 100 percent, enter 1.00; if indexing is not required, enter zero and go to line F8.	0.05
F3.	Amount on line F1 times decimal value on line F2.	500
F4.	Indexing rate, in documents per hour.	2
F5.	Amount on line F3 divided by amount on line F4—the backfile indexing time in hours.	250
F6.	Hourly wage rate for indexing personnel.	$40
F7.	Amount on line F5 times amount on line F6—the labor cost for document indexing.	$10,000
F8.	Average number of characters per database record.	100
F9.	Amount on line F1 times amount on line F8.	1,000,000
F10.	Key-entry rate, in characters per hour.	8,000
F11.	Amount on line F9 divided by amount on line F10—the number of hours required for initial key-entry of database records.	125
F12.	Multiply amount on line F11 by 2.25 if double-keying will be used or by 1.6 if sight verification will be used.	281
F13.	Hourly wage rate for data-entry personnel.	$17
F14.	Amount on line F12 times amount on line F13—the labor cost of data-entry.	$4,781
F15.	Number of operating hours per data-entry workstation per day.	8
F16.	Amount on line F12 divided by amount on line F15.	35
F17.	Desired time, in days, to complete data-entry for backfile conversion.	60

F18. Amount on line F16 divided by amount on line F17; if decimal value, round up to next integer—the number of workstations required for entry of database records.   1

F19. Number of data-entry workstations included in lines A1, A4, B1, B4, D9, D24, D43, and E16.   1

F20. Amount on line F18 minus amount on line F19; if zero or negative value, go to line F23.   0

F21. Cost per data-entry workstation, including hardware and software.

F22. Amount on line F20 times amount on line F21.

F23. Total of amounts on lines F7, F14, and F22. $14,781

F24. Percentage of backfile indexing and data-entry costs to be added for supervision.   0.20

F25. Amount on line F23 times decimal value on line F24. $2,956

F26. Total of amounts on line F23 and line F25. $17,737

F27. Contingency percentage.   0.05

F28. Amount on line F26 times decimal value on line F27. $887

F29. Total of amounts on line F26 and line F28—the total cost of document indexing and data-entry for backfile conversion. $18,624

Worksheet G

Start-Up Costs—Backfile Storage Requirements

G1. Number of backfile pages to be converted to digital images from lines D1 and E1; if zero, go to line G4.   300,000

G2. Number of document images per megabyte.   20

G3. Amount on line G1 divided by amount on line G2—the image storage requirement in megabytes.   15,000

G4. Number of backfile pages to be converted to character-coded text from lines D15, D30, and E1; if zero, go to line G7.   5,500

G5. Number of pages of character-coded text per megabyte.   415

G6. Amount on line G4 divided by amount on line G5—the storage requirement in megabytes for character-coded documents.   13

G7. Amount on line F9 divided by 1,000,000—the storage requirement in megabytes for index database records, excluding full-text indexing.   1

G8.	Percentage of character-coded documents for which full-text indexing will be used entered as a decimal value; if 100 percent, enter 1.00; if full-text indexing is not required, enter zero and go to line G11.	1.00
G9.	Amount on line G6 times decimal value on line G8.	13
G10.	Amount on line G9 times 1.3—the storage requirement in megabytes for full-text indexing of character-coded documents.	17
G11.	Total of lines G3, G6, G7, and G10—the storage requirement for backfile documents and index data.	15,031
G12.	Unused storage capacity in megabytes included in lines A1, A4, B1, and B4.	290,000
G13.	Amount on line G11 minus amount on line G12; if zero or negative value, go to line G16.	-274,969
G14.	Cost per megabyte for online storage of digital documents and index data.	
G15.	Amount on line G13 times amount on line G14.	
G16.	Cost per megabyte for backup media for backfile documents and index data.	$0.02
G17.	Amount on line G16 times amount on line G11.	$300
G18	Number of sets of backup copies to be produced.	2
G19	Amount on line G17 times amount on line G18.	$600
G20.	Total of amounts on lines G15 and G19—the cost of online storage and backup media for backfile documents and index data.	$600

Worksheet H

Annual Variable Costs—Document Conversion

H1.	Number of documents or pages to be converted to digital form per year.	50,000
H2.	Preparation rate in documents or pages per hour.	1,000
H3.	Amount on line H1 divided by amount on line H2.	50
H4.	Disposition rate following conversion in documents or pages per hour.	2,000
H5.	Amount on line H1 divided by amount on line H4.	25
H6.	Total of amounts on lines H3 and H5—the number of hours required annually for document preparation and disposition.	75

H7.	Hourly wage rate for employees performing document preparation and disposition.	$15
H8.	Amount on line H6 times amount on line H7—the annual labor cost for document preparation and disposition.	$1,125
H9.	Percentage of pages to be photocopied; if 100 percent, enter 1.00; if zero, go to line H14.	0
H10.	Amount on line H1 times decimal value on line H9.	
H11.	Photocopying cost, in cents, per page.	
H12.	Amount on line H10 times amount on line H11.	
H13.	Number of annual pages to be converted by in-house scanning; if in-house scanning will not be used, enter zero and go to line H19.	50,000
H14.	Average number of pages scanned per workstation per hour, including make-ready time, image inspection, and image recording.	120
H15.	Amount on line H13 divided by amount on line H14.	417
H16.	Hourly wage rate for scanning workstation operators.	$15
H17.	Amount on line H15 times amount on line H16—the annual labor cost for in-house scanning.	$6,250
H18.	Number of annual pages to be converted in-house to character-coded text via OCR; if OCR will not be used, enter zero and go to line H23.	0
H19.	Number of pages converted to character-coded text per hour, including verification and error correction.	
H20.	Amount on line H18 divided by amount on line H19.	
H21.	Hourly wage rate for OCR workstation operators.	
H22.	Amount on line H20 times amount on line H21—the annual labor cost for in-house document conversion via OCR.	
H23.	Number of annual pages to be converted to character-coded text via in-house key-entry; if 100 percent, enter 1.00; if zero, go to line H31.	0
H24.	Average number of characters per page.	
H25.	Amount on line H23 times amount on line H24.	

H26.   Key-entry rate in characters per hour.

H27.   Amount on line H26 divided by 2.25 if double-keying will be
       used or by 1.6 if proofreading will be used—the number of
       characters that can be key-entered per hour, including
       verification and error correction.

H28.   Amount on line H25 divided by amount on line H27.

H29.   Hourly wage rate for key-entry operators.

H30.   Amount on line H28 times amount on line H29—the annual
       labor cost for document conversion via in-house key-entry.

H31.   Number of annual pages to be converted by a service bureau.   0
       If service bureau will not be used, go to line H40.

H32.   Service bureau charges.

H33.   Packing and shipping costs for sending documents to service
       bureau.

H34.   Percentage of service bureau work to be inspected in-house;
       if 100 percent, enter 1.00.

H35.   Amount on line H31 times decimal value on line H34.

H36.   Inspection rate, in pages per hour.

H37.   Amount on line H35 divided by amount on line H36—the
       number of hours required to inspect service bureau work.

H38.   Hourly wage rate for employees performing inspection.

H39.   Amount on line H37 times amount on line H38—the annual
       labor cost for in-house inspection of service bureau work.

H40.   Total of amounts on lines H8, H12, H17, H22, H30, and H39. $7,375

H41.   Percentage of annual document conversion costs to be added   0.20
       for supervision.

H42.   Amount on line H40 times decimal value on line H41. $1,475

H43.   Total of amounts on line H32, H40, and line H42. $8,850

H44.   Contingency percentage.   0.05

H45.   Amount on line H43 times decimal value on line H44. $443

H46.   Total of amounts on line H43 and line H45—the annual $9,293
       variable cost to convert documents to digital form.

Worksheet I

Annual Variable Costs—Document Indexing and Data-Entry

I1.	Number of documents to be indexed annually; if zero, go to line I6.	0
I2.	Indexing rate, in documents per hour.	
I3.	Amount on line I1 divided by amount on line I2.	
I4.	Hourly wage rate for indexing personnel.	
I5.	Amount on line I3 times amount on line I4—the annual labor cost for document indexing.	
I6.	Number of documents for which index data-entry is required; if zero go to line I14.	1,670
I7.	Average number of characters per index record.	100
I8.	Amount on line I6 times amount on line I7.	167,000
I9.	Data-entry rate, in characters per hour.	8,000
I10.	Amount on line I8 divided by amount on line I9.	21
I11.	Multiply amount on line I10 by 2.25 if double-keying will be used or by 1.6 if sight verification will be used—the number of hours required annually for index data-entry, including verification and error correction.	33
I12.	Hourly wage rate for data-entry personnel.	$17
I13.	Multiply amount on line I11 by amount on line I12—the annual labor cost for data-entry.	$568
I14.	Total of amounts on lines I6 and line I13.	$2,238
I15.	Percentage of annual indexing and data-entry costs to be added for supervision.	0.20
I16.	Amount on line I14 times decimal value on line I15.	$448
I17.	Total of amounts on line I14 and line I16.	$2,685
I18.	Contingency percentage entered as decimal value.	0.05
I19.	Amount on line I17 times decimal value on line I18.	$134
I20.	Total of amounts on line I17 and I19—the total annual cost for indexing and data-entry.	$2,820

Worksheet J

Additional Equipment Costs—Scanning, Inspection, and Data-Entry

| J1. | Number of hours required per year for document scanning, from line H15; if document scanning will not be used, go to line J11. | 417 |

| J2. | Number of scanning hours per workstation per day. | 8 |

| J3. | Number of working days per year. | 250 |

| J4. | Amount on line J2 times amount on line J3. | 2,000 |

| J5. | Amount on line J1 divided by amount on line J4; if decimal value, round up to next integer. | 1 |

| J6. | Number of unused scanning workstations included in lines A1, A4, B1, B4, and D9. | 2 |

| J7. | Amount on line J5 minus amount on line J6; if zero or negative value, go to line J10. | -1 |

| J8. | Cost per scanning workstation, including hardware and software. | |

| J9. | Amount on line J7 times amount on line J8. | |

| J10. | Number of hours required per year for conversion of documents to character-coded text via OCR from line H25; if OCR will not be used, go to line J19. | 0 |

| J11. | Number of operating hours per OCR workstation per day. | |

| J12. | Number of working days per year. | |

| J13. | Amount on line J11 times amount on line J12. | |

| J14. | Amount on line J10 divided by amount on line J13; if decimal value, round up to next integer. | |

| J15. | Number of unused OCR workstations included in lines A1, A4, B1, B4, D24, and J7. | |

| J16. | Amount on line J14 minus amount on line J15; if zero or negative value, go to line J19. | |

| J17. | Cost per OCR workstation, including hardware and software. | |

| J18. | Amount on line J16 times amount on line J17. | |

| J19. | Number of hours required per year for conversion of documents to character-coded text via key-entry from line H28; if key-entry will not be used, go to line J28. | 0 |

J20.	Number of operating hours per key-entry workstation per day.	
J21.	Number of working days per year.	
J22.	Amount on line J20 times amount on line J21.	
J23.	Amount on line J19 divided by amount on line J22; if decimal value, round up to next integer.	
J24.	Number of unused key-entry workstations included in lines A1, A4, B1, B4, D43, J7, and J16.	
J25.	Amount on line J23 minus amount on line J24; if zero or negative value, go to line J28.	
J26.	Cost per key-entry workstation, including hardware and software.	
J27.	Amount on line J25 times amount on line J26.	
J28.	Number of hours required per year for entry of index data, including verification and error correction from line I10; if index data-entry is not required, go to line J36.	21
J29.	Number of operating hours per data-entry workstation per day.	8
J30.	Number of working days per year.	250
J31.	Amount on line J20 times amount on line J21.	2,000
J32.	Amount on line J28 divided by amount on line J31; if decimal value, round up to next integer.	1
J33.	Number of unused data-entry workstations included in lines A1, A4, B1, B4, D9, D24, D43, E16, F20, J7, J16, and J25.	4
J34.	Amount on line J32 minus amount on line J33; if zero or negative value, go to line J37.	-3
J35.	Cost per data-entry workstation, including hardware and software.	
J36.	Amount on line J34 times amount on line J35.	
J37.	Total of amounts on lines J9, J18, J27, and J36—the cost of additional workstations for scanning, conversion of documents to character-coded text, and index data-entry.	$0

Worksheet K

Annual Storage Costs

K1.	Number of digital images to be added per year from line H13; if zero, go to line K4.	50,000
K2.	Number of images per megabyte.	20
K3.	Amount on line K1 divided by amount on line K2—the additional image storage requirement per year in megabytes.	2,500
K4.	Number of pages of character-coded text to be added per year from lines H18, H23, or digital sources; if zero go to line K7.	50,000
K5.	Number of pages of character-coded text per megabyte.	415
K6.	Amount on line K4 divided by amount on line K5—the additional storage requirement per year in megabytes for character-coded documents.	120
K7.	Number of digital documents per year for which entry of index data is required; if zero, go to line K10.	1,670
K8.	Average number of characters per index record.	100
K9.	Amount on line K7 times amount on K8.	167,000
K10.	Percentage of character-coded pages for which full-text indexing will be used entered as a decimal value: if full-text indexing is required and if 100 percent, enter 1.00; if full-text indexing will not be used, enter zero and go to line K13.	1.00
K11.	Amount on line K9 times decimal value on line K10.	167,000
K12.	Amount on line K11 times 1.3.	217,100
K13.	Total of lines K9 and K12.	384,100
K14.	Amount on line K3 divided by 1,000,000—the additional storage requirement per year in megabytes for index data.	1
K15.	Total of lines K3, K6, and K14—the additional storage requirement per year in megabytes for digital documents and index data.	2,621
K16.	Unused online storage capacity in megabytes included in lines A1, A4, B1, B4, and G13.	274,969
K17.	Amount on line K15 minus amount on line K16; if zero or negative value, go to line K20.	-272,347
K18.	Cost per megabyte for online storage.	

K19.	Amount on line K17 times amount on line K18.	
K20.	Cost per megabyte for backup media for digital documents and index data.	$0.02
K21.	Amount on line K19 times amount on line K15.	$52
K22.	Number of sets of backup copies to be produced.	2
K23.	Amount on line K21 times amount on line K22.	$104
K24.	Total of amounts on lines K19 and K23—the cost of online storage and backup media for digital documents and index data.	$104

Worksheet L

Summary of Costs on Annualized Basis

L1.	Start-up cost for purchased digital document hardware and software from line A7.	$289,200
L2.	Cost of computer storage for backfile conversion, from line G20.	$600
L3.	Cost of additional scanning, image inspection, and data-entry equipment, from line J37.	$0
L4.	Total of amounts on lines L1, L2, and L3.	$289,800
L5.	Useful life, in years, of digital document system, including all hardware and software components.	5
L6.	Amount on line L4 divided by amount on line L5—the annualized cost of purchased digital document hardware and software, including storage for backfile documents and index data.	$57,960
L7.	Total of amounts on lines C19, D53, E25, and F29—the total cost of backfile conversion for digital documents and index data.	$104,710
L8.	Useful life, in years, of converted backfile.	10
L9.	Amount on line L7 divided by amount on line L8—the annualized cost of backfile conversion.	$10,471
L10.	Annual fixed costs, from line B10.	$48,216
L11.	Annual variable cost of document conversion, from line H46.	$9,293
L12.	Annual variable cost of document indexing and data-entry, from line I20.	$2,820
L13.	Annual cost of additional computer storage, from line K24.	$104

L14.	Total of amounts on line L2, L3, and L13 .	$704
L15.	Amount on L14 times 0.18.	$127
L16.	Total of amounts on lines L6, L9, L10, L11, L12, L13, and L15—the annualized cost of a digital document implementation.	$128,990

Cost-Justification Examples

Cost of
Paper-Based
Filing System

Table C.1

	Year 1	Year 2	Year 3	Year 4	Year 5	Totals
Equipment	$2100	$2,205	$2,315	$2,430	$2,550	$11,600
Floor space	7,200	8,820	10,560	12,420	14,400	53,400
Preparation of file folders	2,100	2,205	2,315	2,430	2,550	11,600
Document filing	2,820	2,960	3,110	3,265	3,430	15,585
Cross-reference file	6,970	7,320	7,685	8,070	8,470	38,515
Retrieval labor	250,000	262,500	275,625	231,500	243,100	1,262,725
Photocopying reports	60,000	63,000	66,150	69,455	72,930	331,535
Totals	**$331,190**	**$349,010**	**$367,760**	**$329,570**	**$347,430**	**$1,724,960**

Cost of Digital Document Implementation

Table C.2

	Year 1	Year 2	Year 3	Year 4	Year 5	Totals
Equipment and software	$289,200	$0	$0	$0	$0	$289,200
Backfile conversion	104,710	0	0	0	0	104,710
Maintenance contracts	45,215	47,475	49,900	52,350	54,960	249,900
Floor space	3,000	3,150	3,300	3,450	3,600	16,500
Document conversion	9,295	9,760	10,250	10,760	11,300	51,365
Document indexing	2,820	2,960	3,110	3,265	3,430	15,585
Retrieval labor	83,400	87,520	91,900	96,500	101,325	460,645
Printing reports	22,500	23,625	24,810	26,050	27,350	124,335
Totals	**560,140**	**174,490**	**183,270**	**192,375**	**201,965**	**1,312,240**

Cumulative Cost Comparison

Table C.3

	Year 1	Year 2	Year 3	Year 4	Year 5
Paper-Based Filing	$331,190	$680,200	$1,047,960	$1,395,390	$1,724,960
Digital Documents	$560,140	$734,630	$917,900	$1,110,275	$1,312,240

Cumulative Costs: Paper Filing vs. Digital Documents

Figure C.1

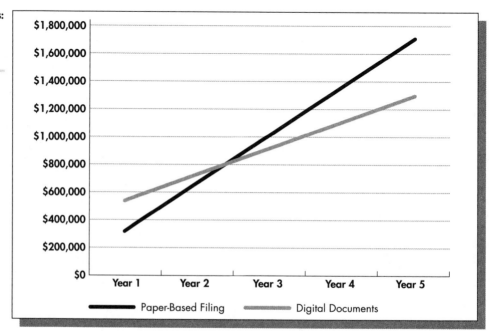

Sources for Finding More Information

The topics covered in this book are discussed in varying levels of detail in thousands of books, journal articles, white papers, technical reports, web pages, and other information sources. These publications can be divided by approach and content into four groups: (1) tutorial treatments of digital document concepts, technology, methods, and standards; (2) descriptions of specific digital document products or services, which are often written by vendors; (3) case studies of specific digital document implementations; and (4) discussions of selected issues and concerns such as the legal status of digital documents, the strategic role of digital document technologies in information management, industry trends, and cost justification parameters for digital document implementations. A comprehensive bibliography of information resources that address these topics is beyond the scope of this book and, while potentially useful, would be quickly outdated. As an alternative, this appendix provides some suggestions for finding pertinent information resources for further study.

A number of book-length studies provide tutorial treatments of digital document concepts, technologies, methods, and implementation issues. The best sources for identifying these publications are the online catalogs of large research libraries, of which the Library of Congress database (www.loc.gov) is one of the most comprehensive and readily accessible examples. Standards for digital imaging, document indexing, computer storage media, and related technologies and methods are published by national and international standard-setting organizations such as the American National Standards Institute (www.ansi.org) and ISO (www.iso-online.org). Digital document standards are also developed and distributed by AIIM (www.aiim.org). In addition to standards, the AIIM web site lists a variety of pertinent books, reports, and white papers, some of which can be downloaded electronically.

Over the past 20 years, many articles about digital imaging, text storage and retrieval, document indexing, content management, and related topics have appeared in business periodicals, technical and professional journals, trade magazines, and other serial publications. Databases that index business and technical periodicals are the best resources for locating these articles. Such databases are available through online and web-based information services, such as Dialog and Lexis/Nexis, and in CD-ROM versions, which are available through many public, academic, and institutional libraries. Useful business databases include ABI/Inform, Business Abstracts, Business Dateline, Business Periodicals Index, Business & Management Practices, Globalbase, Management Contents, PROMT, and the Trade and Industry Database. Technical databases that index articles about digital imaging, text retrieval, and related documents include Applied Science & Technology Abstracts, the Computer Database, Ei Compendex, Information Science Abstracts, Inspec, and Library & Information Science Abstracts. The NTIS database includes indexing information and abstracts for government-generated and government-sponsored reports that deal with digital document technologies and implementations.

Web sites of software developers, scanner manufacturers, imaging service bureaus, data-entry companies, and other vendors are excellent sources of information about the characteristics and capabilities of specific digital document products and services. Some vendor web sites also feature customer lists, case studies, white papers that address technical and implementation issues, and links to other useful sites. Business Wire (www.businesswire.com) and PR Newswire (www.prnewswire.com) are examples of information services that provide convenient access to press releases that deal with digital document technologies and industry developments. Such press releases are also accessible at vendor web sites.

Finally, web search engines, such as Google and Yahoo, are invaluable resources for anyone interested in locating information about digital document terminology, concepts, products, services, and implementations. Similarly, the Wikipedia (www.wikipedia.org) contains hundreds of articles about document imaging, document management, content management, optical character recognition, text retrieval, full text indexing, workflow, and other topics covered in this book. Many of these articles are detailed and include references to pertinent publications. As a notable and useful feature, the Wikipedia also provides informative profiles about specific digital document products and vendors.

A – C

access resolution. Resolution suitable for display or printing.

automatic categorization. A form of automatic indexing in which software analyzes digital documents and assigns them to categories in a predefined file plan or indexing scheme.

backward compatibility. The ability of future software products to read information recorded in particular or formats.

binary-mode scanners. Scanners that do not preserve gray tones and colors within source documents. They encode gray tones or colors as either black or white, depending on their relative lightness or darkness.

bit-mapped images. Bits correspond to specific locations and tonal values within a scanned page, or raster images, because the pixels conform to a rectangular array of parallel lines.

business process. Interrelated activities and procedures that accomplish a specific objective such as the completion of transactions, creation of products, or performance of services.

central files. A consolidation of documents in a designated location where multiple persons can access them.

character-coded digital documents. Documents limited to textual information that can be represented by one of the current coding schemes or by other character-coding schemes that may be developed in the future.

character-coded text. Text generated by word processing programs, e-mail systems, OCR programs, or other software.

concept indexing. A method of indexing subject records in which assigned subject terms represent the indexer's understanding of concepts treated in a document.

cost justification. An analytical procedure that evaluates the costs associated with a particular methodology or technology to determine whether such costs are defensible in terms of the benefits to be derived from them.

D – F

data migration. Periodic conversion of digital documents and index data to new file formats or media.

data validation. A process used to check the appropriateness of field values that are typed correctly. Data validation is performed by software during data-entry.

data verification. A process used for detecting and correcting incorrectly typed characters.

decentralized filing arrangements. Documents are kept in the work areas of individual employees or are otherwise scattered in multiple locations.

derived term indexing. A method of indexing subject records in which subject descriptors are extracted from all or selected portions of a document. The index terms must appear in the document itself; no other words are permitted.

digital documents. Computer-processible records that have *both* of the following characteristics: (1) They are created by computer programs for purposes that would otherwise be served by paper or photographic documents. If a digital document did not exist, the same information would and could be created and maintained in nonelectronic form. (2) They can be printed to produce paper or photographic documents of comparable content, appearance, and functionality.

digitized images. (1) Images that may be produced by document scanners, microfilm scanners, digital cameras, or other devices, including specialized scientific and medical instruments that are outside the scope of this book. (2) Images that replicate the appearance of paper documents from which they were made. They can contain textual and/or graphic information, including signatures, handwritten annotations, and illustrations.

dual-media approach. A digital document implementation that addresses an organization's active reference or workflow requirements while retention requirements are satisfied by paper or microfilm.

duplex scanner. A scanner that can digitize both sides of a page at the same time.

field. *See indexing parameter.*

file plan. A systematic categorization scheme that groups documents pertaining to a given matter. A file plan defines topical or other categories into which documents will be grouped, and a folder is established for each category. Within a given folder, digital documents are stored as individually labeled computer files. Also known as a *file taxonomy.*

flatbed scanner. A scanner that features a flat exposure surface on which pages are individually positioned for scanning.

full-text indexing. A method of indexing subject records that carries derived term indexing to its extreme by using every word in a document as an index term. A computerized indexing method for character-coded digital documents or document surrogates such as abstracts, summaries, and annotations.

G – I

grayscale scanners. Scanners that employ multiple bits to represent gray pixels.

image enhancement. Technologies and processes that improve the quality of digitized images.

index database. A database created to keep track of digital documents that relate to a given person, account, case, claim, subject, or other matter.

indexing depth. The number of indexing parameters and the number of index values per parameter to be applied to individual documents.

indexing parameter. A category of information by which documents will be indexed for retrieval. Also referred to as a *field.*

interface. A device that provides a physical connection between a document scanner and personal computer.

inter-indexer consistency. Agreement in the selection of subject terms when documents of similar content are indexed by different persons.

intra-indexer consistency. Agreement in the selection of subject terms for similar documents indexed by the same person.

inverted index. A computer file that lists words with pointers to the digital documents in which they appear.

K – L

key fields. The most important type of field in digital document implementations, they correspond to the indexing parameters identified for a particular application. They contain names, subject terms, dates, or information by which digital documents will be retrieved.

lossless compression technique. A compression algorithm that reduces image size without omitting any information.

lossy compression technique. A compression algorithm that omits some information from the original image.

M – O

microform scanner. A scanner that produces electronic images from microfilm images, which may be recorded on roll microfilm, microfiche, microfilm jackets, or aperture cards.

name authority list. A variant form of thesaurus, it establishes approved forms for personal and corporate names to be used as index values. It also provides cross-references from unauthorized forms, such as abbreviations and acronyms, to approved forms.

natural language queries. Search queries that consist of questions or instructions entered in a sentence format without regard to formal syntax. The software parses the query to identify search terms and determine the specific retrieval operations to be performed.

nonkey fields. Fields containing descriptive information that is important but will not be used for retrieval; information contained in nonkey fields is displayed when index records are retrieved through searches involving key fields.

nonproprietary file format. A file format supported by multiple vendors and software products. It may be based on published specifications prepared by cooperating software developers. It may be developed by one influential software company and subsequently adopted by others.

optical character recognition (OCR). A data-entry methodology that combines scanning with image analysis to recognize or read characters contained in source documents.

optical resolutions. Resolutions supported by scanning hardware.

output resolutions. Resolutions achieved through the use of interpolation software that employs image analysis algorithms, which add pixels to electronic document images following scanning, thereby increasing their effective resolution.

P – R

picture elements / pixels. Microscopically small units that represent areas of an object or scene in a digitized image.

precision. A measure of the number of relevant documents retrieved by a given search as a percentage of the total number of documents, relevant and irrelevant, retrieved.

preservation resolution. Resolution that provides a very high-quality reproduction of source documents.

production-level microform scanners. Microform scanners that have the primary function of digitization of microform backfiles for input into electronic document imaging systems.

proprietary file format. A file format developed by one vendor for its own software products. It is associated with a specific application program.

rated speed (scanner). The elapsed time required to convert one page to a digitized image from the moment the page is positioned for scanning until digitization is completed.

recall. A measure of the number of relevant documents retrieved by a given search as a percentage of the total number of relevant documents in a given collection.

records management application (RMA) software. A category of computer software that organizes, stores, retrieves, and otherwise manages records. It combines document organization, storage, retrieval, and life-cycle management in a single software platform.

resolution. A measure of the capability to delineate picture detail in document images. An important quality determinant that denotes the sharpness of document images.

S – W

scanning throughput. A measure of the total time required to produce a serviceable digitized image from a scanned page.

sheetfed scanner. A scanner that features a transport mechanism that feeds pages across the exposure surface for scanning.

simplex scanner. A scanner that can digitize one side of a page at a time. Double-sided pages must be turned over and repositioned for scanning.

stability estimates. Estimates that define the time periods during which magnetic or optical media will support reliable retrieval of recorded information. Also termed *lifetime estimates* or *life spans.*

thresholding. A sophisticated form of contrast control available on some document scanners that automatically adjusts the black-white threshold to compensate for colored forms or other documents that contain text printed on a colored background.

vector files. Digital documents that contain mathematical statements that represent images as lines, circles, arcs, rectangles, polygons, or other geometric objects. The statements define a series of points and provide instructions about how they are to be connected to produce geometric objects with specific characteristics, including shape, color, fill, and outline. Vector files can also contain text with information about fonts, sizes, and other attributes.

workflow. A process that automates the routing of documents among designated recipients according to user-defined rules and relationships.

William Saffady is a Professor at the Palmer School of Library and Information Science, Long Island University in New York City, where he teaches courses on information management topics. He previously held similar faculty positions at the State University of New York at Albany, Vanderbilt University in Nashville, TN, and Pratt Institute in New York City.

Dr. Saffady is the author of over three dozen books and many articles on records management, document imaging, information storage technologies, office automation, and library automation. Recent books published by ARMA International include *Records and Information Management: Fundamentals of Professional Practice, Electronic Document Imaging: Technology, Applications, Implementation, Managing Electronic Records,* Third Edition, *Micrographics: Technology for the 21st Century, Cost Analysis Concepts and Methods for Records Management Programs, Knowledge Management: A Manager's Briefing, Records and Information Management: A Benchmarking Study of Large U.S. Industrial Companies,* and *The Value of Records Management: A Manager's Briefing, The Business Case for Systematic Control of Recorded Information.*

In addition to teaching and writing, Dr. Saffady serves as an information management consultant, providing training and analytical services to corporations, government agencies, and other organizations.

ARMA International is the leading professional organization for persons in the expanding field of records and information management.

As of May 2007, ARMA has about 10,000 members in the United States, Canada, and 37 other countries around the world. Within the United States, Canada, New Zealand, Japan, Jamaica, and Singapore, ARMA has nearly 150 local chapters that provide networking and leadership opportunities through monthly meetings and special seminars.

ARMA's mission is to provide education, research, and networking opportunities to information professionals, to enable them to use their skills and experience to leverage the value of records, information, and knowledge as corporate assets and as contributors to organizational success.

The ARMA International headquarters office is located in Lenexa, Kansas, in the Kansas City metropolitan area. Office hours are 8:30 A.M. to 5:00 P.M., Central Time, Monday through Friday.

ARMA International
13725 W. 109th St., Ste. 101
Lenexa, Kansas 66215
800.422.2762 • 913.341.3808
Fax: 913.341.3742
hq@arma.org
www.arma.org